P9-APE-292

ELIZABETH BARRETT BROWNING :
A PORTRAIT

ELIZABETH MOULTON-BARRETT

at the age of 8 years

ELIZABETH BARRETT BROWNING:

A PORTRAIT

BY

ISABEL C. CLARKE

KENNIKAT PRESS
Port Washington, N. Y./London

TO
ALICE PERRIN

ELIZABETH BARRETT BROWNING

First published in 1929
Reissued in 1970 by Kennikat Press
Library of Congress Catalog Card No: 73-103175
SBN 8046-0812-1

Manufactured by Taylor Publishing Company   Dallas, Texas

PREFACE

When I began to write this book I found there had been no authoritative biography of Elizabeth Barrett Browning since the necessarily imperfect one by John Ingram, published in 1888 during the lifetime of her husband, with the exception of the generally brief notices of her in the biographies of Robert Browning and the well-known biographical matter contributed by Sir Frederic G. Kenyon [1] and Mr. Percy Lubbock,[2] in their respective editions of her letters.

My book was just finished, when no less than two admirable works on the same subject were published within a few weeks of each other—*Elizabeth Barrett Browning*, by Miss Irene Cooke-Willis, and the larger and more important biography, *The Brownings*, by Mr. Osbert Burdett.

In the circumstances I feel that some apology is necessary for inflicting another Life of our greatest English poetess—and one that naturally goes over much the same ground as the others—upon a long-suffering public. My excuse is that a narrative-biography—a reconstruction of her story as a whole from extant letters and memoirs—has not so far been attempted, and that having been for many years resident in Italy myself I have been able to follow that part of her life with an intimate knowledge of scenes at once so familiar and so dear to her.

---

[1] *The Letters of Elizabeth Barrett Browning.* Edited with Biographical Additions by Sir Frederic G. Kenyon, K.C.B. (Murray.)
[2] *Elizabeth Barrett Browning in Her Letters.* By Percy Lubbock. (Murray.)

I have consulted all the usual authorities, including those mentioned above, and the indispensable *Browning Love Letters* ; as well as Miss Lilian Whiteing's *The Brownings*, and the respective lives, letters or memoirs of the following :—Mrs. Jameson, Miss Mitford, Mr. William Wetmore Story, Adolphus Trollope, Mrs. Hugh Fraser, Miss Harriet Hosmer, Miss Kate Field and others.

With regard to the disputed date of Robert Browning's first sight of the *Sonnets from the Portuguese* I hope to have set the matter finally at rest, since it is known that they were first published at Reading for private circulation in 1847, a few months after the marriage of Robert and Elizabeth Browning, thus confirming the story told by the poet many years later to Sir Edmund Gosse.

I desire to thank Messrs. John Murray for permission to include many excerpts from the famous *Love Letters*, and also from the *Letters of Elizabeth Barrett Browning*, upon which students must necessarily so largely depend, and also for their kindness in allowing me to quote copyright matter from the Poems of Robert Browning. My very grateful thanks are due to my friend, Mrs. Waldo Story, who has not only kindly lent me some of the photographs included in this book, but has generously permitted me to use the six unpublished letters from Mrs. Browning to Mr. and Mrs. William Wetmore Story which will be found in the Appendix.

Finally, I would add that the very kind reception accorded by the public to my former biographical work, *Haworth Parsonage*, has encouraged me to write the romantic history of Elizabeth Barrett Browning on much the same lines.

ISABEL C. CLARKE.

Rome, 1929.

LIST OF ILLUSTRATIONS

Elizabeth Barrett Browning

CHAPTER I

I

A GARDEN set in park-like surroundings amid the green and characteristically English scenery of the Malvern Hills more than a hundred years ago.

Two children are playing in the garden. The girl, the elder by about two years, is a slim elfin child with dark hair cut short, and great dreamy dark eyes above which the eyebrows are delicately arched. She wears a muslin dress cut low at the neck and sleeveless, and little frilled pantalettes reaching almost to her ankles according to the mode of that day. The boy, her playfellow and constant companion, is her brother Edward.

They run hither and thither often hand in hand, for though he is the younger he is the stronger and sturdier of the two. They gather the wild flowers, for which those fields and woods are famous ; they know the haunts of the birds and of the shy grey squirrels ; they wander at will among the hills and meadows that surround their home. They call each other Ba and Bro, and are inseparable, sharing alike their lessons and their play.

Their love never failed, and the slim dark girl was destined to remember it with mingled happiness and anguish until death closed her eyes nearly fifty years later in Florence. For although she loved her autocratic father and that shadowy invalid figure her mother, it was to Bro that little

Elizabeth Moulton-Barrett's heart was wholly given.

She was often afterwards to think of those serene days of her childhood,

> When summer nights send sleep down with the dew.

She was still quite a young girl when she wrote those charming *Verses to my Brother*, with its quotation from *Lycidas*: " For we were nursed upon the self-same hill."

> I may not praise thee *here*—I will not bless !
> Yet all thy goodness doth my memory bear,
> Cherished by more than Friendship's tenderness—
> And in the silence of my evening prayer
> Thou shalt not be forgot—thy dear name shall be there !

I think there must have been days when she could neither bear to read nor to think of that tender tribute with its crowding, poignant memories —days when she gazed across that treacherously calm sea at Torquay for a boat that never returned.

2

Born at Coxhoe Hall near Durham, the residence of her uncle Mr. Samuel Barrett, in March 1806, Elizabeth was the eldest child of Edward Moulton, afterwards Edward Moulton-Barrett. She was christened two years later at the same time as her brother Edward, receiving the names of Elizabeth Barrett. The family moved to Hope End, Herefordshire, during the following year, shortly after the birth of the second daughter and third child, Henrietta. Although then only about twenty-two years of age, Edward Moulton was thus the father of three children. He had married very young—before twenty, it is said. His wife who was five years his senior, was Mary, the daughter of John Graham Clarke of Fenham Hall, Newcastle-on-Tyne. Although he was still little more than a boy in years, Edward Moulton's life had not been devoid of adventure and experience. Born in the West Indies about the year 1787, he had lost his father while quite a child and was sent to England in the care of Mr. Scarlett, afterwards Lord Abinger. Educated at Harrow, he was summarily removed from thence by his mother, in consequence of a savage punishment having been administered to him by the older boy for whom he was fagging, his crime being the peculiarly heinous one of burning the toast. The culprit was expelled. Young Moulton proceeded to Cambridge at the age of sixteen, and left there a few years later to be married.

It may have been this premature introduction to wedded life, with its consequent heavy cares and responsibilities, that imbued him with that curious anti-matrimonial complex, which was to evince itself in later years with such incredible violence when any of his children wished to marry. But while they were little he seems to have been an unusually indulgent, generous, sympathetic father, sharing in the children's games and not revealing himself as more harsh and tyrannical than it behoved fathers to be in the benighted early years of the nineteenth century. And he had a marked pre-dilection for his eldest child, the vivacious, charming, intelligent little Elizabeth.

3

The house at Hope End had been built upon the site of a much earlier one, which had, however, failed to satisfy the architectural dreams of its new purchaser, the wealthy West Indian plantation-owner, Edward Moulton. The new domain which he caused to be erected, with its domes and minarets, its flamboyant, bizarre, neo-Oriental splendour, must have startled the quiet countryside, so rich in lovely examples of Elizabethan and Jacobean homes. But taste was passing through one of its uncomfortable transition periods. There was a reaction from the delicate if sober stonework of Tudor and Jacobean days, as well as from the palatial solidities of Vanbrugh, whose houses in their echoing immensity seemed to resemble small towns rather than private residences. And there was a tendency towards something less austere, more Oriental and pagoda-like, a desire for something more eccentric, perhaps even more defiant. For had not that period of architectural restlessness produced the strange irrelevant structure, the Pavilion at Brighton, with its queer little domes and turrets and Oriental decorations and mouldings, intended as a pleasure-house for that emphatic pleasure-lover, the First Gentleman in Europe? It was an age to which Oriental architecture especially appealed, although it was perhaps less out of place at Brighton than in the dignified seclusion of the Malvern Hills.

The life at Hope End could never have been at all gay. Mrs. Moulton-Barrett was a delicate, fretful woman, whose married life was almost wholly spent in the bearing and rearing of her many children, ten of whom lived to maturity. Ba and Bro and Henrietta were in due course succeeded by Arabel, Charles (generally known as Stormie), Samuel, George, Henry, Alfred (known as Daisy), Septimus and Octavius.[1] Septimus, or Sette, was a great favourite with his father as a child, his cheerful prattle amused him. George was perhaps the most industrious, ambitious and gifted; he was called to the Bar and was not without a sense of his own importance. The others used to laugh at him sometimes, Elizabeth confessed, for his gravity and absorption in his profession, although they learned to rely on his wisdom and judgment.

They mingled little with the outside world, and indeed they formed a not too small world of their own. Still, there were the Martins at Colwall who remained life-long friends and to whom some of Elizabeth's most intimate and revealing letters

---

[1] A fourth daughter, Mary, died at Hope End at the age of four.

were addressed. And at Great Malvern there was Hugh Boyd, the blind scholar, to whom Elizabeth owed so much of her early love for and knowledge of the classics, and to whom alone she confided the fact of her engagement in 1846. But the children were left a good deal to their own resources for amusement.

It is greatly to Mr. Moulton-Barrett's credit that he early detected the genius of his eldest child. She had no bitter apprenticeship to serve, no family opposition to combat in her self-chosen career. From the first her poetic gift was recognised and encouraged, while her insatiable appetite for learning was duly gratified, at an epoch too when the education of women was commonly of little moment. The one dissentient voice was that of her grandmother, who was fond of visiting Hope End, and not averse to uttering frank criticisms of her numerous descendants. She had been known to remark that she would prefer to see a greater proficiency in hemming on Elizabeth's part than to hear of " all this Greek."

Still steeped in Greek she was, sharing Edward's tutor, and reading Pope's Homer with avidity. Her epic poem the *Battle of Marathon* was written when she was only thirteen, but even then hers was no 'prentice hand, since she had written poetry from the time she was eight.

Mr. Moulton-Barrett (he had added his mother's name of Barrett to his own when he succeeded to his maternal uncle's estates at Cinnamon Hill, Jamaica) was so proud of this performance that he had fifty copies of the poem printed, distributing them among his friends, because, as Elizabeth said, he was bent on spoiling her. In return she dedicated it to him, " as a small testimony of the gratitude of his child, Elizabeth B. Barrett."

The preface, despite its stilted phraseology, is in itself a remarkable composition for a girl of thirteen. She admitted that she had chosen Pope as her model rather than Milton, nor did she apologise for having thus frankly made use of a model. " It would have been both absurd and presumptuous, young and inexperienced as I am, to have attempted to strike a path for myself and to have wandered among the varied windings of Parnassus without a guide to direct my steps or to warn me from those fatal quicksands of literary blunders in which, with even the best guide, I find myself so frequently immersed. There is no humility but rather folly in taking inferiority for a model, and there is no vanity but rather wisdom in following humbly the footsteps of perfection."

This precocious entrance into the world of letters gives Elizabeth a claim to be considered as the contemporary of Keats, Shelley, Byron and Wordsworth, just as later she was to be the contemporary of Tennyson, Browning and the other stars of the Victorian era.

4

Elizabeth had her own little room at Hope End, a small green bower with green carpet and curtains. The hangings of her bed were also green. Honeysuckle and roses clustered on the walls outside and tossed their fragrant blossoms across her window-pane. She looked out on to the garden and across the garden to the park, while the blue profiles of the Malvern Hills rose in the distance against the sky. All of her remembered childhood was passed at Hope End, and it was there she acquired her intimate knowledge of pastoral England, its flowers and trees, its woods and streams and blossoming orchards and meadows. She painted that scenery with an almost poignant accuracy in *The Lost Bower*.

> For you hearken on your right hand,
> How the birds do leap and call
> In the greenwood, out of sight, and
> Out of reach and fear of all ;
> And the squirrels crack the filberts through
>   their cheerful madrigal.

On your left, the sheep are cropping
The slant grass and daisies pale,
And five apple-trees stand dropping
Separate shadows toward the vale,
Over which, in choral silence, the hills look
    you their ' All hail ! '

Far out, kindled by each other,
Shining hills on hills arise,
Close as brother leans to brother
When they press beneath the eyes
Of some father praying blessings from the
    gifts of paradise.

While beyond, above them mounted,
And above the woods also,
Malvern hills, for mountains counted
Not unduly, loom a-row—
Keepers of Piers Plowman's visions through the
    sunshine and the snow.

She remembered too and wrote of the " summer-snow of apple-blossoms running up from glade to glade " ; the little wood, green with hazels, where the sheep had left tufts of their wool on the thorns and brambles ; the open spaces carpeted with grass and moss and the " bluebell's purple presence " ; and, above all, the tall linden-tree with an old hawthorn growing beside it where the ivy climbing from one to the other had made her that bower she still recalled with aching nostalgia from her grey prison in Wimpole Street. The " golden-hearted daisies," the " wind-bells swinging slowly their mute curfews in the dew," came back to her mind like the evocation of some lost treasure as she lay on that couch counting, as she tells us, her memories.

In those early and happy days at Hope End she played and studied with Edward, wrote her poetry, rambled among the hills, rode her pony fearlessly and lived a simple, natural life. Her earnest wish was to please her father who took such delight in her childish poems.

> . . . 'Neath thy gentleness of praise,
> My Father, rose my early lays !
> And when the lyre was scarce awake
> I loved its strings for *thy* loved sake :
> Wooed the kind Muses—but the while
> Thought only how to win thy smile.

Thus, despite all later happenings and the perversity of temper that grew upon him with advancing years, there is abundant evidence to show that Mr. Moulton-Barrett was a kind and indulgent parent to his gifted child. He was a rich man in those days, and could afford to give his children all that wealth could procure. He showed himself especially solicitous for their education, and watched with pride the precocious development of his eldest daughter.

At ten years old Elizabeth wrote tragedies in French and English which the children acted in the nursery. The most important of these was a French hexameter tragedy on the subject of Regulus. But her mind ran on the Greek gods and goddesses, and she went out one day with a bundle of twigs in her little pinafore and a match borrowed from the housemaid, to sacrifice to Minerva, her favourite goddess. She had pretty much the run of the library, though Gibbon's *Decline and Fall* was forbidden as not being " proper," and *Tom Jones* was also on the banned side of the shelves. But among the unforbidden treasures Elizabeth found and read Paine's *Age of Reason*, Voltaire's *Philosophical Dictionary* and Hume's *Essays*, besides Werther, Rousseau and Mary Wollstonecraft—books her father probably never suspected her of reading, and which certainly formed strange mental fare for an imaginative, sensitive child.

She loved animals and kept weird pets, as many less gifted children have done. She liked the little leaping frogs, though she was terribly afraid of the old toad that lived in the hollow of an ancient thorn-tree. And she was afraid too of the bats, of which there were a great many at Hope End, flying into the rooms, " silent, cold, clinging, gliding," never waving their wings. On the other hand, she fed the bluebottle flies and hated their predatory enemies, the spiders. She learned at Hope End to dread thunder, it mattered little to her whether it was on the left or not. Herefordshire has always been known for the violence of its storms, breaking over the Malvern Hills that were only four miles distant from her home. That Turkish house, with its minarets and domes and metal spires, seemed especially built to attract the lightning. Once, in the midst of an unusually violent storm, there was a tremendous crash, and they all believed that the house had at last been struck. Elizabeth was gazing out of window at the time and witnessed the appalling sight of a tree being struck by lightning. " The bark rent from the top to the bottom . . . torn into long ribbons by the dreadful fiery hands and dashed out into the air, over the heads of other trees, or left twisted in their branches—torn into shreds in a moment as a flower might be by a child." The trunk of the tree stood there bare and gleaming, its strange new pallor marked by the crimson track of the lightning that had killed it. Its branches were untouched, and a few hours later birds were singing among the leaves. But there was a more tragic side to the story. Two girls who were picnicking on the hills were killed by lightning only a few miles away. On their breasts there was a little tell-tale mark, not rose-red as upon the tree, but black as charred wood. Elizabeth never in after years lost her fear of a thunderstorm, although her father often scolded her for it and called it disgraceful in anyone who had ever learned the alphabet. She thought of that tree ripped and scarred by the fierce electric fingers, and of the two young girls lying out on the Malvern Hills with the black seal of the lightning upon their breasts. Her terror was thus less unreasonable than her father supposed. . . .

5

Up to the age of fifteen Elizabeth seems to have enjoyed normal health, to which no doubt the good country air and regular simple life contributed. She was very fond of riding, and would catch her black pony, Moses, in the field and saddle him herself. She was about fifteen when she met with the accident that injured her spine and led eventually to those years of ill-health that condemned her to an invalid's couch in a darkened chamber. There are various versions of the accident. Some allege that she overbalanced herself while lifting the saddle on to the pony's back and, falling, injured her head and spine. Others affirm that she strained herself while tightening the girths, but in any case the disaster occurred, and its gravity unfortunately was not immediately recognised. It probably accounted too for her low stature ; she remained from that time physically small and frail.

Debarred from the walks and rides, the old games and amusements, Elizabeth turned her attention to literature with ever-increasing absorption. She read and studied and wrote, and when she was twenty her ambitious *Essay on Mind* was published.

Two years later, on October 1st, 1828, Mrs. Moulton-Barrett died after a long illness. Winter had set in early ; there had been a fall of snow accompanied by a biting wind, and the rigorous weather probably hastened her end. Elizabeth found herself at the head of her father's house, although as she had little liking for housekeeping she relinquished that duty to Henrietta.

Mr. Moulton-Barrett bore his loss with a stoical fortitude. But he became morose and unsociable, never even visiting his old friends the Martins. He ceased to attend the meetings of those religious societies in Ledbury which hitherto he had always so assiduously and punctually patronised. He seemed to shrink from contact with the outside world. He made, however, a pet of little Sette, who always slept in his room.

He had other anxieties on his mind, for he was threatened with the loss of the greater part of his income should the proposed emancipation of the West Indian negroes become law. Perhaps the Turkish house with its weird domes and minarets, that looked so strange amid the quiet Herefordshire scenery, would have to be given up. The proud, austere, reticent man never spoke of these things even to his children, but they saw the ominous change in him, and wondered what fresh calamity awaited them.

The passing of their mother at the comparatively early age of forty-eight made little difference to the lives of these children. Mrs. Moulton-Barrett scarcely comes to life at all in the biographies of her eldest daughter. She remains a shadowy figure—as shadowy as Mrs. Brontë, when she left Haworth Parsonage for her tomb in Haworth church. And like Mrs. Brontë she never knew that she was the mother of an immortal, whose poems were destined to be read and loved as long as English literature survives. She could not foresee that the childish scribblings of Elizabeth were but the prelude to the famous *Sonnets from the Portuguese*, nor that the dreamy, fanciful, delicate girl was to win in the future an undying fame. . . .

Elizabeth felt from that time a new strange responsibility towards her father. She was aware that she loved him better than did his other children ; she knew too that she was closest to him of them all. She had not forgotten his kindness, his never-failing encouragement, his eagerness to bestow upon her that intellectual equipment and training which were to prove such valuable assets to her during her long life as an invalid. And if at the same time she became aware of an increased tendency to exert a harsh authority, a certain perversity in the ruling of his children, she was still too young to resent these untoward complexes. She could not as yet foresee the day when his very step upon the stairs was to bring terror to her heart. . . .

CHAPTER II

I

By most of his daughter's critics Mr. Barrett
has been somewhat erroneously stigmatised as
" Victorian." In reality he was nothing of the
kind, for he belonged to a far earlier epoch. Born
in the reign of George III, his marriage took place
during the lifetime of that monarch, and his youngest
child was born before William IV came to the throne.
No one therefore was less Victorian than he. He
belongs far more to the age of the Fairchild family,
when children were subjected to almost inhuman
chastisements, and lived in a state of continual
rebuke and repression. His despotic temperament
was no doubt hereditary. His own grandfather,
with fifty thousand a year, lived in a patriarchal
manner at Cinnamon Hill, Jamaica, boasting of
his patched garments and ruling his innumerable
slaves in autocratic fashion. His great-grandfather
flogged his slaves " like a divinity," and by them
seems to have been regarded as such. There is
no evidence that Edward Barrett flogged his children,
but in his own boyhood he had seen for himself
how slaves were treated, and his children were all
far too much afraid of him not to have felt the force
of his hand.

For four years after the death of his wife he
continued to live at Hope End, but in 1832, probably
in anticipation of the abolition of colonial slavery
and the consequent serious loss of income to himself,
he sold the great eccentric Turkish house (which

has long since been demolished), and removed with his family to Sidmouth. In the following year the emancipation of the slaves became law.

Elizabeth, although with her liberal ideas she was enchanted at the abolition of slavery, felt the change keenly. Her last days at Hope End were very sorrowful ones. She was never again to return to those scenes, nor to see except in her dreams the blue profiles of the Malvern Hills, of which she was afterwards to write :

" Beautiful hills they are ! And yet not for the whole world's beauty would I stand in the sunshine and the shadow of them any more. It would be mockery, like the taking back of a broken flower to its stalk."

Her sadness was so great at leaving her old home that perhaps she had some premonition that she would never see it again.

Even to her dear friend Mrs. Martin she was unable to dwell upon the pain of those first hours of her journey to Devonshire. She was in charge of the others, only Edward and little Sette having been left behind to keep their father company. It had been arranged that the child should accompany the others, but at the last moment his father felt unable to part from him. He asked him whether he wished very much to go with his brothers and sisters, and Sette, who obviously would greatly have preferred to do so, replied with a child's quick unconscious tact : " Oh no, Papa, I would much rather stay with you ! "

The young Barretts slept at Bath on the first stage of their journey to Sidmouth. The bleak Cotswold scenery, the fields intersected with low stone walls, struck Elizabeth as hideous after the beauties of Herefordshire. Bath was, however, admitted to be a beautiful town as a town, and the part of Devonshire through which they subsequently travelled was pretty in comparison with Somerset.

Still, she was hardly in the mood to be appreciative, for her thoughts were full of the home she had left, and she was unhappy and depressed, although characteristically she allowed nothing of her personal feelings to escape her. She knew too that her father had felt most keenly the hard necessity which had compelled him to dispose of their home of twenty years, and she had not wished to add to his pain. She was just a little surprised that he should have played cricket with his sons on their last evening at Hope End. . . .

They arrived at Sidmouth at dusk, amid scenes of indescribable confusion, for they were immediately besieged by a crowd of tradespeople who followed, them to their new quarters for the ostensible purpose of unloading the carriage. There was no one in the house, which was pleasant and comfortable, although rather dilapidated. It had formerly been occupied by the Grand Duchess Helena. Its windows faced the sea in front and looked out upon pleasant hills and trees at the back. The town of Sidmouth failed at first to make a favourable impression upon the eldest Miss Barrett ; she described it as " not superfluously clean." But she ended by liking it very much. Its beautiful situation entranced her. The garden was full of myrtles, hydrangeas and verbena. The soft Devonshire air revived her and made her sleep more soundly than she had done for a long time. Soon she was able to ride a donkey down to the sea ; to go out in a boat. All her life she needed a warm climate. She came of a family that for generations had lived and flourished beneath the burning rays of a tropical sun.

A few weeks later Mr. Barrett, accompanied by Bro and Sette, arrived at Sidmouth. He was in good spirits and was delighted with the place. People who had connections in the West Indies called upon them. Their life was far less secluded than it had been at Hope End, for here in Sidmouth they were surrounded by friendly neighbours, among whom was that well-known figure, their cousin, Mr. John Kenyon.

Elizabeth, perhaps more than the rest, felt the charm of Devonshire, its shady lanes, its thatched cottages, the tracts of heather, the glimpses of blue sea, the rosy cliffs dipping down to the waves. Her health improved wonderfully ; she lost her cough, and acknowledged that she felt stronger. Books were obtainable from the library, and she read Bulwer's novels, Mrs. Trollope's " libels " and many others. She was delighted with Bulwer, though her exalted opinion of him was one that later generations have failed to endorse. " He has all the dramatic talent which Scott has, and all the passion which Scott has not."

Rowing on the sea was a favourite pastime with the young Barretts in fine weather ; they went on one occasion as far as Dawlish. The younger boys were fond of shrimping. Between the fishing and the boating, they managed to get wet three times a day, and nobody seemed any the worse for it. Except for an epidemic of influenza during the following winter they all enjoyed excellent health. Arabel, Henrietta and Daisy (Alfred) were the chief sufferers during the outbreak of influenza ; Elizabeth escaped more lightly, and her health continued to show a marked improvement.

Her description of their life at Sidmouth definitely shows that these high-spirited and energetic children had ample liberty and little restraint or repression. While the younger ones fished and boated and shrimped, Elizabeth found leisure to continue the work that always came first with her. During those first weeks at Sidmouth she completed her translation of the *Prometheus Bound* of Æschylus in twelve days. Published in the following spring, it received two sentences of contemptuous notice in the June number of the *Athenæum*, in which she was held up as a warning to those who might be tempted to translate that Greek poet. She was so dissatisfied with it herself, afterwards that she endeavoured to withdraw it from circulation, and many years later she published a revised version of it.

While they were at Sidmouth they became acquainted with a Miss Katherine Cockell, an invalid, who lived at Livonia Cottage about a mile from the town. She sent word begging Elizabeth to go and see her. It was to her that Miss Barrett said she would refuse to know anyone, man, woman, or child, whom she was likely to love and be loved by intensely. " Oh," said Miss Cockell, " is it possible you can say so ? I would walk like a pilgrim to the end of the world to find one who would love me and whom I could love ! " Elizabeth, astonished, recognised in this the " true feeling, generous and worthy of love." But she had been warned once by her devoted uncle never to love, for if she ever loved anyone it would be with nothing less than her whole self, a prognostication which was to be literally fulfilled. Perhaps, too, she was aware of that capacity for loving within herself, and shrank from putting it to the test.

2

Mr. Barrett grew restless at Sidmouth. The occupations and amusements that appealed to his children were less suited to a man who was approaching his forty-sixth year. Moreover, he saw the impracticability of remaining much longer in their present abode, since the house evinced unmistakable signs of disintegration. During a storm the wind blew the tiles from the roof while the Barrett family were at dinner, and when the workmen came to repair the damage they found it necessary to remove a chimney which threatened to collapse. They further entreated the inhabitants not to lean too much out of the windows lest the walls should give way. And as it was not an easy matter to discover a house in Sidmouth sufficiently spacious to shelter his large family, Mr. Barrett began to contemplate departure.

Now that the famous Anti-slavery Bill had become law he was much less wealthy, and he was wont to declare that no sane person would henceforth dream of planting sugar in Jamaica. The consternation among their West Indian friends was naturally very great ; they saw ruin staring them in the face.

Edward Barrett, the eldest son, and heir after his father's death to the property at Cinnamon Hill, had now gone to Jamaica to study the new conditions and look after the estates. Stormie, the second son, and George, were now at Glasgow University and doing well there. With these absentees it was no longer necessary to rent so large a house, and in the following year—1834—they moved to a thatched cottage in Sidmouth.

In October Mr. Barrett went to London on business and while there was laid up with a sharp attack of rheumatism. A family council was held at Sidmouth, and with many misgivings as to the results of so bold and unprecedented a step they decided to send Henry—then the eldest son at home—to his father's assistance. Initiative on the part of his children was a thing that Mr. Barrett severely discouraged, and they lived in fear and trembling for the news of their brother's reception. Mr. Barrett, however, appears to have shown no displeasure on this occasion—perhaps he was too ill to do so—but when Elizabeth begged to be allowed to follow her brother and go and nurse him, he emphatically refused his consent.

She therefore remained at home, and with the help of Henrietta and Arabel looked after their three youngest brothers, Alfred, Sette and Octavius. Samuel had by this time faded out of the picture, probably he had died before they left Hope End.

Despite her visits to relations at Torquay and her drawing and sketching lessons with Arabel while she was at home, Henrietta Barrett was far less contented at Sidmouth than her elder sister,

who had learned to love the " nest among elms,"
as she called the cottage.

In the following spring George Barrett took
his degree at Glasgow, his subjects being Latin and
Greek, Logic and Moral Philosophy. The examination
was held in public, and so brilliant were his answers
that they elicited applause from the onlookers.
Stormie, who stammered, shrank from the *viva voce*
ordeal, although it was believed he could have
acquitted himself with equal credit.

It must be remarked that Mr. Barrett was quite
exceptionally fortunate in his children. Beyond
the dreadful fact that three of them ventured to
commit matrimony during his lifetime, not one of
his many sons and daughters appears ever by their
conduct to have given him an hour's anxiety. It
may safely be said that few families, owning in their
midst a great celebrity, could have emerged so
triumphantly unscathed from the searching scrutiny
to which, during the last sixty years, theirs has been
so relentlessly exposed. Not a shadow of a skeleton
has been unearthed. The ten Moulton-Barretts
have come through the ordeal with flying colours.

Suddenly the news reached them that Mr. Barrett
had taken a furnished house at 74 Gloucester
Place, and he now bade his family join him
in London. They remained there for three
years, from 1835 to 1838, when they finally took
up their abode at 50 Wimpole Street, which has
ever since been associated with Elizabeth's name
and with the story of one of the most wonderful
love-affairs the world has ever seen.

It was winter when they reached London, and
the city was wrapped in a thick yellow curtain of
fog. Elizabeth's health, which had improved so
conspicuously at Sidmouth, broke down before
this untoward change. Something of bitterness
escaped her in a letter to Mrs. Martin. Half her
soul, she confessed, seemed to have been left behind
on the sea-shore at Sidmouth; she loved it more
than ever now that she had been compelled to leave

it. But perhaps in time she would grow accustomed to her dungeon and begin to find amusement in the spiders. . . .

3

There were, however, compensations. She formed fresh friendships and renewed others, of which the most intimate was with her father's cousin and old school-fellow, John Kenyon, who was to play such a prominent part later on in bringing herself and Robert Browning together. But there was no thought of love or marriage in Elizabeth's mind just then. She was twenty-nine years of age, and with her slight, small form looked even less, but she was practically an invalid.

It was difficult for her to breathe in the damp, foggy air ; she coughed continually, sometimes she spat a little blood. But she was not idle. She wrote several poems and sent them to magazines. In July of that year—1836—the *Romaunt of Margret* was published in Colburn's New Monthly, and in the following October the *Poet's Vow* appeared. Her name was beginning to be known. The poems, especially the *Romaunt of Margret*, possessed an unusual quality that attracted attention.

Mr. Barrett's principal object in settling in London was to provide careers for his sons. George was to be called to the Bar, where it was prophesied he would have a brilliant future.

Later in the year Edward returned from Jamaica, to Elizabeth's great joy. Despite the separation which had lasted some years they were as close and intimate as ever. There was a tenderness in his demeanour towards her which perhaps the others lacked, though they were never wanting in kindness to their delicate sister until she took the almost incredibly courageous step of leaving home ten years later.

Edward joined them in Gloucester Place, but this house, like the one at Sidmouth, also showed alarming signs of disintegration. He and Elizabeth were discussing shipwrecks one day during a violent storm, when a chimney crashed through the skylight into the hall. The bricks smashed the stone stairs, so fierce was the impact, and twenty-four panes of glass were shattered. Elizabeth confessed that she was terrified out of all propriety. " Bro " had a narrow escape, for he had been on the stairs only a few moments before. A housemaid was actually ascending them when, chancing to look up, she saw the nodding chimneys and rushed for shelter into the drawing-room. She escaped except for a trifling injury to one hand caused by a falling brick.

Mr. Barrett, who had long been in treaty for an unfurnished house in Wimpole Street, began to see that a removal from their present abode was clearly indicated. After his two recent experiences of unsafe houses and peripatetic chimneys he must have taken pains to ascertain that No. 50 Wimpole Street was in good structural condition. Elizabeth, although she longed to have her own furniture and books about her again, disliked the gloomy look of Wimpole Street, the walls of which resembled " Newgates turned inside out." Nothing was, however, decided, and they did not finally move to Wimpole Street until 1838, when Elizabeth was thirty-two years old.

4

Her health had improved, and her new friend Miss Mitford, who had already attained to literary fame, took her to see Wordsworth at Chiswick. It was like a dream to her. Wordsworth's manners were simple, his conversation not—to use her own word—prominent ; she contrasted him with the brilliant Landor whom she saw at the same time, little foreseeing the trouble that old gentleman was to prove to her and her husband much later on in Florence. Still, there was something a little . . . disappointing . . . about Wordsworth. She would never have singled him out as a great man. "His eyes have more meekness than brilliancy." She confessed, however, that she trembled in soul and body when she spoke to him. The great man, who did not look like a great man, was very kind to her. He talked to her for some time, and recited a translation by Cary of some of Dante's sonnets by way of amusing her. Landor, on the other hand, intrigued her. He talked brilliantly and " prominently," thereby arousing the anger of Edward, who considered that he had displayed an " ambitious singularity and affectation."

Elizabeth thoroughly enjoyed her evening. " I never walked in the skies before and perhaps never shall again when so many stars are out," she wrote to her friend Mrs. Martin, then the recipient of some of her most charming letters. And perhaps those stars that to her seemed so brilliant were not unaware of this new planet in the sky who arrived chaperoned by Miss Mitford and " Bro." Elizabeth is said to have looked charming that night with her pale face, her shower of dark curls, her great deep eyes fringed by the long lashes, and her quick bright smile. Her aspect was indeed so youthful that Miss Mitford had some difficulty in persuading the friend who drove them down to Chiswick that this woman who had passed her thirtieth year was old enough to go to a party !

Elizabeth was always daintily and fashionably dressed, as were her sisters. The choosing of a new bonnet was a serious business not to be lightly undertaken. Yet she was never extravagant, for she told Robert Browning in the days of their secret engagement that she had never spent more than twenty pounds a year on her clothes.

She now studied German with her two brothers, Edward and Henry. Arabel, who had learned to draw at Sidmouth, took up painting in oils. Henrietta, the sociable and admired member of the family, was often away from home paying visits. It must have been about this time that she first contemplated marriage. But when she approached her father on the subject there was a scene which was as incredible as it was devastating. She was the first of his children to discover that lamentable complex which made marriage in his eyes an unforgivable offence. She was flung with violence to the ground, her knees being made to ring on the floor. Elizabeth, who tried to accompany her hysterical sister from the room, was so overcome herself that she fell down in a dead faint. And Henrietta renounced her lover as a child might give up a holiday. But the episode provided a useful lesson to the other members of the family. They were no longer in any doubt as to how similar intentions on their own part would be received. What had been said with such vehement anger to Henrietta would be said to them all. And supposing that Edward or George or even Elizabeth . . . ?

After their removal to Wimpole Street, Elizabeth's health broke down once more. She ruptured a blood-vessel in the lungs and became an almost complete invalid. But from her prison in that gloomy street she put forth a new book of verse that May—*The Seraphim and other Poems*. It was, on the whole, favourably received.

In the autumn of 1838 it was apparent to all that she would never survive another winter in London. Remembering the beneficial effect Devonshire had had upon her health, Mr. Barrett arranged for her to go to Torquay, where they had relations—an uncle and aunt—living at that time. Edward accompanied her, and she was visited too by her sisters. Sometimes her father went down to see her, looking very well and " astonishing every one with his eternal youthfulness." While at Torquay Edward developed a passion for sketching in water-colours. He made many friends among the young men of his own age in the place. Despite her illness, her appalling physical weakness, and the fact that for months she was unable to leave her bed, Elizabeth was not unhappy. She had Edward with her, and he was dearer to her than anyone else in the world.

Meantime George was called to the Bar at the Inner Temple. Perhaps it was this fact that made Mr. Barrett uneasy on the score of leaving Edward so long in idleness at Torquay. He did not, however, suggest his leaving the place to take up work in London just then, because Elizabeth was so very ill all through the autumn and winter of 1839—1840. Her weakness was now very alarming. When lifted from her bed to the sofa she frequently fainted. The slight hæmorrhage from the lungs still continued, and she was blistered every few days.

But she still had strength to write to her friends, to Mrs. Martin at Malvern, to John Kenyon and Hugh Boyd in London, to Miss Mitford in her Berkshire home. In November 1839, she was very anxious to know what Hugh Boyd thought of Prince Albert, whose engagement to Queen Victoria had just taken place.

The most the physicians could hope for was that she might recover her strength sufficiently to go about in comfort and independence, although it was unlikely that she would ever be fit for anything like exertion. And in the meantime there seemed no possibility of her leaving her bed. She lay there, never completely idle, for the urge to write poetry was always too strong within her, and she wove many ambitious schemes for work that was still to be accomplished. Yet to look at her frail and wasted form, the great eyes shining like dark stars from the pallid whiteness of her face, one would have supposed that the fragile body, already diseased with phthisis, had little to look forward to but the grave.

CHAPTER III

I

ELIZABETH seems to have survived that winter as if by a miracle. The doctors feared the worst for her, but with the warmer weather she began to revive. The improvement was so marked that Mr. Barrett regarded it as an opportune moment to warn Edward that, now his sister was so much better, he could not permit him to remain in idleness at Torquay any longer.

Elizabeth was weakened by illness, and at this decision she broke down completely both in health and spirits. She wept, and her aunt comforted her, assuring her that she would not allow her to be grieved. With singular temerity this lady thereupon wrote to Mr. Barrett, telling him that it would break Elizabeth's heart if Edward were to be taken away from her. "As if hearts were broken *so*! I have thought bitterly since that my heart did not break for a good deal more than that. . . ."

With a rare and, as it proved, fatal leniency, Mr. Barrett rescinded his decision. He wrote, however, saying that though in such circumstances he did not refuse to suspend his judgment, he considered it to be "*very wrong* in Elizabeth to exact such a thing."

The doctors also declared they would not answer for her life if she were in any way agitated, and for the moment there was no further talk of a separation. Edward, too, holding his sister's hand, assured her that he loved her better than them all, and that he would not leave her till she was well.

A few days later, on July 11th, 1840, Edward, accompanied by two of his friends, went out for a sail in a boat, *La Belle Sauvage*. His companions were Charles Vanneck, who was only twenty-one, and Captain Carlyle Clarke. When night came they did not return, and it was impossible to hide the sinister fact from Elizabeth. Her anguish during the days that followed can only be compared to that of Mary Shelley when her husband's boat failed to return to Lerici. In vain did her sisters try to reassure her. There was really no danger . . . absolutely no wind was blowing . . . the sea was beautifully calm. They had gone out of their course and would soon return. But to Elizabeth the bright sunshine, the calm sea, were treacherous things that mocked her. The other boats came back, but not her one. She could have said with a later poet :

Never for me that sail on the sea-line. . . .

There was a rumour that a boat similar to *La Belle Sauvage* had been seen to founder in Babbacombe Bay, but nothing definite was known until a week later, when Captain Clarke's body was washed ashore. He was not in the least disfigured, and the buttonhole he had worn was still in his coat. After that there could be no reasonable doubt as to the nature and extent of the disaster, although it was not until August 4th, more than three weeks later, that Edward's body was found off Torbay. It is believed that Charles Vanneck's body was never recovered at all.

And Elizabeth ? Five years later, when she was trying to give some account of it to Robert Browning, she quoted those lines from his own poem *Gismond* :

What says the body when they spring
Some monstrous torture-engine's whole
Strength on it ? No more says the soul.

C

Never had Browning written anything that lived with her more than that. It was such a dreadful truth. For in those weeks that followed the disaster, she lay there unable to speak or shed a tear, half-conscious, half-unconscious, her mind weak and wandering, " too near to God under the crushing of His hand to pray at all." Yet they were all very gentle and forbearing. Even her father never by word or look reproached her. No one apparently had the courage to say to her : " You have done this," or, " If he had not been here. . . ." So deep was her measure of self-reproach that she was grateful for this extraordinary clemency. . . .

The shock very nearly killed her. For the remainder of her life, the loss of this beloved brother, who was " above us all, better than us all, kindest and noblest and dearest to me," was an abiding grief to her. There were even moments when she shrank from bestowing any of her love upon Robert Browning, because it seemed in a sense an act of disloyalty, almost of treachery, to the dead. . . .

" It was a heavy blow (may God keep you from such !) " she wrote later to Horne, whom she had never seen, but with whom she had for some time past kept up a literary correspondence. " I knew you would be sorry for me when you heard. It was a heavy blow for all of us, and I being weak, you see, was struck down as by a bodily blow in a moment, without having time for tears. I did not think indeed to be better any more, but I have quite rallied now—except as to strength, and they say that on essential points I shall not suffer permanently, and this is a comfort to poor Papa."

In time she was able to find consolation in the thought that she would have made any sacrifice, died any death, for Edward. The love that had existed between them ever since they had played together in the garden at Hope End, had only grown deeper and more devoted with the lapse of years and despite the test of protracted separation. She could remember, too, that once when Edward had wished to marry, and was unable to do so because he was completely dependent upon his father—who would never have countenanced such a step—she had wished to endow him with all the money that had been left her by the uncle, who had once told her to her dismay that he loved her better than her father did. She found, however, it was impossible for her to transfer the money to her brother— perhaps, indeed, it had been left in trust for any children that might be born to her—but she would gladly have given every penny of it to " Bro."

In her poem *De Profundis,* which was not published until long after her marriage, she was able to show how a sense of real resignation to the Will of God had gradually come to her.

> Whatever's lost, it first was won ;
> We will not struggle nor impugn.
> Perhaps the cup was broken here,
> That heaven's new wine might show more clear.
> I praise Thee while my days go on.
>
> I praise Thee while my days go on ;
> I love Thee while my days go on ;
> Through dark and dearth, through fire and frost,
> With emptied arms and treasure lost,
> I thank Thee while my days go on.

But for years she was able to bear no reference to the tragedy, and when Miss Mitford, with an astonishing lack of discretion considering their long intimacy, published some details of it in her *Reminiscences,* Elizabeth could not bring herself to read it nor even to glance at the reviews lest there should be any mention of it. This was twelve years later, when she was spending the winter with her husband in Paris. She wrote thus to Miss Mitford :—

" Now let me tell you the truth. It will prove

how hard it is for the tenderest friends to help paining
one another, since *you* have pained *me*. See what
a deep wound I must have in me to be pained
by such a hand. Oh, I am morbid I very well
know. . . . You cannot understand ; no, you cannot
understand with all your wide sympathy (perhaps
because you are not morbid and I am), the sort
of susceptibility I have upon one subject. I have
lived heart to heart (for instance) with my husband
these five years ; I have never yet spoken out in
a whisper, even, what is in me ; never yet could
bear to hear a word of reference from his lips. And
now those dreadful words are going the round of
the newspapers to be verified here, commented
on there, gossiped about everywhere, and I, for my
part, am frightened to look at a paper as a child in
the dark—as unreasonably as you will say—but what
then ? what drives us mad is our unreason."

Sensitive and susceptible as she was, it was
unlikely that she should ever fully recover from the
effects of that shattering tragedy. It was one of
those griefs that leave the heart raw and shrinking,
as exposed nerves will quiver beneath the menace
of accidental touch.

From that moment Elizabeth hated Torquay,
hated the very sound of the waves that had robbed
her of her beloved " Bro." The thought of a heaven
" where there shall be no more sea " made a significant appeal to her. A year later it was believed
that she had only a short time to live, and indeed
all wish to live had long since left her.

Then, as before, health and a measure of strength
crept back, albeit grudgingly, to this woman who
only desired death. Reviving energy imbued her
with but one wish, and that was to leave her
ghastly prison at Beacon Terrace, Torquay, made
additionally terrible to her by the moaning waves
beyond her window. In her own words she " forced
back the current of rushing recollection by work,
work, work." Yet there were still moments when

bitterness escaped her. " My spring is broken."
She became thenceforward much more of a recluse,
as some natures are apt to do after a crushing sorrow ;
she dreaded to encounter fresh faces or, indeed, any
faces save those of her own family. This unsocia-
bility grew upon her, as a habit of the kind always
does. Once formed it is extremely difficult to break
through that implicit rule of " never seeing anyone."

Elizabeth remained at Torquay for more than a
year after the death of her brother. The doctors
were even then reluctant to consent to her leaving
the place, and explained all the risks entailed with
unusual frankness. But her two urgent motives for
departure eventually prevailed. She wanted to
" rescue " herself from the dreadful associations of
Torquay, and also to return to London because she
was " breaking up poor Papa's domestic peace into
fragments by staying away from home." He would
not permit her sisters to leave her, thus the number of
faces around his table was sensibly diminished.
It was true that Stormie had returned home after
a sixty days' voyage—presumably from Jamaica—
during the winter following their bereavement, but
despite this joyous event there were vague hints in
her father's letters that all was not going smoothly
in Wimpole Street. " Something about Sette and
Occy being unknown or misknown, through the fault
of their growing," she told Mrs. Martin in a letter.
However, the doctor assured her then that if she
attempted the journey she would die on the road,
and the project was postponed until the following
summer.

In August, when she was " gasping " for leave
to go home, " Papa " suddenly disappeared into
Herefordshire, so that the journey was again deferred.
Her anxiety to return to London was now acute.
" Enough has been done and suffered for me. It
is an instinct of self-preservation which impels me
to escape—or try to escape." Yet her last letter
to Hugh Boyd just before her departure betrays a
certain nervousness as to the result of the experiment.

A patent carriage upon innumerable springs was despatched from London, and in this she performed the journey quite safely, and with as little shaking as possible, in the early days of September 1841. She returned to Wimpole Street after an absence of nearly three years, to all intents and purposes a confirmed invalid. She was greatly changed by both sickness and grief, and had aged a good deal. She who had always looked young now looked old for her thirty-five years.

She was a prisoner all through the winter that followed. She refused to receive visitors. " I can't see anyone," she wrote to Mr. Boyd, " and if I could it would be very bad for me. Part of me is worn out, but the poetical part—that is, the love of poetry—is growing in me as freshly and strongly as if it were watered every day."

And it was not only poetry that occupied her time. She contributed a series of papers on the Greek Christian Poets to the *Athenæum* of February and March 1842, and these must have been the work of that first melancholy winter in London. Mr. Dilke, who was at that time editor of the *Athenæum*, begged her to abstain as much as possible from theological discussion, and to use the names of God and Jesus Christ as little as she could.

Elizabeth Barrett never spent a single night away from Wimpole street for five years after her return from Torquay. During the winters all her worst symptoms of cough, fever and spitting of blood manifested themselves, but in the warmer weather she always revived, and was even able to go out occasionally for a drive with Arabel.

How this woman of surpassing genius, unbounded spirit, and extraordinary intellectual energy, was induced to spend five long years practically immured in a back room in Wimpole Street I do not pretend to explain. Perhaps the doctors were then less insistent upon the claims of fresh air and beneficial climate than they are now. Perhaps they believed that in any case she couldn't live very long, so it

wasn't a matter of great moment where and how she spent the remaining time allotted to her. But the fact remains as an almost inexplicable enigma.

Her brothers and sisters were very kind to her. Arabel was constant in her attentions, Henrietta less so perhaps, for she was often away from home. The young Barrett brothers visited her on their return from their various ploys every evening. Mr. Barrett, who spent all day in the City, where he was engaged in numerous financial enterprises, never failed to go up and see his daughter the last thing at night, to pray with her and bless her. And she had for a constant and faithful companion the little spaniel Flush, given to her by Miss Mitford.

You can hardly form any mental picture of Elizabeth without including Flushie, surely one of the most adorable dogs ever sent to comfort an afflicted invalid woman. It is interesting to know that he died in honoured old age at Florence, and was buried in the vaults of Casa Guidi, an end which few prophets could have ventured to foretell !

Slowly, slowly, life came back to her ; the wish to live stirred anew within her " from under the crushing foot of heavy grief." The unusually hot summer of 1842 proved of great benefit to her. It completely arrested the hæmorrhage from the lungs, which up till then had been such a frequent and disquieting symptom. This improvement did little, however, to diminish the alarming physical weakness.

Outside interests forced themselves upon her, and though she still saw only her own family and relations and such old friends as John Kenyon and Miss Mitford, she corresponded with quite a number of people whom she had never seen. For instance, Haydon submitted his portrait of Wordsworth to her, and this elicited a sonnet from her. Haydon forwarded the sonnet to Wordsworth, who was justifiably flattered, although he had the temerity to suggest a slight alteration in it. (Being a poet himself, he should have known better than to take such an unpopular step.) He, however, availed himself of the opportunity to thank her again for two copies of her poems.

Few authors accept criticism in a spirit of meekness, and Elizabeth warned Robert Browning at a very early stage of their friendship that she was not of them. Perhaps in the long run it is as well, for suggestions are only confusing, and if followed tend to ruin the spontaneity and individuality of the work. And no one would, I think, admit that Wordsworth's

> By a vision free
> And noble, Haydon, is thine art released,

is an improvement upon Miss Barrett's

> A vision free
> And noble, Haydon, hath thine art released.

Elizabeth finally altered it to please herself, though she did not substantially improve the poem, which was at best only an intellectual exercise.

> A noble vision free
> Our Haydon's hand has flung out from the mist.

2

I am sure they did all they could to relieve the tedium of Elizabeth's existence, but then she had strength for so very little, and sometimes was even too weak to receive her own brothers when they came home in the evening. She was tended by an excellent maid, Wilson—who eventually died in her son's service—an expensive servant who then received the almost unheard-of wages of sixteen pounds a year. And she had the constant companionship of Flush, to whom she wrote that tenderest

tribute ever penned to a canine friend : *To Flush :
My Dog*.

> But of *thee* it shall be said,
> This dog watched beside a bed
>   Day and night unweary,—
> Watched within a curtained room,
> Where no sunbeam brake the gloom
>   Round the sick and dreary.
>
> Roses, gathered for a vase,
> In that chamber died apace,
>   Beam and breeze resigning ;
> This dog only, waited on,
> Knowing that when light is gone
>   Love remains for shining.
>
> Other dogs in thymy dew
> Tracked the hares, and followed through
>   Sunny moor or meadow ;
> This dog only, crept and crept
> Next a languid cheek that slept,
>   Sharing in the shadow.

They were what she called " cobweb verses,
thin and light enough," but Miss Mitford declared
they were as tender and true as anything she had
written. And although Elizabeth herself did not
think highly of them she was " humbled " by Mr.
Boyd's hard criticism of her " soft rhymes about
Flush." They have, however, secured a degree of
immortality for her little spaniel that other dogs
might envy.

There was, of course, a likeness between them.
She was quite aware of it, and on one occasion, when
Mr. Horne asked for a portrait of her to reproduce
in his *New Spirit of the Age*, she drew a little
sketch of Flush at the top of her letter in which she
wrote : " Here I send you one of the Spirits of the
Age, strongly recommending it to a place on your
frontispiece. It is Flush's portrait, I need hardly
say, and only fails of being an excellent substitute
through being more worthy than I can be counted."
The little drawing was made to resemble herself.

But she laughed at the thought of his wanting to illustrate his book with her " darkness." It was true, however, that a Mrs. Carter had painted a miniature of her in the Sidmouth days, producing a portrait of a very pretty little girl with unexceptionable regularity of features, which Mr. Barrett had flung down with a contemptuous " Pshaw ! "

Elizabeth's bright, fanciful humour always emerges in her letters whenever she writes of Flush. When Mr. Barrett gave her an Æolian harp the little dog was frantically jealous of it, believing it to be alive. She used to say that he disapproved of her calling anything beautiful except his own ears. He shared her delicate meals, the cups of coffee and sponge cakes, the invalid dainties of which she could only partake so sparingly. He was jealous too of the little brown dogs he could see nestling against her in the mirror, and would tremble and bark at the unwelcome vision thus proffered. And later on he was jealous both of John Kenyon and Robert Browning ; it is indeed on record that he flew at them and bit them.

A great deal of her time during the next five years was dedicated to that wonderful correspondence which gives us so many details of her daily life. She wrote to Mrs. Martin, Miss Mitford, Mr. Boyd, Mr. Kenyon, and to Richard Hengist Horne, the author of *Orion*, from which Mr. Kenyon declared he had derived the same sort of pleasure he had received from *Endymion* and *Hyperion*. This is a criticism which few people would be prepared to endorse at the present day.

It is interesting to remember that both Elizabeth Barrett and Robert Browning—who were still unknown to each other—collaborated with Horne in his venture, *A New Spirit of the Age*.

Perhaps of all her letters at that time the most amusing and spontaneous were those addressed to Hugh Boyd. She was astonished and even annoyed, however, to discover that he believed in Ossian, and told him that Flush didn't ! . . .

3

The winter of 1842—1843, following that exceptionally hot summer, was very mild. Elizabeth's
health suffered no serious relapse, and the more
ominous symptoms of her disease ceased to manifest
themselves.

It is significant that about this time she began to
resent the harsh criticisms meted out to Robert
Browning's *Dramatic Lyrics* in England, and to his
Blot in the 'Scutcheon in America. " There is truth
on both sides, but it seems to me hard truth on
Browning. I do assure you I never saw him in
my life—do not even know him by correspondence,"
she wrote to Cornelius Mathews, the editor of an
American publication, *Graham's Magazine*, to which
she had been invited to contribute, " and yet
whether through fellow-feeling for Eleusinian
mysteries, or whether through the more generous
motive of appreciation of his powers, I am very
sensitive to the thousand and one stripes with which
the assembly of critics doth expound its vocation
over him, and the *Athenæum*, for instance, made me
feel quite cross and misanthropical last week."

She contributed in all four poems to *Graham's
Magazine*, for which she received fifty dollars.

She had an intense admiration for Browning's
poetry, though it was a far cry from Byron—who
had been her earliest literary hero—to Browning,
whom the critics accused of being wilfully obscure.
As a little girl she had even dreamed of dressing as
a boy and running away to be Byron's page. She
must have been about eighteen when she wrote her
Stanzas on his death, and spoke of " that generous
heart where genius thrilled divine."

Meanwhile, reading and writing and a voluminous
correspondence occupied her time. Mr. Kenyon
sent her a note from Browning in May 1843, just
two years before their first meeting. Elizabeth was
delighted to possess it and insisted upon keeping it.
She paid the poet a charming tribute in *Lady*

Geraldine's Courtship—published in 1844—which delighted him.

> Or from Browning some " Pomegranate," which, if cut deep
> down the middle,
> Shows a heart within blood-tinctured, of a veined humanity.

It seemed in a sense prophetic that she should have written thus about him.

Mr. Kenyon, who had also had interests in the West Indies in former days as had the Barretts and the Brownings, was a friend of them both, and thus they were aware of each other, although the moment for their fateful meeting had not yet arrived.

Elizabeth was busy that summer in transforming her bedroom into what we should now call a bed-sitting-room, that is, she was trying to make her prison look as little like a bedroom as possible. The wardrobe proved to be the only piece of furniture that could not be successfully camouflaged. The bed was of the divan kind ; the sofa and the arm-chair were placed opposite to each other, and during the daytime she always lay upon the sofa, which seems to have been Arabel's bed at night. Sette made her some shelves of papered deal and crimson merino for her books. The washing-stand was enclosed in a cabinet and crowned with some more shelves, and near the window there was a deep box filled with soil in which scarlet-runners, nasturtiums and convolvulus were beginning to spring up. She had green blinds placed in her windows, a choice against which all her family loudly protested. But probably some memory of her little green room at Hope End prompted the idea. Mr. Kenyon sent her an ivy plant which was intended to embower her window with its green leaves, but it did not flourish at first, and Mr. Barrett was wont to exclaim every morning when he visited his daughter before going down to the City: " Why, Ba, it looks worse and worse ! " Still, it eventually grew, and its leaves made a green frame for that dull back window.

She was growing used to her prison (or was she ?) and was beginning to take an interest in the spiders.

Her passion for novels was satisfied by Balzac, George Sand, and " the like immortal improprieties," although Mr. Kenyon told her that no woman ought to admit having read such books. But in this, as in many other things, Elizabeth was in advance of her times. Like Charlotte Brontë she satisfied her craving for romantic literature with French novels, and was never any the worse for it.

In the summer of 1843, George spent his holiday on the Rhine, accompanied by Stormie. They were neither of them very young, and George was a barrister of some years' standing, still Papa's permission had to be obtained. Elizabeth, who had supported the project and even pleaded for them, could not witness their departure without emotion. Her love for her own family was always of a very deep quality, and on this occasion she seems to have had some kind of superstitious fear for their safety. A letter from Ostend, however, relieved her anxiety, and she began to think less of the fatal influence of her own star. The thought of their crossing the sea that had proved so treacherous to her in the past was evidently the cause of her misgivings.

Soon, however, she was plunged into a fresh and unlooked-for tribulation. Flush was stolen by professional dog-thieves for the first, but not, as it proved, the only time. The thought of her dog's misery in strange, rough, unfriendly hands tortured her, the more so because she was too ill to take any steps towards finding him herself. The episode was kept a profound secret from Mr. Barrett for two very good reasons. The first was in order to shield the unfortunate Arabel, who had imprudently taken Flush out without a lead, from his anger, and the second and more serious one was that he would not have countenanced the paying of any ransom in order to redeem him. And when all was said and done Arabel was hardly to blame. She was waiting for admittance outside their own door, when he was snatched up from almost under her very eyes.

Elizabeth refused to be comforted. Flush, who always slept on her bed and refused to eat from any other hand, to be seized in this way ! . . . "And then he loves me heart to heart ; there was no exaggeration in my verses about him, if there was no poetry."

However, the thieves were bribed into surrendering their victim, and Flush was restored to her, only to be stolen again two years later, when Robert Browning also unsympathetically evinced a great dislike to the thought of her paying the exorbitant ransom demanded.

Nothing else disturbed the current of her life that year. She might as well, indeed, have lived in a desert, " so profound is my solitude and so complete my isolation from things and persons without. I lie all day, and day after day, on the sofa, and my windows do not even look into the street." But, as she added in a letter to another American correspondent, Mr. Westwood, " Books and thoughts and dreams and domestic tenderness can and ought to leave nobody lamenting. Also God's Wisdom, deeply steeped in His Love, is as far as we can stretch out our hands."

So little indeed did any word of her escape into that outside world that a fellow-barrister said to George Barrett about this time : " I suppose your sister is dead ? " George was amazed and startled. " Dead ? " he repeated. " Dead ? "

" Why yes," replied his friend. " After Mr. Horne's account of her being sealed up hermetically in the dark for so many years one can only calculate upon her being dead by this time ! "

One can but wonder why this little speech did not open their eyes to the fact that such a death-in-life existence was a wholly abnormal and unnatural one for a brilliant, gifted woman who was still less than forty years old. But they had grown accustomed to their immured prisoner ; they had done their best to make her dungeon look as little like a bedroom as possible. She seemed quite resigned and happy too, with her books and Flush and an occasional visitor.

They had forgotten the little girl who once had roamed freely among the gardens and woods and fields at Hope End, and who had loved the sunshine, the soft wind, the flowers, and had made herself a green bower roofed by thick ivy-leaves that stretched between two trees. But Elizabeth had not forgotten that other care-free happier self, and that was perhaps why she had tried to make her gloomy London window into a pathetic simulacrum of that lost bower where once she and Bro had played together. . . .

CHAPTER IV

I

THE long-awaited *Poems* were published in 1844, and were dedicated to her father in words that plainly show there had so far been no least rift in their harmonious relations.

" When your eyes fall upon this page of dedication, and you start to see to whom it is inscribed, your first thought will be of the time far off when I was a child and wrote verses, and when I dedicated them to you who were my public and my critic. Of all that such a recollection implies of saddest and sweetest to both of us, it would become neither of us to speak before the world ; nor would it be possible for us to speak of it to one another with voices that did not falter. Enough that what is in my heart when I write thus will be fully known to yours.

" And my desire is that you, who are a witness how, if this art of poetry had been a less earnest object to me, it must have fallen from exhausted hands before this day—that you who have shared with me in things bitter and sweet, softening them or enhancing them every day—that you, who hold with me over all sense of loss and transiency, one hope, by one Name—may accept from me the inscription of these volumes, the exponents of a few years of an existence which has been sustained and comforted by you as well as given. Somewhat more faint-hearted than I used to be, it is my fancy thus to seem to return to a visible personal dependence upon you as if I were indeed a child again ; to conjure

ELIZABETH BARRETT-BROWNING

From a painting by Gordigiani

p. 48

your beloved image between myself and the public so as to be sure of one smile—and to satisfy my heart while I sanctify my ambition, by associating with the great pursuit of my life its tenderest and holiest affection."

Few fathers can ever have received a more touching and devoted tribute from a daughter. There is something wistful in the gratitude she gives him, something that would convey her implicit thanks for the bitter hour when he failed to utter a single word of reproach. The old friendship between them, the old sympathy, had grown perhaps more close and profound since that day, four years before, when Edward's barque had foundered in a serene summer sea.

The *Poems* were published in two volumes, and included the *Drama of Exile, A Vision of Poets, The Romaunt of Margret, To Flush: my Dog, The Cry of the Children, Lady Geraldine's Courtship,* and many more. Perhaps of all these *The Cry of the Children* made at the time of its publication the most instant appeal, and is even now the best known. Written in 1843, she told Mr. Boyd (who criticised the rhythm somewhat severely) that the first verse " came into her head like a hurricane," and the succeeding stanzas had perforce to follow the same pattern. It was an epoch-making poem, drawing public attention to one of the crying scandals of the age, the employment of little children in mine and factory. I think that few would now venture to find fault with its stirring, arresting rhythm, even though the captious might complain of a certain looseness of rhyme.

Do you hear the children weeping, O my brothers,
    Ere the sorrow comes with years ?
They are leaning their young heads against their mothers,
    And *that* cannot stop their tears.
The young lambs are bleating in the meadows,
    The young birds are chirping in the nest,
The young fawns are playing with the shadows,
    The young flowers are blowing toward the west—

D

But the young, young children, O my brothers,
　　They are weeping bitterly !
 - They are weeping in the playtime of the others,
　　In the country of the free.

Do you question the young children in the sorrow,
　　Why their tears are falling so ?
The old man may weep for his to-morrow
　　Which is lost in Long Ago ;
The old tree is leafless in the forest,
　　The old year is ending in the frost,
The old wound, if stricken, is the sorest,
　　The old hope is hardest to be lost.
But the young, young children, O my brothers,
　　Do you ask them why they stand
Weeping sore before the bosoms of their mothers
　　In our happy Fatherland ?

When the poems were ready for the press it was found that the first volume was unequal in length to the second. Additional pages were required, and Elizabeth took up an unfinished ballad poem, *Lady Geraldine's Courtship*, and completed it in a single day " like one in a dream." The task was an exceptionally heavy one, for she wrote no less than one hundred and forty lines, each containing fifteen syllables. This poem, thrust in thus as a make-weight at the eleventh hour, strangely enough proved to be for a long time one of her most popular achievements, though I doubt if to-day this estimate of it would be very readily endorsed. Such widely different people as Carlyle and Harriet Martineau preferred it to all the rest. And there is no doubt that the introduction of Robert Browning's name was destined to affect Elizabeth's whole future life. It was probably on the strength of it that he ventured to write her that first and highly significant letter. *I do, as I say, love these books with all my heart, and I love you too. . . .*

The publication of these poems (so long delayed that the impression of her death was thereby deep-ened) assured Elizabeth Barrett of her permanent place among the English poets. Written during those bitter years of grief, illness, mortal weakness, and imprisonment within that back room of a gloomy London house, they won immediate appreciation and fame. An American edition was called for and published, and for this she wrote another preface. But to remember the bleak periods of grief and despair, of physical suffering and disability through which she was passing when she wrote those poems, so rich in thought and music, so tender and sensitive in feeling, is to evoke a parallel with the " mattress-grave " of Heine.

2

John Kenyon had read the *Drama of Exile* in manuscript, and his comments had been encouraging. Elizabeth was just then inclined to be despondent, both on account of her own weakness and because she was dubious of the success of this ambitious poem. His praise coming at such a moment touched her to the heart.

" The good you have done me " she wrote, " and just at the moment when I should have failed altogether without it and in more than one way, and in a deeper than the obvious degree—all this I know better than you do, and I thank you for it from the bottom of my heart. I shall never forget it as long as I live to remember anything . . . I was falling to pieces in nerves and spirits when you came to help me."

She had indeed put it into his hands in fear and trembling, fully expecting him to advise against its publication. But on the contrary he had the wisdom to see that it was superior as a whole to any of her past achievements, " more sustained and fuller in power."

Kenyon was, however, a perfectly frank critic.

He did not hesitate to tell her of her faults. He condemned her careless rhythms, her loose rhymes, calling them " Barrettisms." And indeed, most of her critics down to the present day have cavilled at her poems on this score. *Silence* and *islands*, *children* and *bewildering*, and a host of others do doubtless grate upon the accurate, sensitive ear, but it is only just to Elizabeth to say that she used them deliberately, and that this dissyllabic rhyming was with her in the nature of an experiment.

Both Kenyon and Boyd were old friends who held the doubtful privilege of candid speaking, but Elizabeth was never meek beneath their criticism. Her own purpose was too considered and assured for her to submit to being lightly turned from any chosen path. And then, as she said in her pathetic preface, her poems, although full of faults, had her heart and life in them ; they were not empty shells. " Poetry has been as serious a thing to me as life itself, and life has been a very serious thing ; there has been no playing at skittles for me in either. I never mistook pleasure for the final cause of poetry nor leisure for the hour of the poet."

And already London was beginning to know something of the life of this woman—of her imprisonment in an upper chamber, guarded from light, almost from air—the woman who had so long been immured that already she was believed to be dead. There was a young poet called Robert Browning, who lived with his parents at Hatcham, and who from time to time put forth a modest sheaf of verse in pamphlet form under the title of *Bells and Pomegranates*, who had once asked Kenyon to obtain for him the privilege of seeing her. He was told that she was too ill, and even now when he read her poems—sent by Kenyon to his sister, Sarianna—he wondered whether he dared to write and tell her what he thought of them. He would, of course, ask Kenyon, and abide by his decision.

3

Mr. Boyd drank Cyprus wine, and sent some to Elizabeth as a present. She thoroughly appreciated it, although Flush fled in terror from the proffered glass. Never could there have been in modern days such wine—she hardly knew whether she ought to accept such a present from him !

Mr. Barrett held a very different opinion on the subject of this nectar, and Elizabeth, who always wrote admirably frank and delightful letters to Mr. Boyd, described a little scene in which she induced her father to taste it.

" What is this ? " he asked.

" Taste it."

His face of recoil as he did so was accompanied by a shudder of deep disgust.

" Why, what most beastly and nauseous thing is this ? Oh, what detestable drug is this ? Oh, oh, I shall never get the horrible taste out of my mouth ! "

Elizabeth, who had really enjoyed the sweet stuff, explained that it was Greek wine, Cyprus wine of great value.

" It may be Greek twice over, but it is exceedingly beastly," he retorted, feeling no doubt as insulted and resentful as Flush at being offered a drink of the kind.

Elizabeth timidly suggested that it could hardly be beastly, since the taste was that of oranges mingled with orange-flower and mixed with the honey of Mount Hymettus.

" He took me up," she wrote, " with stringent logic, that any wine must positively be beastly which pretending to be wine tasted as sweet as honey ! "

It is certain that up to the end of 1844—the year that established her fame as a poet and gave her a permanent place in English literature—there was no cloud of any consequence between the father and daughter. She confessed in her preface that she still liked to feel a child's dependence upon him—

a graceful admission when we remember that she alone of all his children was not financially dependent upon him. She had been left about £400 a year by her uncle, and this sufficed to pay the expenses of her maid, her clothes and books—the latter always a heavy item—and for those drugs necessitated by her illness. Of these the laudanum cost her most. She was in the habit of taking, by the doctor's orders, about forty drops of it a day.

Stormie and Henry went to Egypt in the autumn of that year. Mr. Barrett had bought a ship, the *Statira*, which was employed in his own commercial and speculative activities. He appointed a captain and crew, and the vessel was first sent to Odessa with a freight of wool. Her next destination was Alexandria, to which port she was to carry coals. Stormie, eager for adventure, and perhaps even more desirous to escape for a time from the paternal vigilance, entreated to be allowed to go on this cruise. Mr. Barrett reluctantly gave his consent, and Henry was permitted to accompany his brother. But the plan was kept from Elizabeth until a few days before their departure. It was feared that it might have a deleterious effect upon her health. Although she was glad for their sakes, she confessed to a deep anxiety for their safety. She was afraid of the sea . . . and small wonder.

Mr. Barrett was full of plans at that time for retrieving his fallen fortunes. Besides the *Statira* he had bought shares in a Cornish quarry, and after his sons' departure he went down to visit it, intending to extend his trip to the Land's End. During his absence the frivolous Henrietta indulged in a little " polka " on her own account, not however without some fear lest it should bring the ceiling down. Elizabeth chose this opportunity for putting up a transparent blind in her room. Mr. Kenyon sent her a new table with a little rail round it to protect her vanities from Flush's predatory paws.

Mr. Barrett returned after an absence of some weeks, as pleased with his quarry as his daughter was to see him again. They were at that time on the most affectionate and intimate terms.

Meantime, the two voyagers reached Malta after a three weeks' cruise from Gibraltar. This good news cheered Elizabeth.

The autumn passed pleasantly: She made a new friend, Mrs. Jameson, whose first book, the *Diary of an Ennuyée*, had attracted a good deal of attention. They had corresponded since the publication of the *Poems*, and Mrs. Jameson ventured to call. She was admitted to that legendary chamber and sat with Elizabeth for nearly an hour, kissing her when she left. It was what her sisters called one of her sudden intimacies.

Among her few visitors was the devoted Kenyon, now a widower for the second time. He was a very well-known figure in the literary London of that day, associating with many of its most prominent men. Despite the relationship, Mr. Barrett refused to invite him to dinner when Elizabeth suggested it. The only person who ever seems to have been honoured with such an invitation was another cousin, Captain Surtees Cook, who was secretly courting Henrietta.

Flush was jealous of Kenyon, and on one occasion snapped at him—as later on he snapped at and actually bit Robert Browning. Elizabeth was always ready to make excuses for her favourite. It was his nervous system that betrayed him rather than his temper, she averred, in a charming little note of apology to Kenyon. " In that great cloak he saw you as in a cloudy mystery. And then when you stumbled over the bell-rope he thought the world was come to an end ! " Kenyon bore no malice, for he presented Flush with the famous purple cup out of which he always drank his water.

About this time she wrote in a letter to Kenyon : " Can it be true that Newman has at last joined the Roman Church ? " (As a matter of fact he did not do so till a year later, in October 1845.) " If it is true it will do much to prove to the most illogical minds the real character of the late movement. Miss Mitford told me that he had lately sent a message to a Roman Catholic convert to the effect— ' You have done a good deed, but not at a right time.' "

The Oxford Movement was then causing a considerable stir among the more moderate members of the Church of England, who beheld the conversion of many well-known men to Catholicism with something of dismay. To Elizabeth, as to many more, it was the only logical outcome of a movement that aimed at a revival of Catholic practices in a Church essentially and historically Protestant.

Elizabeth often lamented the dearth of women-poets in England. In a letter to Mr. Chorley she averred that prior to Joanna Baillie there had been none, nor had England ever produced a name to rival those of Marie of Britanny in France and Vittoria Colonna in Italy. Chorley put in a word for his own favourite, Anna Seward, whose poems had been edited by Sir Walter Scott in 1810, after her death. In this connection Elizabeth's beautiful little poem on the death of Felicia Hemans, and which was addressed to " L.E.L." [1] must not be overlooked :

> Nor mourn, O living One, because her part in life was mourning.
> Would she have lost the poet's fire for anguish of the burning ?–
> The minstrel harp, for the strained string ?   The tripod, for the afflated
> Woe ? or the vision, for those tears in which it shone dilated ?
>
> .   .   .   .   .
>
> Be happy, crowned and living One ! and, as thy dust decayeth,
> May thine own England say for thee, what now for Her it sayeth—
> "Albeit softly in our ears her silver song was ringing,
> The footfall of her parting soul is softer than her singing ! "

It has always seemed to me that Felicia Hemans, so many of whose charming, fluent poems have become classics in our language, deserves a higher

---

[1] Letitia   Elizabeth Landon, 1802-38.

place, a more conspicuous niche, than that which posterity has allotted to her. Her verses may not have been great poetry, but they were full of a certain singing music that makes them easy to memorise. Her short, unhappy life ended in 1835, and the remembrance of her seems to be growing a little faint, although its fragrance is undiminished, and some of her poems can never be forgotten.

Elizabeth Barrett wrote from personal experience when she said : " Would she have lost the poet's fire for anguish of the burning ? " Her tributes to her fellow poets are always beautiful and generous. She seemed to divine their sufferings, to measure them by her own. Her poem *Cowper's Grave*, published in the volumes of 1844, is perhaps one of the most wonderful tributes ever paid by one poet to another.

It is a place where poets crowned may feel the heart's decaying ;
It is a place where happy saints may weep amid their praying.
Yet let the grief and humbleness, as low as silence, languish :
Earth surely now may give her calm to whom she gave her
        anguish.

O poets, from a maniac's tongue was poured the deathless singing !
O Christians, at your cross of hope, a hopeless hand was clinging !
O men, this man in brotherhood your weary paths beguiling,
Groaned inly while he taught you peace, and died while ye were
        smiling !

And now what time ye all may read through dimming tears his
        story,
How discord on the music fell, and darkness on the glory,
And how when, one by one, sweet sounds and wandering lights
        departed,
He wore no less a loving face because so broken-hearted.

Her critical faculty was always keen and even shrewd. She never let her admiration get the better of it. Even her wholehearted appreciation of Wordsworth could not blind her to the fact that he had " insulted his own genius "—as no other poet had ever done—by writing poems " the vulgarity of which is childish and the childishness vulgar." When she compared him with others she admitted that Byron had more passion and intensity, Shelley more fancy and music, and Coleridge the power of seeing further into the unseen. This praise of Shelley is perhaps a little inadequate according to our present-day estimate of him, and I have often wondered whether Keats had no place in her library, since there is but little mention of him in any of her letters, and the allusion to him in her *Vision of Poets* is hardly satisfying :

> And Keats the real
> Adonis, with the hymeneal
> Fresh vernal buds, half sunk between
> His youthful curls, kissed straight and sheen
> In his Rome-grave, by Venus-queen.

Still, later in Casa Guidi a replica of his death-mask had an honoured place.

He had perhaps hardly come into his own in the late thirties of the last century, when he had not been dead twenty years and the brief tragedy of his life was less well known than it is now.

Both he and Shelley were somewhat eclipsed in their own day by their great contemporary Byron, who had both wealth and notoriety to aid him in his swift passage to fame. And Byron, together with Pope, had been among Elizabeth's earliest loves. She confessed once that the two women she most hated were Lady Byron and Marie Louise !

But her sympathy for her fellow-poets was unfailing. She knew the hardships so often involved in the poet's life. " His work is no light work. His wheat will not grow without labour any more than other kinds of wheat." She tried—as she has herself told us, in her preface to the *Vision of Poets*—to express her view of " the mission of the poet, of the self-abnegation implied in it, of the great work involved in it, of the duty and glory of what Balzac has beautifully and truly called *la patience angélique du génie* ; and of the obvious truth, above all, that if knowledge is power, suffering should be acceptable as a part of knowledge."

She was always a great believer in regular and steady work, the daily tale of bricks. And even in those years of physical disability, both before and after her brother's death, her output was astonishing. Work was to her an anodyne. There was little else to relieve the monotony of her life. She had few visitors from outside since, beyond Mr. Kenyon and Miss Mitford, and later Mrs. Jameson, no one except relations ever penetrated to that upper room. There had been nothing so far to give her any hint of the destiny that awaited her, was even now approaching her door on swift feet. It never occurred to her that the year 1845 was to add anything to her scanty store of interests, or to bring her any event more joyful than the anticipated return of Stormie and Henry from their perilous voyage to Alexandria. The former had just written to tell her that he was bringing back a little gazelle for her, as a companion to Flush. . . .

CHAPTER V

I

MR. KENYON sent Elizabeth's *Poems* to Sarianna Browning, probably as a Christmas present. Early in January 1845 the volumes fell into the hands of Robert Browning, and made such a profound impression upon him that he forthwith approached Kenyon as to the desirability of writing to the author of them. Once before he had tried ineffectually, through Kenyon, to invade that penetralia, and there is no doubt that he was aware of the mystery that shrouded at that time the almost legendary figure of Elizabeth Barrett.

Those significant lines in *Lady Geraldine's Courtship* showed him too that this woman, so closely guarded from the eyes of strangers, was aware of him and of his capacity to " tear the heart from a fact," as a later critic said of him. Here at any rate were knowledge, sympathy, understanding. . . .

The chances of admittance to that upper chamber might be as remote as ever, but at least he could write, and Kenyon encouraged him to do so. He knew that one of Miss Barrett's greatest pleasures lay in the writing and receiving of letters, and he believed that a correspondence between these two poets could not but have the most gratifying results.

On January 10th, 1845, Browning wrote the first of that immense series of letters which, more than fifty years later, when the fame of both was securely established, was given—bravely as we think—by their son to the world. When reproached for his action in publishing them, Robert Barrett Browning said to a friend of the writer : " *They were too beautiful to destroy. . . .*"

Elizabeth was in the habit of receiving letters from unknown admirers and critics, both English and American, and since the publication of the *Poems* her circle of correspondents had appreciably widened, but it would be safe to say that never in her life had she received such a letter as the one that now reached her. Its very beginning was unconventional. " I love your verses with all my heart, dear Miss Barrett. . . . Since the day last week when I first read your poems I quite laugh to remember how I have been turning and turning again in my mind what I should be able to tell you of their effect upon me, for in the first flush of delight I thought I would this once get out of my habit of purely passive enjoyment, when I do really enjoy and thoroughly justify my admiration—perhaps even, as a loyal fellow-craftsman should, try and find fault and do you some little good to be proud of hereafter !—but nothing comes of it all—so into me has it gone, and part of me has it become, this great living poetry of yours, not a flower of which but took root and grew." He went on to speak of the " fresh strange music, the affluent language, the exquisite pathos and true new brave thought." And then, with increasing and even astonishing temerity, " I do, as I say, love these books with all my heart—and I love you too." He referred to the fact of his single abortive attempt to see her through the instrumentality of Mr. Kenyon. " You were too unwell, and now it is years ago, and I feel as at some untoward passage in my travels, as if I had been close, so close, to some world's wonder in chapel or crypt, only a screen to push and I might have entered, but there was some slight, so it now seems, slight and just sufficient bar to admission, and the half-opened door shut, and I went home my thousands of miles and the sight was never to be."

The sight was never to be. But he knew when

he wrote those words that he wasn't quite sincere. He meant, sooner or later, to have that hitherto frustrated glimpse of his world's wonder, for hadn't he, as he subsequently told her, always got what he wanted in the long run ?

In a letter to Miss Mitford written on the following day, Elizabeth mentioned that she had had a letter from Browning, " the author of Paracelsus and king of the mystics."

She wrote to him at once. " Such a letter from such a hand ! " The sympathy of a poet—and of such a poet—was to her the quintessence of sympathy. She told him that the most frequent general criticism she received was : " If she would but change her style ! "

. . . And then, was it true that once she had been so near the pleasure and honour of making his acquaintance ? " Can it be true that you look back upon the lost opportunity with any regret ? But you know, if you *had* entered the crypt, you might have caught cold or been tired to death. . . ." Still, she held out hope of some future meeting. Not yet—not certainly before the spring. She hibernated in winter. . . . She admitted that she was better, that she seemed to be turning round to the outward world again. For the end of the letter she kept a graceful little compliment of which, after those lines in *Lady Geraldine's Courtship,* he could hardly question the sincerity. " I will say that while I live to follow this divine art of poetry, in proportion to my love for it and my devotion to it, I must be a devout admirer and student of your works."

He read the letter with renewed hope. Some day he would have his wish and meet her face to face. " I will joyfully wait for the delight of your friendship, and the spring, and my Chapel-sight after all ! "

His foot was on the first rung of the ladder. And on her side she confessed to a friend that she was getting deeper and deeper into correspondence with

Robert Browning, poet and mystic. . . . "We are going to be the truest of friends."

Elizabeth's letters were always delightful ; there was a sparkling vivacity, an epigrammatic wit about them which Browning, slower of foot though deeper of vision, could never emulate. " If nobody likes writing to everybody, yet everybody likes writing to somebody," she wrote, in reply to his entreaty that she should no write to him if she hated doing so as much as he hated writing to nearly everybody. And she was able to show him that letters were a paramount interest and pleasure in her secluded life. " I have done most of my talking by post of late years—as people shut up in dungeons take up with scrawling mottoes on the walls." It was in this letter that she made use of her famous phrase—that he would find her an honest man on the whole.

2

Reading them to-day, thirty years after their first publication, when they have become almost historical, and the sensation caused by their appearance, unabbreviated, unabridged, has long since been forgotten, it must be said that the famous letters seem now to resemble fiction of an exalted quality. For these two people had never seen each other face to face ; they knew each other only through the written word, letter or poem ; they were in fact strangers. Yet daily there crept into those letters a warmer and more personal and intimate note— a precursor of the mutual love that was one day to burst into bright flame.

Browning was at this time about thirty-three years of age, and Elizabeth was thirty-nine. But the difference was not only in years. He was strong and vigorous, except for occasional headaches ; she was an almost complete invalid. Fame she had dreamed of and tasted, but love she had never known. Perhaps she had put all thought of it aside as a thing that was never likely to come her way. And in place of it she had pleasant wholesome friendships with both men and women ; intellectual people such as Kenyon, Boyd, Mrs. Jameson and Miss Mitford, with whom she could talk and correspond freely. But she must have foreseen almost from the first that if and when she saw Browning it would not be on those terms. Always one sees her trying, as it were, to keep their letters on the same simple, intellectual level to which she was accustomed in writing to her other friends. But it was of no use —almost from the first she was aware of a difference, as if this man whom she had never seen were already a little in love with her.

For already in February he was writing :   " Real warm Spring, dear Miss Barrett, and the birds know it, and in Spring I shall see you, surely see you— for when did I once fail to get whatever I had set my heart upon ?   As I ask myself sometimes with a strange fear . . ."

It must have seemed to her that he was counting the days.   Quite evidently he believed in the continual dropping, for hardly one of his early letters is devoid of some allusion to the Spring that shall bring with it their meeting. But Elizabeth was perfectly firm. Her Spring seldom came before May, and she said so. To her the snowdrop was much the same as the snow. But when the warm, settled weather came she would perhaps find herself more fit to enjoy certain pleasures.

She wrote a good deal about Prometheus (such a safe subject !) and told him that Kenyon had said she ought to write her poems at least twelve times. "Not that I do it.   Does anybody do it, I wonder ? Do *you*, ever ? "   She asked him once if he knew Tennyson with a face-to-face knowledge ?   She had, she confessed, an immense admiration for him. " In execution he is exquisite—and in music a most subtle weigher-out to the ear of fine airs "—a scrap of criticism that could hardly be bettered. Still, both of them expressed wonder that Tennyson should be so sensitive to the opinions and suggestions of his critics, even submitting to them. " For Keats or Tennyson to go softly all their days for a gruff word or two is inexplicable to me, and always has been," wrote the man who was afterwards to describe himself as ever a fighter. Byron, it will be remembered, shared this view ; he held that a man should count the cost before venturing into the arena. But both he and Browning combined with their poetic gift a certain robust contempt for those not similarly endowed.

Browning was able to give her glimpses of that London literary world to which the author of *Paracelsus* and *Bells and Pomegranates* was welcome. He knew Carlyle, who had recently turned upon him, *à propos de bottes*, with the abrupt, rather strange question : " Did you never try to write a *song* ? Of all the things in the world *that* I should be proudest to do." Turning to his wife he added, " I always say that some day in *spite of nature and my stars* I shall burst into a song ! "

Sometimes Elizabeth gave him glimpses of herself as a little girl, of how she took the little clasped books in which she wrote her poems and put them away tenderly, kissing them, sometimes even carrying them away with her to give them the pleasure of the change, and all this out of gratitude to them. " But between me and that time the cypresses grow thick and dark."

And was it true, she asked a little wistfully, that his wishes fulfilled themselves ? And when they did were they not bitter to his taste—did he not wish them unfulfilled ? It was as if she were trying to tell him not to expect too much from that meeting, even perhaps to warn him against possible disillusionment. " The brightest place in the house is the leaning out of the window, at least for me."

Browning laughed that implied suggestion of disillusionment to scorn. " If my truest heart's wishes avail as they have hitherto done you shall laugh at east winds as I do." He admitted that he

E

had been spoiled. But already she was his dear friend, and he begged her not to lean out of the window when his foot was on the stair.

There was an exaggeration of the kind in almost every letter. How much did he mean of it all? Was it only to herself that he wrote in this eager, half-friendly, half-loverlike manner? She did not know him, and often the written word must have puzzled even while it thrilled her.

" How kind you are," she wrote early in March— " how kindly and gently you speak to me. Some things you say are very touching, and some surprising, and although I am aware that you unconsciously exaggerate what I can be to you, yet it is delightful to be broad awake and think of you as my friend."

But she realised that he had been spared " the great afflictions " that had been hers or his step would not be quite so lightly on the stair.

This letter made him very happy, and he told her so. He begged that in future her letters might always contain a little bulletin such as " I am better " or " still better." And then his impatience broke out again, for the cold March days and piercing east winds seemed to make the prospect of their meeting ever more remote.

" Do you think I shall see you in two months, three months ? "

Again she made that rather reluctant promise to see him when the warm weather revived her. She saw that he realised that something more than the bitter winds and keen airs were responsible for her reluctance to receive him. " I observe that you distrust me, and that perhaps you penetrate my morbidity and guess how when the moment comes to see a living human face to which I am not accustomed, I shrink and grow pale in the spirit." There seems to have been a little fear too, as if her heart already warned her that she could never be wholly indifferent to this man who had thus captured her imagination, and whose desire to enter her life was expressed with a force and determination against

which her frail barriers must needs break down.
" For if you think I shall not *like* to see you, you
are wrong for all your learning. But I shall be
afraid of you at first—though I am not in writing
thus. You are Paracelsus, and I am a recluse with
nerves that have been all broken on the rack, and
now hang loosely, quivering at a step, a breath."

He tried to reassure her. He could not believe
that the thin white face he saw in the mirror could
evoke fear in anyone. He made, however, scarcely
any allusion to the tragic note of her letter, in which
for the first time she had alluded to the great calamity
of her life. Perhaps she felt that hers had been too
long and too intimate, and his reply too short and
perhaps even a trifle too jocose, for she did not
write again until three weeks later, not indeed until
he had sent her another letter, wondering perhaps
a little at her unusual silence. He confessed that
he had had occasion on the preceding day to go
past the end of Wimpole Street, but that he had
not felt as if he had her leave to walk down it,
" much less count number after number till I came
to yours—much least than less look up when I did
come there." It was a delicate reassurance on his
part of his complete submission to her will in the
matter of their meeting. The writer of those profoundly subtle psychological poems revealed himself
in the letter, in that confessed hesitancy so much
as to pass her door without leave. She had not
written for an unusually long time, and he must
have feared that she was ill and had longed, just as
any other of her friends might have done, to call and
ask for news of her.

" How glad I was to see your letter. . . ." That
sentence in her postscript must have renewed hope
in his heart.

3

So far, she had refrained from admitting him to
any knowledge of her private life, and except for

that single allusion to the great tragedy that had overwhelmed her with its waves she had told him little of herself except in regard to her own health. Thus the homecoming of the wanderers, Stormie and Henry, in April, was never mentioned in her letters to Browning, although she wrote of it in considerable detail to Mrs. Martin, and indeed it was to her a very important event. The *Statira* had been a hundred days at sea when she put into Plymouth. Even then the voyage was not over, for the two brothers were detained off Sandgate for three or four days' quarantine before being allowed to land. Stormie had such bad chilblains on his hands that he could hardly write to her, and he was in miserable plight, being entirely destitute of shirts and sheets. Elizabeth hoped that these hardships would damp his enthusiasm for sea voyages, and indeed it is not on record that any of the brothers again ventured their lives in the *Statira*. Wimpole Street, as she had hoped, proved more desirable than the prolonged battling with Mediterranean storms.

The correspondence with Browning continued, flagging a little at times it is true, almost as if some invisible barrier had arisen between them, checking the fluent rapture of those first letters. Browning was evidently ill-at-ease and restless, and when May came he admitted that for the past two months he had not felt well ; he had suffered from constant headaches which only " very rough exercise " could benefit. He was better now, " thanks to polking all night and walking home by broad daylight to the surprise of the thrushes in the bush here." *Luria* had suffered from his indisposition, for Browning never adopted that habit of regular daily work which Elizabeth, despite her ill-health, so rarely relinquished. She reproached him for this revelation of dancing and late hours. " Do tell me how Lurias can ever be made out of such ungodly imprudences." It was already May, and her brother and sister—probably George and Henrietta—had been invited to meet him at Mr. Kenyon's. Browning could not fulfil the

engagement on account of his head ; he had been
seized with sudden illness just as he was going out
one evening to dine with a friend, and was obliged
to see a doctor. This news alarmed her ; she was
disappointed too at not seeing him " with my sister's
eyes for the first sight."

He was able to reassure her ; the " ungodly
imprudences " were now at an end. " And one day ;
oh, the day, I shall see you with my own, own eyes ! "
Not an hour sooner than she willed—he reminded
her that her power of giving or withholding didn't
end with the mere shutting of the door of her
room. Hadn't he refrained from walking down
Wimpole Street, past her very house, when an
engagement had led him in that direction ? And
often as he saw Kenyon he limited his mention of
her to the most conventional inquiries about her
health.

This extraordinary delicacy was not lost upon her.
May had come, but he was less insistent about seeing
her than at first. He was waiting for her to speak
the word, but it is easy to see that in the meantime
his preoccupation was so intense that he could think
of nothing else, and his very nerves were reacting to
the delay.

And on Thursday, May 16th, she gave him permission to come. It mustn't be before next week,
and if he preferred to come with Mr. Kenyon for the
first time, he would have to wait until that mutual
friend returned in June. Her sister would be there
to bring him up to her room. " And you will
try to be indulgent and like me as well as you
can."

And again it was as if she would have warned him
of that disillusionment which to her seemed so inevitable. " There is nothing to see in me, nor to
hear in me. I never learned to talk as you do in
London, although I can admire that brightness of
carved speech in Mr. Kenyon and others."

Did he remember that letter when he wrote those
famous stanzas in *James Lee's Wife* ? :

There is nothing to remember in me,
　　Nothing I ever said with a grace,
Nothing I did that you care to see,
　　Nothing I was that deserves a place
In your mind, now I leave you, set you free. . . .

" You are extravagant in caring so for a permission which will be nothing to you afterwards. . . . Not that I am not touched by your caring so at all ! I am deeply touched now ; and presently . . . I shall understand. . . . Come then. . . ."

Browning in his reply said that he would come on the following Tuesday at two o'clock, the earliest possible hour at which she could receive him.　The envelope of this letter was endorsed by him as follows : Tuesday, May 20th, 1845.　3—4½ p.m.

There is no record of that first and momentous meeting.　Both were perhaps a little shaken with emotion.　But we know that as he stood there looking down upon the slight frail form on the sofa, with the white face " spirit-pure," the dark poetical eyes, the beauty and brilliancy of the smile, and listened to the low soft voice, he believed that she was unable to stand up, and more, that she would never be able to do so again.

His letter written that same evening showed that he was not too happy about the impression he must have made.　Did he, for instance, talk too loud ? People had sometimes told him that he did.　And did he stay too long ?　At the end he wrote : " I am proud and happy in your friendship.　May God bless you."

But she reassured him.　Indeed there was nothing wrong—she had heard no loud speaking.

When her father visited her on the following morning she told him that the idea of Mr. Browning beset her.　It haunted her—it was like a persecution. She attributed it to her being so unaccustomed to seeing strangers.

One would have thought that this spontaneous admission would have put Mr. Barrett on his guard, but he only smiled and told her it was not grateful of her to use such a word as persecution. Both were perfectly unconscious that Elizabeth had already fallen a little in love with Browning; she didn't understand the nature of her own obsession.

But she was alarmed, as she subsequently confessed after the barriers had been swept aside and their love stood revealed between them. She felt even then that he had a power over her and intended to use it. His letters had prepared the way; they had influenced her, made her almost see him. "Then when you came you never went away. I mean I had a sense of your presence constantly."

And Browning for his part had come ready—as she told him later—to love whatever he should find. And not all her warnings of probable disillusionment had been of any avail. He did fall in love with what he found that day at No. 50 Wimpole Street.

Afterwards she was glad that it had been so. " I am glad now, yes glad, as we were to have a miracle to have it so, a *born* miracle from the beginning. I feel glad now that nothing was between the knowing and the loving . . . and that the beloved eyes were never cold discerners and analyzers of me at any time. . . ."

He was the stronger of the two, and as she told him much later, she had felt the mastery in him " by the first word and the first look."

CHAPTER VI

I

ROBERT BROWNING was more than six years younger
than Elizabeth Barrett. He was the only son of
Robert Browning and Sarah Anna Wiedemann, the
daughter of a German shipowner settled in Dundee.
His father was a clerk in the Bank of England.
Like the Barretts, the Brownings had West Indian
connections, but the poet's father had relinquished
an appointment he had been given at St. Kitts in
early manhood because of his abhorrence of the slave
system that prevailed there. This lucrative post on
the sugar plantation of his late mother would probably have made him a rich man had he stuck to it.
His grandfather was so angry with him that when his
marriage to Sarah Wiedemann was being arranged
he called upon the uncle, with whom she was then
living at Camberwell, and told him that " his niece
would be thrown away on a man so evidently born
to be hanged ! "

There were two children of the marriage, both
born at Camberwell. Robert, the elder, was born
on May 7th, 1812, and Sarah Anna—usually known as
Sarianna—on the 7th January, 1814. She survived
the poet for many years, dying at Asolo at the age
of ninety.

The elder Browning worked hard at an uncon-
genial occupation in order to keep his wife and children
in comfort. He was a great reader and knew the
Odes of Horace by heart. He taught his little boy
the Latin declensions by means of rhymes, and many,
many years later adopted this method with his

ROBERT BROWNING

From a drawing by Field Talfourd
Rome, 1859

grandson, the little Penini, when instructing him in the rudiments of anatomy. Of vigorous constitution, he lived until he was eighty-five. " I fear I am wearying you, dear," were his last words to his son, who was fanning him.

As for the poet's mother, Carlyle called her " the true type of a Scottish gentlewoman," and her son's devotion to her was deep and sincere. Indeed, the two households could hardly have shown a more vivid contrast. In the house at Hatcham, whither the Brownings moved when Robert was about twenty-eight, there was no coercion, but a complete freedom that was rarer in those days than it is now. Having early discerned his son's gifts as a poet, the elder Browning would not permit him to become a bank clerk, but allowed him to live at home and work at his self-chosen if unremunerative career. He had a profound faith in him, which the years were destined amply to justify. He had wished to be an artist himself in his youth, and this had been forbidden, just as his request to go to the University had been refused. His own thwarted and frustrated youth made him exceptionally lenient and sympathetic in his dealings with his son. At one time he imagined the boy would become an artist, and he treasured a little sketch of a cottage and some rocks, executed in lead pencil and black-currant jam by the child at the age of two, when he was still too young to be permitted the use of poisonous paints !

Robert's education was largely supervised by his father, but he went also to a Mr. Ready's school, where he gained no prizes and made no friends. The boy was an omnivorous reader, and in a house overflowing with six thousand books he had plenty of opportunity for indulging his hobby. Byron was his chief adoration, but he early developed an admiration for Elizabethan poetry. He had, too, a passion for drawing.

He wrote poetry at a very early age, and at twelve had produced a little volume of poems called *Incondita*, which his parents wished to have

published, only that no publisher could be found
to undertake the task.   One of the poems, *On
Bonaparte,* was so beautiful that, had it not been
written in his unformed script, his father said he
could not have believed it to be the work of a child.
But Browning destroyed his Juvenilia and nothing
remains to us of his early work.

2

His first published poem was *Pauline,* written
when he was in his twenty-first year.   His mother's
sister, Mrs. Silverthorne, gave him thirty pounds,
which paid all the expenses of its publication, including those of advertisement.   It appeared in
1833.   His father with ready generosity paid the
expenses of *Paracelsus, Sordello,* and the eight parts
of *Bells and Pomegranates.*   It was when *Paracelsus*
appeared that he became known in literary circles.
Good-looking, with his slim upright form, pale face,
dark, flowing, " sculptured " hair and burning dark
eyes, he was a fluent and agreeable talker, and was
soon a popular member of the literary group that
included Horne, Leigh Hunt, Monckton Milnes,
Procter, Dickens, Wordsworth and Landor, with
occasional glimpses of Tennyson.   At a supper
given by Talfourd, both Wordsworth and Landor
drank to the young man's health.   He was already
one of the acknowledged poets of the day, although so
far his publications had brought him no monetary
return.

For eleven years he always put " By the Author
of Paracelsus " on all his publications, though it
will be remembered he refused to allow it to be
inserted in the announcement of his marriage to
Miss Barrett.

Browning travelled in those early years.   He
went to Russia in the spring of 1834, and four years
later visited Venice, the city where he was destined
to die.   He went by sea from London to Trieste,

the voyage, a sufficiently unpleasant one, occupying seven weeks. His object in going to Italy was to study the scenes for *Sordello*, a poem about which his admirers have ever remained divided. Tennyson declared that he only understood two lines of it, the first and the last, and that both were lies, while Jane Carlyle, a woman of abounding intelligence, said that after two attentive readings she was unable to discover whether Sordello was a man, a city, or a tree ! But then, it is on record that she didn't like Browning ; when she told him to put the kettle down the foolish young man had placed it on the floor ! . . .

During the voyage to Trieste, Browning wrote two short poems, *Home Thoughts from the Sea* and *How They Brought the Good News from Ghent*. The latter has always been one of his most popular achievements. Venice inspired *In a Gondola*, while Asolo, which he visited for the first time, supplied the scenery for the beautiful *Pippa Passes* which he planned long afterwards while walking in the Dulwich woods. This poem made such an impression on Miss Mitford that she urged Elizabeth Barrett to read it, and one can picture the emotion produced upon her by those oft-quoted words :

> God's in His Heaven—
> All's right with the world !

They must have sounded like a clarion cry in the ears of the pale invalid writing her own immortal poetry in that darkened upper room in Wimpole Street.

3

Browning paid a second visit to Italy in 1844. He went to Naples and Rome, and thence to see Trelawny at Leghorn. Perhaps he had Trelawny in his mind when he wrote :

> Ah, did you once see Shelley plain ?
> And did he stop and speak to you ?
> And did you speak to him again ? . . .
> How strange it seems and new !

There is no record of this visit when the younger poet saw that " last of the Pisa gang," the man who had known Shelley and Byron and had once been in love with the pathetic Claire Claremont.

That was, in brief, Robert Browning's life until he met Miss Barrett in 1845, if we except his dramatic ventures, *Strafford*, which was produced in 1837 with Macready and Helen Faucit in the leading parts, and which despite its initial success only ran for a few nights, and *A Blot in the 'Scutcheon*, which was brought out at Drury Lane in February 1843, and in which Macready threw up his part at the eleventh hour, thus causing a breach between himself and the poet.

It was not a very stirring or adventurous life, but it had held a fair measure of success and appreciation, a modicum of fame among the London intelligentsia, not so swift nor so startling as Tennyson's, but well worth having. There had been travel, too, and amusement, despite the want of wealth. The background was supplied by the quiet home life amid the fields of Camberwell and Hatcham. And apart from a boyish admiration for Miss Flower, there had been apparently no love affair of the slightest importance. Elizabeth, it is true, was told that Browning had once been engaged to be married, a report which he neither confirmed nor denied, although his slightly cryptic reply gives some credence to the story.

Perhaps his knowledge of women was not very extensive, or he would not have made such a false step, two days after their first meeting, when he wrote Miss Barrett the only letter which has not been preserved and which she returned, begging him to destroy it. Its content can best be gleaned from her answer, and also from her allusion to it much later when she told him that it was read in pain

and agitation. " I could not sleep night after night
—could not . . . and my fear was at night lest
the feverishness should make me talk deliriously
and tell the secret abroad. Judge if the deeps of
my heart were not shaken."

But at the time she handled a difficult situation
with considerable skill. She did not answer at
once, but waited for two days before replying,
which must have flung Browning into an agony of
suspense and caused him to apprehend the nature of
her answer.

That it was a love-letter is not open to doubt,
although whether he actually spoke of marriage
we shall never know. No one read the letter
except Elizabeth, and she returned it to him.

" You do not know what pain you give me
in speaking so wildly . . . you have said some
intemperate things . . . fancies which you will
not say over again, nor unsay, but *forget at once*
and *for ever having said at all,* and which (so) will
die out between *you and me alone* like a misprint
between you and the printer. And this you will
do *for my sake* who am your friend (and you have
none truer)—and this I ask because it is a condition
necessary to our future liberty of intercourse.
You remember—surely you do—that I am in
the most exceptional of positions ; and that just
because of it I am able to receive you as I did on
Tuesday, and that for me to listen to ' unconscious
exaggerations,' is as unbecoming to the humilities
of my position, as unpropitious (which is of more
consequence) to the prosperities of yours. Now if
there should be one word of answer attempted to
this ; or of reference ; *I must not . . . I will not
see you again*—and you will justify me later in your
heart. So for my sake you will not say it—I think
you will not—and spare me the sadness of having
to break through an intercourse just as it is
promising pleasure to me ; to me who have so
many sadnesses and so few pleasures."

She told him that his influence and help in poetry would be full of good and gladness to her, for with many to love her in that house there was no one now to judge her. And his friendship and sympathy would be dear and precious to her all her life, if indeed he would leave them with her " so long or so little."

The letter betrayed her pain and agitation. He had told her of his love—this man whose mastery she had felt in the first look, the first word. The " unconscious exaggerations " of his former letters made it plain to her that he had fallen in love with her before he had ever seen her. And what could she give him in return—this invalid, older than himself, imprisoned in her bleak, gloomy London room ?

Browning, who had shown himself extraordinarily delicate and subtle in his approach shots, was at his worst when he found himself—as now—completely bunkered.

He has been blamed for his answer, and it would have been better for him if he had adopted the course she indicated, of not trying to unsay his words. For unsay them he did in a manner she little anticipated. She had misunderstood him, was the gist of his reply, concealed beneath a mass of uncouth and rather obscure verbiage. There were cryptic allusions to the specks of Vesuvius and Stromboli and huge layers of ice and pits of black cold water in his microcosm. A little over-boisterous gratitude had perhaps caused all the mischief. He asked her to return his letter, which she did, though after their engagement she tried to recover those first words of love that now could pain and agitate her no more. But Browning had destroyed it.

He did not see her again till the following Saturday week. In the meantime she had written to offer her apologies for having spent so much solemnity on so simple a matter. She had never made a mistake of the kind before, had never attached any importance to indefinite compliments. She told him she had not read the letter again and was returning it to him, advising him, however, to burn it, although it was admittedly very beautiful and worthy of the rest of its kin in the portfolio, " Lays of the Poets," or otherwise. " After which friendly turn you will do me the one last kindness of forgetting all this exquisite nonsense and of refraining from mentioning it, by breath or pen, to me or another."

This letter was extraordinarily skilful and it evidently abashed Browning. Yes, he would come to see her on Wednesday as she suggested, and would enter as boldly as he suspected most people did after they had been soundly frightened. It was his second letter, not the first, that she must have found so difficult to forgive. In a clumsy endeavour to extricate himself he had put her in the wrong. Any woman can forgive a man for telling her that he loves her, but few could forgive him for saying afterwards that he hadn't meant it.

It was inevitable that there should be something of embarrassment in their first attempts to know each other after their long and in so many respects intimate correspondence. But the interval between their first two meetings was of sufficient length to dispel any slight awkwardness caused by this incident.

There were things, however, she wished to change. She disliked having always—at his request—to fix the hour and day of their next meeting. It was enough for her that he cared to come, wished to come. And if here her reasoning was a little subtle, and the expression of it somewhat diffuse, we must remember how unaccustomed she was to receiving any young man who wasn't a brother. She shrank, too, from any chance of being thought exacting. If any of her brothers failed to visit her, or if her father omitted his good-night call, she never inquired the reason. Elizabeth had a passionate love of liberty both for herself and for others. Her secluded life made her the more sensitive; she didn't wish people to come just out of pity. And as yet it was difficult for her to believe that any other motive could actuate Browning.

" I am like Mariana in the moated grange and sit listening too often to the mouse in the wainscot. Be as forbearing as you can—and believe how profoundly it touches me that you should care to come here at all, much more, so often ! "

Her letters were slightly more affectionate than his at this juncture, as if to assure him that her friendship was unalterably his, at least as long as he should desire it. She had shown him she wanted nothing more than friendship, and with this *situation nette* between them she could afford to end her letters, " And may God bless you, my dear friend," while he contented himself with his usual " Ever yours."

On June 9th he wrote, " I do believe we are friends now and for ever." But he told her frankly that he did not seek her friendship to do her good— any good—only to do himself good. Still, if there was any fetching or carrying to be done he eagerly offered his services, since her brothers were probably occupied with their own business and Mr. Kenyon was in New York. This suggestion evidently touched her, and she told him that if ever she wished for anything done or found she would not scruple to ask him. Only at this moment she wanted nothing but his poems—a gentle reminder that he too, like her brothers, had his work to do. And then Mr. Kenyon didn't happen to be in New York—she had seen him only a few days ago.

After the misunderstanding which had imperilled their friendship at the outset, things went smoothly. The old warm note which he had not hesitated to use before their meeting crept back insensibly into Browning's letters.

" You do not understand what a new feeling it is for me to have some one who is to like my verses or I shall not ever like them after !   So far differently was I circumstanced of old that I used rather to go about for a subject of offence to people ; writing ugly things in order to warn the ungenial and timorous off my grounds at once. . . . As it is, I will bring all I dare, in as great quantities as I can—if not next time after then—certainly.

"To bring ! Next Wednesday—if you know how happy you make me !   May I not say *that*, my dear friend, when I feel it from my soul ? "

There was a postscript with an allusion to one of her poems. " You let flowers be sent you in a letter every one knows, and this hot day draws out our very first yellow rose."   The little rhyme he made could hardly have escaped her.

The " flower in the letter," she hastened to tell him, was from her sister Arabel, though many of her poems were ideal.   But his rose came quite alive and fresh. . . . " I thank you for this and all, my dear friend."

His continued headaches alarmed her, and she begged him to seek medical advice, although she had not a great deal of faith in it herself.   They gave her digitalis to make her weak when her pulse was above a hundred and four with fever, and when she was so reduced that she could not move without fainting they gave her quinine to make her feverish again.   It seems to me that Elizabeth made a mistake in this and reversed the remedies thus applied.   Probably they gave her quinine to reduce the fever and digitalis to restore the action of the heart.

There was a chance of Browning's visiting her on the following Wednesday, but if he heard that she was expecting Mr. Chorley to call with Miss Mitford on that day he would know that it was entirely at that lady's suggestion, and that as far as she herself was concerned it would certainly not be acceded to. Elizabeth felt vexed about it, for she had already refused to see Chorley, and Miss Mitford had once before had to receive him downstairs without her. But of course she would call her perverse and capricious. Elizabeth still sedulously hid from the outside world that Browning was in the habit of coming to see her. If people heard of it others would wish to come, and she still shrank, as she had always done, from the intrusion of strange faces.

" *So till to-morrow—my light through the dark week.*" That was what he wrote on June 24th, growing a little bolder.

Alas, Wednesday was taken, not by Miss Mitford and Mr. Chorley, but by no less a person than Kenyon himself. Besides, her aunt, Mrs. Hedley, who was supposed to have been comfortably relegated to Brighton for two months, had announced her intention of arriving at midday. " Take away the doubt about Miss Mitford, and Mr. Kenyon remains, —and take away Mr. Kenyon and there is Mrs. Hedley—and thus it *must be for Friday*, which will learn to be a fortunate day for the nonce—unless Saturday should suit you better. I do not speak of Thursday because of the doubt about Miss Mitford."

His answer was abrupt but characteristic.

" Pomegranates you may cut deep down the middle and see into, not hearts—so why should I try and speak ? "

It was beginning to be a minor tragedy to both of them, when well-meaning friends or relations caused them to postpone their meetings. And after all it must be Saturday, because one of Mrs. Hedley's children was ill and she had to come up again—from Eltham this time—on the Friday. Browning let nothing interfere with his visits to her ; it is doubtful whether he made any engagement just then that was not altogether unavoidable.

So he would come on Saturday, promising, however, not to stay so long nor talk so loud, and if she were tired after seeing so many visitors she must not hesitate to tell him; or even to send down word if she were indisposed and would prefer not to receive him.   Monday or Tuesday was not so far off, after all. . . .

Miss Mitford stayed for hours on the Thursday, little guessing how ill-timed and even unwelcome her visit was.   And on the preceding day Elizabeth acknowledged that she had been tired by the confounding confusion of so many voices in her room.

Browning came on the Saturday, and brought her some roses from the garden at Hatcham.   There were trees and fields, and thrushes singing in Hatcham in those days. . . . So engrossed were they in their conversation that she quite forgot to tell him the news Mr. Kenyon had brought her—namely that Harriet Martineau was practising mesmerism. The occult always had a peculiar attraction for Elizabeth.   But Browning too had a friend, an old French friend, who was practising that same art.   He was going to dine with him.

4

The old visitors still came punctually to see her, unaware of this new and passionate interest that was colouring her life with fresh wonderful hues. Mrs. Jameson shared the honours with Miss Mitford, although at that time she had hardly become the intimate, sympathetic friend she was to show herself later on.   Elizabeth had a sensation of cold blue steel from her eyes, and acknowledged that she was a coward to her, for when Mrs. Jameson denounced carpet-work as " injurious to the mind," because it led the workers into fatal habits of reverie, she defended it.   Whereupon Mrs. Jameson told her that she could do it with impunity, because she could be writing her poems all the time !   " Think of people making poems and rugs at once. There's complex machinery for you ! "

She had never dared to disclose to Mrs. Jameson that she believed women's minds as a rule to have quicker movement but less power and depth than those of men. . . .

It was July now, the weather was bright and warm. Browning was very anxious that she should profit by it and go out. His insistence was rewarded, and on July 7th she did actually venture out, although she did not attain to either of her principal objectives, of going in the Park or of calling upon Mr. Kenyon. She got as far as Devonshire Place, and then turned back because Arabel told her to do so. But there had been no other reason—no faintness or anything of that sort. And in reply he showed his delight that she had made the effort, and begged her not to defer her drive for the reason that he was to come on any particular day.

She confessed then to her own terror of thunderstorms. " Dr. Chambers, a part of whose office it is, Papa says, to reconcile foolish women to their follies," assured her that she was peculiarly susceptible to electrical influences. It was the first time she had quoted her father to him, and Browning frankly confessed that he agreed with Dr. Chambers, rather than with Mr. Barrett. But he gave her a vivid description of the " bora " at Trieste—the sudden storm that springs up on a calm and beautiful summer's day.

For the first time the desirability of sending Elizabeth abroad to a warm climate was being seriously discussed by Mr. Barrett and Mrs. Hedley. Malta and Alexandria were mentioned as places that were likely to suit her. Of course it might come to nothing, Elizabeth told Browning in her next letter, and in any case nothing could happen before September or October. She was not likely to be consulted, but any place seemed to her more desirable than Madeira, which had sometimes before been suggested by the doctors. The news evidently took him a little aback. In her next letter she said that Malta was more probable than Alexandria. And would he come on Thursday or Friday instead of Wednesday because she was going out in the carriage on that day?

His hopes were renewed, not only by the present improvement in her condition, but also by the thought of that still greater improvement which a winter abroad might effect. "And now—surely I might dare say you may if you please get well, through God's goodness—with persevering patience surely—and this next winter abroad—which you must get ready for now, every sunny day, will you not?"

Elizabeth rebuked him for the mistakes in this letter. He had written fennel for hemlock, four o'clock for five o'clock, and other things of more consequence. And so he might not be quite right about her getting well if she pleased! It reminded her of what her father was fond of telling her, that there was nothing the matter with her except obstinacy and dry toast, and that if she would only have porter and beefsteaks instead she would be as well as ever in a month. However, as if to soften the reproach, she came nearer to telling him what he had become to her than she had ever before ventured to do. " If I get better or worse . . . as long as I live and to the last moment of life, I shall remember with an emotion which cannot change its character, all the generous interest and feeling you have spent on me. . . . I shall never forget these things, my dearest friend, nor remember them more coldly." And in return he offered: " May God bless you, and let you hold me by the hand till the end. Yes—dearest friend! "

He brought her gifts of flowers both from his sister and himself. Sometimes, too, there were little cakes for Flush. Any attention shown to Flush was a sure road to her heart. And once when Browning sent her some flowers enclosing no letter, she was disappointed and showed it. " Not a word even under the little blue flowers ! ! ! "

Of course he was delighted and flattered that she should have noticed the omission. But the carrier was waiting—there had been no time for him to put in even a word.

About this time her brother Henry confessed with shame that he had taken Browning's umbrella by mistake, thinking, when he saw it in the hall, that it belonged to a cousin who was staying with them. And he saw him without conjecturing who his sister's visitor was. Mr. Barrett was out all day, but the others came in and went out and she saw them only at certain hours, because she wasn't able to bear much talking around her. And there was no disposition on their parts to rush in when Browning was there, because he had a reputation and was supposed to talk in blank verse !

A little later she told him that there would soon be a decision, either for or against Malta, and that she was afraid of them both. . . .

CHAPTER VII

I

THEIR intimacy had progressed to such a degree
by August that Elizabeth for the first time permitted
Browning a glimpse of the domestic conditions
and difficulties that prevailed in Wimpole Street.
She felt that he could not be a friend of hers for
very long without learning something of what lay
so palpably on the surface.

She had said something about her father's autocratic temperament at one of their many meetings,
and afterwards she had a scruple lest he should not
perfectly have understood her. It wasn't that she
was weak-willed, but sometimes it was easier to
give way than to vex a person of whom you were
very fond and to whom, when all was said and done,
you owed a great deal. " It is possible to get
used to the harness and to run easily in it at last."
She had, besides, her own " side-world " of literature
and poetry in which to take refuge, and where she
was potentially free ; there was also the carpet-
work which Mrs. Jameson had called immoral.
And so far her own sense of right and happiness
had never been pitted against that formidable
authority, that autocratic will which ruled over
50 Wimpole Street and its numerous adult denizens.
Sometimes, however, she, like the rest of them,
acted secretly without the permission or knowledge
of that supreme authority. But submission was
necessary in all cases except her own, for she alone
of all the Barretts was not financially dependent upon
her father.

Having said so much she proceeded to interpret her father more tenderly, and surely that filial *apologia* must have touched the man who had been too hasty perhaps to condemn that tyranny, since in his own life he had known only tenderness and nothing of coercion.

" But what you do *not* see, what you *cannot* see, is the deep tender affection behind and below all those patriarchal ideas of governing grown-up children ' in the way they *must* go ! ' and there never was, under the strata, a truer affection in a father's heart . . . a worthier heart in itself . . . a heart loyaller and purer and more compelling to gratitude and reverence than his, as I see it ! The evil is in the system—and he simply takes it to be his duty to rule, and to make happy according to his own views of the propriety of happiness—he takes it to be his duty to rule like the Kings of Christendom, by divine right."

In this same letter—one of the longest of the many long ones she wrote to Browning—she told him graphically the history of her brother's death at Torquay. She had not, she assured him, ever said so much to any living being—she had never been able to speak or write of it. And she asked him in return not to notice it or make mention of it. Browning wrote a beautiful answer, short and delicate. He thanked her for telling him, for her invitation to participate, as it were, in the supreme grief of her life. He must have known of the tragedy from Kenyon, but so far Elizabeth had told him nothing of it, and this exhibition of her confidence could not but renew the hope that had never died in h s heart from the hour of their first meeting.

" I will write no more now ; though the sentence of ' what you are expecting—that I shall be tired of you, etc.'—though I *could* blot that out of your mind for ever by a very few words *now*—

for you *would believe* me at this moment close on
the other subject :—but I will take no such
advantage—I will wait."

This letter crossed one from her, and for three
days he did not write again. She wrote to him on
August 30th, asking the "alms of just one line."
She had taken it into her head that something was
wrong . . . perhaps she had offended him in her
last letter. Again their letters crossed, for he
sent her quite a short note that plainly indicated
he had something of importance to tell her, which
must wait until he saw her on the following Monday.

I think that her letter in which she craved the
" alms of one line " was wrongly dated by her
" Friday evening." Probably it was written on
Thursday evening, and in her agitation she put the
wrong day. For Browning received it and answered
it on Friday evening, August 30th, which was the
date of the postmarks on her letter and his reply.
His note had gone, but he was no longer able to
wait until the following Monday to tell her what
was in his heart. They had known each other now
for three months and more ; their intimacy had been
rapid and engrossing ; their frequent meetings had
been supplemented by even more frequent letters.
And he must have felt that when she had admitted
him to her confidence on those two subjects—her
brother's death and her father's tyranny—she had
admitted him also to a degree of friendship that was
but the precursor of love.

He reminded her that she had forbidden him to
speak of love to her again, and he had obeyed her.
She could not have known at that time the power
he had over himself, that he could sit and speak and
listen as he had done ever since. But now he would
tell her this once that he had loved her from his
soul, had give her his life then, as much of it as she
would take. It was done and could not be altered.
But he would not speak of it again. When he came
on Monday she would find his manner unchanged.

Elizabeth was stupefied. What had she said or done to provoke such a letter ? But the question was not one that could again be shelved. It was no longer within her power to refuse to admit him, since his visits were at least as dear to her as they were to him. But she saw one thing very clearly, too clearly perhaps for her own peace of mind. He must not love her. She had nothing to give, nothing, that is to say, that she dared to give. But she told him frankly that his had not been, of the two, the harder part. Yet she could never regret her share in the events of that summer, and his friendship would always be dear to her to the last.

"And as to what you say otherwise you are right in thinking that I would not hold by unworthy motives in avoiding to speak what you had any claim to hear. But what could I speak that would not be unjust to you ? Your life ! if you gave it to me and I put my whole heart into it what should I put but anxiety and more sadness than you were born to ? What could I give you which it would not be ungenerous to give ? "

But when he came to see her on the following Monday it was not possible to leave the matter undiscussed between them. They frankly envisaged the love that had sprung up between them, even though she felt so passionately that to bind him to any engagement would be to do him too great a wrong.

Although the plan of her going to Malta had been temporarily dropped, the question of her spending the winter at Pisa was being seriously discussed. Browning's evident intention was to follow Elizabeth and her sister to Pisa—he said that he might even arrive there before them. Elizabeth regarded this plan as of doubtful expediency.

On the Tuesday night he wrote a few lines :

"I rather hoped, with no right at all . . . to

hear from you this morning or afternoon—to know
how you are—that ' how are you,' there is no
disguising, is—vary it how one may—my own life's
question."

The same night he wrote an even shorter note :

" Before you leave London I will answer your
letter—all my attempts end in nothing now."

2

Meanwhile Dr. Chambers held out every hope
that if Elizabeth were to winter in the mild climate
of Pisa her present improvement would continue.
To her relief, however, he vetoed the beefsteak and
porter prescribed by Mr. Barrett.

Elizabeth was full of the Pisa project. She
induced her brother George to find out the probable
dates of sailings. The direct Leghorn steamer
did not leave till about the middle of October,
which she considered too late, but there was one for
Malta that left on September 20th. By going in
it she could change at Gibraltar and take a French
steamer thence to Leghorn. She appealed to
Browning for help. For in the midst of it all there
was a little deadly fear at her heart, caused by her
father's ambiguous silence. Now that the time
for starting was drawing near the whole project
seemed too impossibly fantastic to one who for
years had not slept a single night away from home,
and whose longest excursion had been a drive in the
Park.

Mr. Kenyon urged her to go. It was arranged
that one of her sisters should accompany her. She
began to wish that it were either July or November,
so that the journey could be out of sight. For
it had always been planned that she should go in
September, and it was already the 9th of that month,
and Elizabeth, so unused to travelling, dreaded the

exertion it entailed. She needed all her courage to cling to the slender chance of complete recovery thus offered her.

Her brothers all supported her, and George especially counselled her unhesitatingly to go. Her father wrote a little note of consent, and on seeing this both George and her aunt, Mrs. Hedley, advised her to spend the winter at Pisa. She forwarded George's letter on the subject to Browning, begging him to burn it. It was addressed to "Ba," and she explained to him that this was her nickname in the house.

In the same letter she enclosed two sonnets, written to her sisters, which would help him, she hoped, to distinguish between them. The one about Arabel was especially tender. Henrietta, she told him, was the elder, and the one who had first brought him up to her room, and Arabel was the one who would accompany her to Pisa if she went. Arabel was her favourite, though to acknowledge it seemed to savour of disloyalty. Browning in his answer replied that he remembered the light hair, which was Arabel's. It pleased him to be told of her little name, "Ba." He had known so far very little of her family, had heard them spoken of more or less collectively, though lately the names of George and Alfred had emerged with more clearness of outline. These signs of a deepening intimacy, a desire on her part to admit him to a closer knowledge of her surroundings, were perhaps the reason of his writing to her with an even greater lucidity on September 13th. Already he was addressing her as dearest, although he had not as yet begun to call her Ba. And in this letter he approached the subject of ways and means. In Pisa, he believed, it was possible to live on £100 a year. For himself, he had lived for two years on bread and potatoes, probably at the time when the knowledge of Shelley's vegetarianism had inspired him to a similar experiment. His wants were small, were easily supplied, but now that he saw her so close to the life he had planned all was changed. In fact he would try to earn some money. . . .

The obstacles, she told him, were not connected with money, inasmuch as she had three or four hundred a year of her own, of which no one could dispossess her. But if her father knew that he had written to her in that way, and that she had answered him so, he would not forgive her at the end of ten years. This had nothing to do with Browning's name and position, it was unaffected by his lack of means, or by the fact that he had not adopted a remunerative career. It was simply that he did not approve of his children falling in love. He did not, in fact, tolerate in his children, either sons or daughters, the development of a certain class of feelings. . . .

So far, they had regarded this idiosyncrasy with tolerance and a certain sense of humour. Elizabeth had once said to her sisters :

" If a prince of Eldorado should come with a pedigree of lineal descent from some signory in the moon in one hand, and a ticket of good behaviour from the nearest Independent chapel in the other ? . . ."

" Why, even then it would not *do* ! " was Arabel's rejoinder.

Perhaps it had been easy enough to laugh at it in the past, but neither Elizabeth nor Henrietta was able to accept it so lightly now. They were both being sought in marriage, and the utmost secrecy had perforce to be maintained. Mr. Barrett so far suspected nothing, but he was without doubt subconsciously aware of the conspiracies that possessed his household in the autumn of 1845.

3

During the eternal discussions about Pisa, Mr. Barrett's silence was obstinate if a trifle ominous. Although nothing was said in his presence, he was aware that his children were solidly united against him in the matter. Mrs. Hedley, too . . . but he had listened to her advice and remonstrances already once too often, and it was unlikely that she would be able to influence him now. And Elizabeth . . . there was something about her demeanour which intrigued him. During the past six months a great change had come over her ; she was no longer such a complete invalid . . . she seemed to gain in strength and vitality every day . . . she often drove out with Arabel. He did not enquire too closely into this strange regeneration of one who had once been given only a few months to live. It is certain that at this juncture he never discovered the real cause, nor traced it to the regular visits of the " Poet of the Pomegranates," as he was wont to call Browning. Indeed, that Elizabeth, whom he had once described as the purest woman he had ever known, should be thinking of love and marriage never entered into his wildest imaginings.

Still, the matter of Pisa pressed heavily. Dr. Chambers expressed his belief that if she spent the winter in a warm climate she might be cured. Perhaps Mr. Barrett passed in review those phthisical patients whom Italy had failed to save. Keats, for instance—what had the climate of Rome done for Keats ? He had lived a few miserable months in a moribund condition after his arrival there. To send Elizabeth to Italy was at least a hazardous experiment, and who could tell if she would even survive the journey ? Had Torquay—so confidently recommended seven years ago—proved of any permanent benefit ? On the contrary, she had returned home from her disastrous sojourn there with death in her face and at her heart. . . .

Notwithstanding Mr. Barrett's silence, the secret preparations went forward. George, whose practice at the Bar must by now have procured him a certain measure of independence, occupied himself with finding out the probable sailings of Mediterranean-bound vessels. When everything was settled he

determined to approach his father and break down
that perverse and ambiguous silence.

Elizabeth herself was torn between conflicting
emotions. Always doubtful of the expediency and
even of the desirability of Browning's plan of joining
her at Pisa, she felt the bitterness of the approaching
parting from him.   Yet matters had so far progressed
between them that she could no longer blind herself
to the fact that he loved her and wished to marry
her, and that nothing but her own delicate health
constituted a real barrier to their union.   It was
thus her duty for his sake to go abroad in the hope
of regaining her health.   She could not throw away
this chance of recovery upon which all their future
happiness depended.

They were all discussing it, for journeys in those
days were not only expensive, but difficult, and were
by no means to be undertaken lightly.   Mr. Kenyon
paid them one or two visits, coming up from Brighton
to see what he could do.   Mr. Boyd, Miss Mitford,
Mrs. Jameson, and Mrs. Hedley all championed
the project.   Only the Oracle of Wimpole Street
remained dumb. . . .

But behind this silence he showed his displeasure.
He no longer visited his daughter at night.   He
ceased to address her as " my puss " and "my love."
He must have been painfully aware that he stood
alone.   Even Kenyon, his cousin and contemporary,
was against him.

" I had expected more help than I have found,"
Elizabeth wrote to Mrs. Martin about this time,
" and am left to myself, thrown so on my own sense
of duty as to feel it right for the sake of future years
to stand by myself as I best can."

Towards the end of September she had a scene
with her father.   The simple act of putting on
her gloves evoked his wrath.   He complained
of the undutifulness and rebellion of every one in
the house.   He did not even exempt his eldest
daughter from this general charge ; he meant it
for them all, one with another.

Elizabeth pointed out to him that her health, her very life, depended on the step, and that although she was willing to sacrifice it out of affection for him, she must feel that he exacted the sacrifice, and that it was no idle one, made blindly or through any misapprehension. He refused to answer. He would not say that he was either pleased or displeased. She could do what she liked—he washed his hands of her. . . .

George declared that she had done all that was possible, and advised her to go on with her preparations. What should she do ? She appealed to Browning for advice. There was her dread of involving Arabel and Stormie (who were to accompany her) in a project that was so obviously unpopular, although George believed that even if she renounced it altogether there would be displeasure just the same. " Shall I give it up at once ?   Do think for me."

4

These revelations must have seemed almost incomprehensible to Robert Browning, whose own parents were so amiable and tender, and whose home-life was one of such harmonious tranquillity. Elizabeth was to him the victim of the veriest slavery, and he who could free her from it, now and for ever, scarcely dared to write, " though I know you must feel for me and forgive what forces itself from me . . . what retires so mutely into my heart at your least word . . . what shall not again be written or spoken if you so will . . . that I should be made happy beyond all hope of expression by."

When he first knew her he had believed that she was not only incurable, but absolutely dependent upon her father ; but now he knew she could never be poor, and that there was hope of her regaining a measure of health and strength, he made an astonishingly unselfish offer. He would marry her at once, and for the rest things should remain as they were. He would come and go only at her bidding ; he would be no more to her than her own brothers. " I deliberately choose the realisation of that dream (of sitting simply by you for an hour every day), rather than any other, excluding you, I am able to form for this world or any world I know."

This letter left her in no manner of doubt as to the profundity and durability of his feeling for her. She told him that it did her good and took away all the little bitternesses from her life. He had touched her more profoundly than she had believed to be possible, yet when he had been with her that day her heart was deeply touched. She added that she left him perfectly free, but should she ever get better she would be to him whatever he chose.

" *My own* now ! " he wrote in answer.

Difficulties arose which baffled even George. The cabins on the two Malta-bound steamers in October were all engaged, thus she was faced with the dismal alternative of Madeira or Cadiz unless she went to Gibraltar and changed steamers there.

The moment had now arrived for George to obtain some definite statement from his father. He himself was going away on Sessions, and there was no time to be lost. Thus confronted by his son, Mr. Barrett said Elizabeth might go if she liked, but it would be under his heaviest displeasure. George was angry and indignant and pressed the point, but Mr. Barrett was obdurate. Elizabeth was thus left to decide the matter for herself.

The stars in their courses were fighting against her, for at this critical juncture Octavius, the youngest son of the house, was taken seriously ill with fever of a typhoidal nature, and it would thus have been almost impossible for Elizabeth to add in any way to her father's anxiety. Kenyon, too, told her that while she had every right to decide for herself, she was hardly justified in exposing Arabel and Stormie to their father's displeasure.

G

A little natural bitterness escaped her as she saw her one chance of recovery thus frustrated, for no adequate reason, but simply from motives of caprice. "Do you think," she wrote to Mrs. Martin, "that I was born to live the life of an oyster, such as I do live here? Do you know what it is to laugh that you may not cry?"

She had been told that if she had gone abroad years ago, she would have been well by now, as only one lung was slightly affected. But her nervous system was shattered (and perhaps Wimpole Street was hardly the best place for a nervous invalid!) and she took by the doctor's orders forty drops of laudanum a day to quiet her pulse.

To Hugh Boyd she wrote: "I do not go to Pisa, my dear friend. It is decided that I remain in my prison. It was my full intention to go."

And in the meantime she was comforted by those constant letters that now concealed nothing of Browning's love for her. "My life is bound up with yours, my own first and last love," he wrote to her in the midst of it all.

"Can you care so much—*you*?" she wrote. "Then that is light enough to account for all the shadows." In proportion as she realised that her father's love had failed her, so did she learn to appreciate this deeper and more passionate feeling that was being offered to her. The bitterest fact that emerged from the episode was the knowledge that her father had not loved her as much as she believed, yet she never regretted knowledge.

"My cage is not worse but better since you brought the green groundsel to it," she wrote to Browning about this time, "and to dash oneself against the wires of it will not open the door."

From this time, however, she became more careful. Not in her letters, for on both sides now that their ove was openly declared a gradual crescendo is ndicated, so that she dared to write to him: "You have come to me as a dream comes, as the best dreams come." But because of their acknowledged love, and what really amounted to a secret engagement between them, precautions were absolutely necessary. Supposing, for instance, Robert came too often and his visits were noticed, " difficulties and vexations " would inevitably ensue. It would be wiser to run no risk. The settled weekly visit was an established thing, and every now and then he might come twice in the same week, but there must be no fixed habit. " Let Pisa prove the excellent hardness of some marbles."

" I love you because I love you," was his answer. " I see you once a week because I cannot see you all day long. . . . Let me have my way, live my life, love my love."

And she, on her side :   " You do not know what my life meant before you touched it."

<h1 style="text-align:center">5</h1>

She knew in her heart that Browning blamed Mr. Barrett bitterly for his recent action in denying her what might have meant health and even life. Elizabeth often tried to modify his view. She begged him to understand that there might be " an eccentricity, an obliquity, in certain relations and on certain subjects," while the general character was worthy of both esteem and regard. Mr. Kenyon, however, averred that his friend's attitude towards marriage amounted to monomania, and indeed he was hardly exaggerating when we remember the immortal occasion upon which Mr. Barrett harangued his assembled children on the duty of passive obedience, especially in regard to marriage. One by one his sons left the room, and only Captain Surtees Cook, who was secretly engaged to Henrietta, remained. When Mr. Barrett had finished his oration he mildly inquired, as if asking for information, whether children were to be regarded as slaves ?

But although Mr. Barrett must seem to us, and to all admirers of his brilliant, gifted daughter, a harsh, austere man, utterly insensitive to the spiritual needs of his children, exercising even when they were grown-up a tyrannical authority sustained by his almost complete control of the family finances, there were traits in his character which under more favourable conditions might have achieved greatness.

His fortitude in adversity frequently elicited his daughter's admiration. Like herself, he was dumb in the presence of calamity, permitting nothing of pain to escape him. And at a certain period of his life successive misfortunes overwhelmed him like waves. The death of his wife, the loss of fortune consequent upon the emancipation of the West Indian negroes, the appalling disaster that robbed him of his eldest son, that rare spirit Edward Barrett, the grave malady that reduced his favourite child to a condition of absolute invalidism—all these calamities elicited from him neither complaint nor outward rebellion. But his heart was embittered. It seemed, indeed, to undergo a process of figurative ossification. Having suffered so much, he took the perverse view that henceforward his children must yield and submit to him in all things. While giving them all that was necessary on the material side, he denied them such essentials as love and light and laughter. They must not wish for anything that lay outside the gloomy precincts of No. 50 Wimpole Street, although his passionate temper, menacing anger, sarcastic comments, and the scenes to which he subjected his sensitive daughters wrecked the peace of that house. And although he reacted insensibly to those rebellious undercurrents that affected, albeit imperceptibly, the atmosphere of his home, he little dreamed that even at that moment two of the prisoners were actually beating their wings against the bars in an agonising desire for freedom and escape to the wider horizons that lay beyond.

This condition of things not only perplexed

Browning but it also rendered him almost unduly anxious. His own home was so different, and while Elizabeth had once frankly acknowledged that had her father known the content of her letters to him he would not have forgiven her at the end of ten years, Browning could offer by way of contrast that had he taken his letter to her downstairs and expressed a wish that it should be delivered that same night at her address his father would have at once declared that he " wanted a walk," or that he " had just been wishing to go out." And his mother, he added, loved him just as much more as must of necessity be. . . .

This " involuntary contrast," as he called it, between the two households rendered it even more difficult for him to appreciate the complete dominion Mr. Barrett exercised so ruthlessly over his daughters. But realising how deeply and almost dumbly Elizabeth suffered beneath that tyrannous rule, he was determined to remove her from her present environment as soon as ever it was possible to do so.

CHAPTER VIII

I

" I am yours—your own—only not to hurt you."

The first sharpness of disappointment was over, and Elizabeth, when she wrote those significant words to Browning, was already making plans for the winter. They were both to be busy and cheerful. He would come and see her all through the dark months when she was a prisoner indoors, unless, of course, he decided upon going abroad. Occy was better, and was developing the usual enormous appetite of the starved typhoid patient. The clouds that had gathered and hung over Wimpole Street were beginning to disperse.

Meantime, Elizabeth received a letter from a firm of American publishers offering her liberal terms for permission to reprint her prose papers which had appeared in the *Athenæum*. The volume was to be published both in England and America. She felt a little disinclined to revise those essays for the press and to supplement them with the additional matter required. She asked Browning's advice, and he considered the opportunity most favourable for every reason and urged her not to hesitate, but to accept the offer at once.

He sent her, too, the proofs of his new book of poems. These included *The Lost Mistress, Saul, Pictor Ignotus, The Ride, The Last Duchess*, and many more. *Luria* was submitted to her in instalments, as he wrote it, and met with her eager appreciation and encouragement. She was working, too, she assured him, and it was probably during that winter that many of the *Sonnets from the Portuguese* were written.

She told him once that in her hour of bitterest sorrow she had never been tempted to ask, " How have I deserved this of God ? " She had always felt there was cause enough for the chastisement. But in this very different hour " when joy follows joy " she could not repress the thought : " How have I deserved this of Him ? " She had not deserved it ; she did not deserve it. . . .

Then came one of the most beautiful passages in all her many letters :

" Could it be that heart and life were devastated to make room for you ?—If so, it was well done, dearest ! They leave the ground fallow before the wheat. . . . "

Her letters alone place Elizabeth Barrett among the great prose-writers of the nineteenth century. They possess a certain careless grace of language that makes them at once unstudied and of a delicate individual quality. Browning's letters could never attain to that same perfection, although when he wrote of his love for her there was a depth of poetic passion that even she could never surpass, and which atones for the hesitating, stumbling sentences, tortured with many a parenthesis and not always too happily worded, which form the greater part of his missives.

George was to meet Browning at dinner, and was properly " indoctrinated," inasmuch as before going to chambers he looked in and inquired with a smile if Elizabeth had a message for her friend. " That was *you* . . . and so he was indoctrinated."

The two men met and liked each other. Browning did not ask after Elizabeth, because he heard Moxon, the publisher, doing so. George applied the epithet " unassuming " to Browning, who was certainly never one to adopt the conscious pose of a celebrity. He was, however, a little hard on Mr. Chorley, who was present on the same occasion, considering his affectation "bad." There was, too, he assured his sister, a touch of vulgarity about Chorley.

Browning thought that George was over-hasty in condemning the famous editor and critic. His verdict was, however, no unusual one. Many writers of that day disliked him. Miss Mitford called him a coxcomb ; Harriet Martineau picked a quarrel with him ; Charlotte Brontë, although afraid of him as a critic, was disdainful in her allusions to him.

" Chorley is of a different species to your brother," Browning wrote, " differently trained, looking different ways. Your kind brother will alter his view, I know, on further acquaintance." It would be impossible, too, he added ,as if in deprecation of that praise of himself, for anyone to be assuming under Mr. Kenyon's hospitable roof, "where every symptom of a proper claim is met half-way."

In December Elizabeth gave him—not without some hesitation—a ring containing a lock of her hair. It was the fashion of lovers at that date to exchange such trophies, as a cursory glance at one's great-grandmother's treasure-case will reveal. Woven hair played a not inconsiderable part in the bracelets, rings, lockets and other love-tokens of the day. One may wonder if such relics will ever acquire a marketable value, but to our more modern eyes they seem to possess a forlorn and rather pathetic quality. This particular one was sold with the other Browning relics at Sotheby's in 1913, when the famous letters realised the sum of £6,550.

George further evinced his partiality for Browning by going to a party at Mr. Talfourd's on purpose to see the author of *Paracelsus* dancing the polka. The polka was not a success, for of his two partners, one had not the head to dance and the other was an indifferent performer. Still, he talked a little to George, whom he liked more and more. " It comforts me that he is yours."

2

But in spite of this promising friendship with her brother and their mutual liking for each other, Elizabeth was not unmindful of the growing danger of her own situation. She had nothing to fear from her brothers, who were delighted that she should have this new interest in her life, and probably they imagined she was too old to be sought in marriage, and that her friendship with Browning was a purely intellectual one. From her sisters she had even less fear of betrayal, for Henrietta was engaged in a secret affair of her own with Captain Surtees Cook, who was permitted to come to the house and was even occasionally invited to dinner because he was a cousin. The danger lay exclusively in the possible awakening of Mr. Barrett. . . .

Despite her early love-affair which had ended so disastrously, Henrietta, who trembled at the mere bending of her father's brows, had embarked like her sister upon a clandestine engagement. For her there was even less prospect of marriage, inasmuch as she was entirely dependent upon her father, and Surtees Cook had little private means. At one time she had had three suitors. One of them who withdrew from the contest nicknamed the others Perseverance and Despair. Perseverance, who was Surtees Cook, drove Despair from the field, and it was said that he subsequently consoled himself with a new horse and some music-lessons. " I always persevere about everything," Surtees Cook used to announce airily. And persevere he did, waiting every morning until Mr. Barrett had departed for the City, and then appearing to lay siege to Henrietta's heart.   He cared nothing for the rudeness of the Barrett brothers nor for the obvious hesitancy of the sisters, but remained there for four hours until Henrietta declared she was " taken by storm and couldn't help it."

Arabel slept in the same room with Elizabeth, and in January 1846 she was admitted to her sister's confidence. She, however, shrank from involving her brothers in the matter lest they should suffer for it, but they tacitly accepted the situation and sometimes expressed their conjectures and suspicions, although never unsympathetically. Yet the danger always remained. Mr. Barrett left the house every morning after breakfast and did not return until six o'clock at night, but did it never occur to him to wonder how his sons and daughters were employed in the interim? Always Elizabeth knew that she stood on the brink of a precipice. One false move, and the ground would crumble beneath her feet. And then Browning would be forbidden ever to enter No. 50 again, his letters would be stopped and destroyed, even perhaps opened and read. . . .

3

" From out of the deep dark pits men see the stars more gloriously, and *de profundis amavi*." . . .

Elizabeth wrote thus to Browning as Christmas approached. Almost she wished that she might die that winter—die before she had ever disappointed him. For when he came to know her well, how could he help being displeased and disappointed? His very extravagance of affection frightened her. . . .

The winter proved an astonishingly mild one, and although a prisoner indoors, Elizabeth suffered little from actual illness. The letters " rained down " as usual, and Browning's visits were as frequent as prudence allowed.

Once on a marvellously warm January day— the thermometer stood at 68° in her room—Elizabeth ventured down to the drawing-room. It was the first time she had walked downstairs, for even in the autumn when she had gone out for a drive one of her brothers had invariably carried her. Everyone was as astonished as if she had walked out of the window instead of down the stairs. Stormie, the shy, awkward one with his stammering speech, who possessed the most loving of hearts, told her eagerly he was *so* glad to see her. The little episode cheered her, though she paid for it with a restless, feverish night.

She sometimes imagined they had ceased to pity her, believing her to have become accustomed to her entombment, which they now took for granted. It needed some such trivial incident to demonstrate that they were less indifferent than she had supposed.

As the weeks wore on, Browning's restiveness increased. Disliking the secrecy, he became ever more desirous of confronting Mr. Barrett. The two men had never met, and Elizabeth had once apologised to Robert for her inability to draw him into the family circle so that he might make his own way with her relations. Such a feat would have been impossible. Even her brothers were not permitted to invite their friends. So far George was the only one of her family with whom Browning had any acquaintance, and that was solely due to Mr. Kenyon's kindness ; it had not been of Elizabeth's seeking.

She wrote now quite frankly of her father, because it was necessary to deter the impulsive, fearless Browning from approaching him. It wasn't that she didn't love him ; from first to last she clung to that pitiful assertion. She could discern all that was good in him, could hear the fountain within the rock, could admire his great qualities of fortitude, courage, endurance. Notwithstanding the miserable system which made him seem even harder than he was, she loved him and clung to him. But even before her illness people had told her that she looked broken-spirited, and it was because she was made to suffer through the sufferings imposed upon others. Yet after her return to London from Torquay she could remember that he had been so kind and gentle to her that once she had told him her best hope was "to die beneath his eyes." "After all, he is the victim. He isolates himself—and now and then he feels it . . . the cold dead silence all around him which is the effect of an incredible system. If he were not stronger than most men he could not bear it as he does."

Browning, however, shrank from the mere contemplation of her being exposed to a tyranny from which he could at any moment release her. He told her that it could not be for her good that this state of things should continue, and frankly said that in the autumn he should claim her promise, since his one good in the world was to spend his life with her and to be hers. After their marriage they could live for a year or two in Italy, in the hope that a milder climate would restore her health.

Incredible as the thought had been when it was first presented to her—that she was absolutely necessary to his happiness, and that the undue delay, the devastating uncertainty, were even affecting his health—Elizabeth was now compelled to envisage this side of the question. She was all his world. He wanted to take her away from the storms and scenes, the slavery and oppression that prevailed in Wimpole Street, to that calmer and more serene life he was able to offer her. But it was not only for her sake; it was in far greater measure for his own.

I suppose she never wrote a more beautiful and tender letter than the one she sent in reply.

"Let it be this way, ever dearest. If in the time of fine weather I am not ill, then, not now, you shall decide and your decision shall be duty and desire to me both. I will make no difficulties. . . . That I love you enough to 'give you up for your good' is proof (to myself at least) that I love you enough for any other end—but you thought *too much of me in the last letter*. Do not mistake me. I believe and trust in all your words—only you are generous unawares, as other men are selfish.

"More I meant to say of this ; but you moved me

as usual into the sunshine yesterday; and then I am dazzled and cannot see clearly.   Still, I see that you love me and that I am bound to you and ' what more need I see ' you may ask; while I cannot help looking out to the future, to the blue ridges of the hills, to the chances of your being happy with me. Well!   I am yours as you see. . . . You shall decide everything when the time comes for doing anything. . . ."

It was about this time that she asked him to return the letter he had written after their first meeting, wishing to possess once more that first expression of his love.   But he had burnt it, as she had requested him to do at the time.   It was apparent that his letter of repudiation still rankled, for she once more alluded to the " deep black pits of cold water," and said she was glad to think that his liking for her did not come and go.   As for herself, she sometimes felt that her own letters were cold, but her feelings were near to overflow and she had perforce to try to " hold the cup straight."

" You understand—you will not accuse me of over-cautiousness and the like.   On the contrary you are all things to me . . . instead of all and better than all!   You have fallen like a great luminous blot on the whole leaf of the world . . . of life and time . . . and I can see nothing beyond you, nor wish to see it.   As to all that was evil and sadness to me I do not feel it any longer—it may be raining still, but I am in the shelter and can scarcely tell.   If you *could* be *too dear* to me you would be now—but you could not—I do not believe in those supposed excesses of pure affections—God cannot be too great.   Therefore it is a conditional engagement still—all the conditions being in your hands, except the necessary one of my health. . . . "

She signed the letter for the first time, *Your own Ba*.

4

Their betrothal, although secret and, to her, conditional, was now an accomplished fact, and that they continued to conceal it from everyone in the house except Henrietta and Arabel speaks well for their caution and prudence. Yet they had some narrow escapes, and even outsiders were becoming suspicious.

Sam Barrett—a cousin—openly chaffed Henrietta about the withdrawal of "Despair" before the superior attractions and more obstinate persistence of Surtees Cook. Everyone knew all about it, he declared, except her father, and he didn't blame her for keeping it a secret, as it was well known that Mr. Barrett would never consent to the marriage of any of his sons and daughters. Sam did not stop there. Not contented with attacking Henrietta, he boldly continued :

"And what's this about Ba ? "

"Who has been persuading you of such nonsense ? " her sisters asked.

" Oh, my authority is very good ! It's perfectly unnecessary for you to tell any stories, Arabel. A *literary* friendship, is it ? "

It was a relief to hear that Sam had gone to Paris. . . .

Mr. Barrett came into his daughter's room one morning and found Robert Browning there. This was apparently their first meeting, and perhaps the fact of her receiving a visitor at such an unusual hour aroused his suspicions. His displeasure was visible to her when he went up to see her that evening. Robert was told, however, that he mustn't feel uncomfortable about it for she wasn't scolded. It was just his manner. . . . But his deadly obstinate silence possessed a more sinister quality than any words, and it confirmed her bitter belief that it would be futile to hope for any yielding from that quarter. This was in February, and the episode must have brought home to her how desperate was the game in which they were engaged, how slender were their chances of ultimate success.

She told Browning frankly that she was compelled by the doctors to take opium to quiet her pulses. He said in one of his letters that he had never dared nor would dare inquire into her use of it, but obviously the knowledge imbued him with a certain anxiety.

" Knowing you utterly as I do I know you would only bend to the most absolute necessity in taking more or less of it.   Increase must signify increased weakness, a diminution diminished illness.   And now there is diminution."

But all the kind explaining about the opium made him happier.   He was evidently a little startled at the admission, and perhaps he felt that the administration of this drug accounted for something wavering, uncertain, vacillating in her character, for an occasional rather undue excitement, as well as for her inability on certain days to receive him. And perhaps thenceforward he waited with an increased impatience for the time when he could take her away from those exhausting scenes and apprehensions which rendered the use of morphine necessary.

5

Miss Mitford was still a constant visitor, less welcome now, perhaps, than when there had been no Browning whose afternoons she unconsciously stole. Nor was she always sympathetic, for she was a lady of very pronounced likes and dislikes.   Poor " Orion " Horne, who stayed for a few days in her neighbourhood in Berkshire, was severely trounced to Elizabeth.   He asked to be called at four and did not get up until eight.   He poured water on his bare head from the finger-glasses at great dinners. In the society of sportsmen, those rural aristocrats who discoursed learnedly of horses and dogs, he had

been heard to exclaim in a loud mocking voice :
" If I were to hold up a horse by its tail ? " He
threw himself full length on satin sofas ; he giggled ;
he thought he could talk, whereas his ignorance on
all subjects was astounding. He had an unpleasant
habit also of proposing to heiresses, and thought no
one's poetry any good but his own. There was much
more besides, for Miss Mitford discoursed copiously
and acidly on the subject.

Browning considered that this description was
a gross misrepresentation of Horne, if not an actually
false one. He did know a good deal about horses,
and although he might fling himself upon sofas
he could talk admirably when thus recumbent.
Browning didn't believe a word about his proposing to
heiresses, and added that he was singularly generous
in his praise of other people's poetry. . . .

Browning was not at all well that winter, and in
February he suffered more than usual from headaches. Elizabeth suggested the remedy of putting
his feet into hot water at night ; she was always
perhaps unduly anxious when anything ailed him.
Once, after one of his visits, she asked her maid,
Wilson, how she thought he was looking, and was
evidently comforted by her answer. Wilson declared
she hadn't noticed, but Mr. Browning certainly
ran upstairs instead of walking as he did the time
before ! . . .

Perhaps Mr. Barrett's suspicions were momen-
tarily lulled, for he told his daughter one evening
that Mr. Kenyon had invited George to meet
Mr. Browning and Mr. Procter.

Browning enjoyed the party. They were discussing Mrs. Jameson, and he let the talk go on by itself
until he suddenly heard his own voice utter the
words, " Miss Barrett." He added hastily, " Mrs.
Jameson says," for his visits were still a secret from
such men as Procter, and only George understood
the significance of his speech or even perhaps noticed
the gaucherie.

Whatever fears Browning might once have

entertained as to her lack of reciprocation must
have been by this time set completely at rest. When
Henrietta asked her if she ever regretted posting a
letter because she felt it had not been very kind, her
answer was that she had only regretted them for
the very reverse of that reason, because when once
posted they seemed to her too kind. Both her
sisters laughed at the admission.

" You are all to me, all the light, all the life ;
I am living for you now.   And before I knew you
what was I and where ?   What was the world to
me, do you think, and the meaning of life ? . . . My
claim is that you are more to me than I can be to
you. . . . "

It seemed to her now that all the time she had
loved him unawares. Yet indeed it had never
entered her head when he first came to see her that
she was destined to love him. She was a hero-
worshipper, had cared for his poetry for many
years, and afterwards it was a pleasure and pride to
receive his letters and to write to him. And then
there had been for her a curious psychological but
quite understandable difficulty—that of reconciling
the two personalities—the man who had written to
her and the man who had subsequently come to
see her.

6

The spring came early, and at the end of February
he sent her a sprig of hawthorn (or was it blackthorn ?)
to give her a practical proof of its progress.   Elizabeth, too, lured by the warmer weather, had put on
her cloak and descended to the drawing-room, where
she found Henrietta awaiting Captain Surtees Cook,
who had promised to come in, after a levée at St.
James's Palace, in his regimentals. Although he
was a cousin, Elizabeth had never seen him, but,
conquering her dislike of meeting strangers, she

complied with her sister's request that she should stay with her to receive him. He failed to appear, and Elizabeth teased Henrietta by saying that Queen Victoria must have been so enchanted with the regimentals that she had invited him to stay and dine! The minutes passed, and Elizabeth, fearing other visitors, was anxious to return to her room, but Henrietta held her almost by force, with the result that she was called upon to confront the unlikely person of Mrs. Jameson.

Henrietta took the visitor upstairs, where Elizabeth joined her. She was extraordinarily kind, offering to accompany her to Italy. Elizabeth wanted desperately to hear her speak of Browning and even praise the last " Bell." But she herself could not summon up courage to introduce his name. Mrs. Jameson in common with the rest of her friends, with the solitary exception of Kenyon, knew nothing of her friendship with the poet.

Indeed, she had kept the fact a secret so long that it would have embarrassed her to divulge it now. But sometimes after Mrs. Jameson's visits she felt half ashamed, and accused herself of being a hypocrite because she had discussed Browning as if she did not know him personally. She was led on to speak of him, to utter her complete appreciation and admiration of his work, until Mrs. Jameson exclaimed : " I am really glad to hear you speak so ! " But the scene disturbed Elizabeth ; her hands were " marble-cold " when her visitor took leave of her, and she felt almost on the brink of tears. The two women had, however, become friends, and Elizabeth could no longer detect the steely glance that had troubled her at first. Browning had been anxious that they should like each other.

As Mrs. Jameson was leaving London for a month there was no chance of seeing her again for the moment, and Browning, despite his liking for her, found relief in the thought. For if she began to talk about " Ba " to him he knew that if his hands did not turn cold, his ear-tips would certainly turn red.   The wonder is that they were able to keep the secret of their friendship so long from the outside world.

For these people who came regularly to see her, Miss Mitford, Mrs. Jameson, Mr. Kenyon and the rest, must have noticed the change in Elizabeth ; the increased vitality, the happier look, as well as the flowers that always filled her room with their light and colour, and which were brought or sent regularly from the fertile little garden at Hatcham. Were the constantly remitted proofs of *Luria* and the *Soul's Tragedy* always sedulously and effectively concealed when these " people of importance " were conducted by Henrietta to the mysterious, darkened upper chamber where one of England's most famous women lay on her sofa with Flush beside her ?

Even her brothers on coming up would look round and say :   " So Mr. Browning has been here again ! " when their eyes fell on the fresh spring flowers.

It was a shock to Elizabeth to hear at the end of March that Miss Mitford had postponed her visit to Paris and intended to spend a fortnight in London, with the intention of coming to see her every day. " I look a little aghast.   *Am I not grateful and affectionate ?*   Is it right of you not to let me love anyone as I used to do ? "

Even Miss Mitford and Mr. Kenyon, dear friends as they were, were less welcome than they used to be, because so often Browning's visits were made to give way before theirs, lest their suspicions should be in any way aroused.

CHAPTER IX

I

" I SEEM now always to hear the sea in the wind,
voice within voice! But I like a sudden wind—
not too loud—a wind which you hear the rain in
rather than the sea—and I like the half cloudy,
half sunny April weather such as we have it here in
England, with a west or south wind— I like and enjoy
that ; and remember vividly how I used to like to
wade nearly up to my waist in the wet grass or weeds,
with the sun overhead, and the wind darkening or
lightening the verdure all round."

She looked back thus on the old childish days at
Hope End, when she had roamed at will in field and
wood, and felt the wind blowing against her face and
heard the rain pattering on the leaves. But even that
seemed no longer happiness to her. " None of it
was happiness, dearest, dearest. Happiness does
not come with the sun or the rain. . . . Now I know
life from death . . . and the unsorrowful life for
the first time since I was a woman ; though I sit
here on the edge of a precipice in a position full of
anxiety and danger."

April had come ; they had known each other for
nearly a year, and for fifteen months they had
corresponded regularly and punctually. It was a
relief to her that her father kept so far from her now,
she told Browning. He had almost given up coming
to see her in the evening. Had he been affectionate, or made her feel for a moment that she was
necessary to him, it would have been difficult for

her even to contemplate giving him pain. The Pisa episode had taught her many things—hard and even bitter things—but it had made her way seem clearer.

Browning became impatient. She had told him that it would be dreadfully natural if he were to leave off loving her. " Like the sun's setting. No more wonder, only more darkness, more pain."

His answer was characteristic. " Oh, dearest, let us marry soon—very soon—and end all this ! . . . *Can* you now, by this time, tell me or yourself that you could believe me happy with any other woman that ever breathed ? I tell *you*, without affectation, that I lay the whole blame on myself . . . that I feel that if I had spoken my love out sufficiently, all this doubt could never have been possible."

His letter, she said, went to her heart and stayed there and seemed to mix with the blood of it. She had never felt towards him as she had done when she read it. " No words but *just your own*, between heaven and earth, could have persuaded me that one such as you could love me ! and the tongue of angels could not speak better words for that purpose than just yours. Also I know that you love me . . . I do know it, my only dearest, and recognise it in the gratitude of my soul :—and it is through my want of familiarity with any happiness—through the want of use in carrying these weights of flowers, that I drop them again and again out of weak hands."

But he had convinced her at last that with him this was no passing infatuation, but a love that could only cease with life. When she told him frankly that she was not worthy of him—for was she not six years his senior and a frail invalid at that ?—he only answered that for him all power of choice was past. She might be right or he might be right, he could not decide (although the suggestion that she was not worthy of him met always with a scornful disclaimer). He only knew that he loved her and would continue to do so till his last hour. And he made her see, too, that for him life without her would be desolate.

" All the other doors of life were closed to me," she was to write later to Mrs. Martin, " and shut me in as in a prison, and only before this door stood one whom I loved best and who loved me best and who invited me out through it for the good's sake . . . I could do him." He had loved her—to use her own words—" heart to heart persistently," and drawn her back to life and hope again, and this at a time when she had believed that both were at an end for her for ever. " My life seemed to belong to him and to no other at last, and I had no power to speak a word. I shut my eyes sometimes and fancy it all a dream of my guardian angel."

2

They were never unmindful of the edge of the precipice. Sometimes she had to warn him not to come ; at another an unexpected packet from Jamaica would arrive and necessitate her father's presence in the City, so that the field was clear for Browning.

There were other perils, for Mr. Kenyon's suspicions were by this time thoroughly aroused. Once or twice he had encountered Browning there ; they had gone downstairs together. One April evening he appeared, and fixing his " detestable spectacles —like Greek burning-glasses"—upon Elizabeth, remarked : " I suppose now that Mr. Browning's book is done and there are no more excuses for coming, he will come without excuses ! "

They were near to quarrelling on this occasion, for Mr. Kenyon repeated a remark of Mrs. Procter's to the effect that it was a pity Browning hadn't got a settled occupation which would give him seven or eight hours' work a day. Elizabeth replied indignantly that he didn't need an occupation either as a means of living or as an end, since he had found one in the exercise of his genius. She added that if

Mr. Procter had looked as simply to *his* art as an end he would have achieved more.

"Now you are spiteful," said Kenyon, "and you need not be, for there was nothing unkind in what was said." He tried to smooth matters over by speaking of Browning and his family in "the best and most reverent words."

She seemed to discern, however, at the back of his speech the suggestion that if Browning had a more settled and remunerative profession he would be in a better position to marry her. For in the same letter she told him that when next they discussed the subject of their marriage she wanted him to understand that as long as they had enough between them to live upon it was not of the least importance whether the money were hers or his. That they had sufficient she had already proved to him. There seems never to have been any question of their deciding to remain in England after their marriage, and in Italy one could live at that time cheaply enough.

She looked out of the window one afternoon, on one of her rare excursions to the drawing-room, and saw someone walking down the street. She was too near-sighted to see him very distinctly—she could only discern a shadow in the dimness, but the shadow had some trace or sign of Browning, and she wrote to ask him if he had passed down Wimpole Street on that day and at that hour. "I looked after it till it vanished. No, it was not you. I feel now that it was not you, and indeed yesterday I felt it was not you. But for the moment it made my heart stop beating."

Kenyon came again a few days later and his first question was: "Have you seen Mr. Browning? And what did he come for again, pray?"

It is easy to see that he wanted to force Elizabeth's confidence, but she on her side was equally resolved that he should be told nothing, lest by occupying himself in the matter he should forfeit Mr. Barrett's friendship.

They talked of *Luria* and *The Soul's Tragedy*. He " saw the goodness and the greatness, the art and the moral glory." Their conversation diverged to other poets, to Wordsworth and Coleridge, both of whom Kenyon had known. Then presently, leaning up against the mantelpiece, he said quietly : " Do you not think—oh, I am sure I need not ask you !—in fact I know your thoughts of it—but how strikingly upright and loyal in all his ways and acts Mr. Browning is ! "

Elizabeth did not record her own answer ; perhaps she had not felt the need to speak at all. But it must have been difficult for her to withhold her confidence then from her old and kindly friend.

Kenyon no doubt guessed a good deal and so did her brothers. Forster had written a laudatory article in the *Examiner* about Browning's new book of poems, and for some reason or other Elizabeth had not seen it. She was " in high vexation, reproaching them all," when Stormie informed her that only their father had seen the paper and that " he had of course put it away to keep her from the impropriety of thinking too much about . . . about . . ." Yes, Stormie had really had the impertinence to say that ! The episode ended amicably by Mr. Barrett's bringing the paper himself to Elizabeth that afternoon.

Then George met Tennyson at a friend's house, and when Elizabeth inquired if he had found him agreeable and pleasant in conversation, he answered in the affirmative, adding, however, that he was quite inferior to Browning, he neither talked so well, nor had he so open and frank a manner. The advantages, affirmed George, were all on Browning's side. George was often a little criticised in the house for his official dignity and gravity, Henrietta and Arabel being especially wont to cavil at these qualities in him, but his judicial opinion on this occasion delighted Elizabeth.

But both Elizabeth and Henrietta were worn to death by the perpetual fear of discovery. Lady

Carmichael, a cousin, met Henrietta about that time and commented upon her altered looks, urging her to act for herself. Browning, who must have despaired of ever obtaining his heart's desire, was anxious to confide in Kenyon, who had always proved such a good friend to them both. But Elizabeth was obdurate on the point. It would only involve him in the eventual odium, for " Papa " would certainly never speak to him again while he lived. He might, indeed, attribute the whole blame to his old friend.

It was unlikely that Henrietta would take any active steps during that year (1846), Elizabeth told Robert, since the lack of means stood in the way of her marriage.

Disturbing gossip reached Elizabeth's ears. It was Miss Heaton, a lady from Leeds, only recently admitted to Wimpole Street, who told her that Browning had once been engaged—a very strong attachment on both sides—but that it had been broken off on account of religious differences. She stayed three hours on that occasion, and after she had gone Wilson told her mistress that she looked like a ghost.

Unsuspected dangers revealed themselves from unlikely quarters. Mr. Kenyon called, and turning his horrible spectacles upon Elizabeth asked suddenly :

" Does Mrs. Jameson know that Mr. Browning comes here ? "

" No," Elizabeth answered abashed.

" Well, then, I advise you to give directions to the servants that when she or anyone else asks for you that they should not say, ' Mr. Browning is with you,' as they said the other day to Miss Bayley who told me of it ! "

So the secret of their friendship and of his visits was beginning to leak out. It could only be a question of time before everyone knew of it, and then the gossip would be certain to reach Mr. Barrett's ears. . . .

3

One of the Barrett brothers attended a Flower Show, where he was informed on good authority that Browning was engaged to a Miss Campbell. Robert, however, denied it categorically, saying that he knew no lady of that name. The matter was not allowed to rest there, for on the following Sunday —a day when Elizabeth always had a gathering of her brothers and sisters for half an hour in her room —Alfred repeated the story and gave her the opportunity of denying it. Someone said : " Of course Ba must know, because she and Mr. Browning are such very intimate friends ! "

Alfred ended by flinging himself on the sofa " with an exceeding impertinence," and declared that he felt inclined to be *very* ill in the hope that some charming young lady would come to visit him. But the chaff was always good-natured, and Elizabeth knew she had nothing to fear from them.

Her letters at this time were charming. There had been some interchange of pleasantries between herself and Browning regarding the throwing of coffee-cups, and she related a story—which was probably current gossip of that day—to the effect that Queen Victoria had been guilty of throwing a tea-cup at the Prince Consort. " Whereupon Albertus Magnus, who was no conjurer, could find nothing better to do than to walk out of the room in solemn silence. If I had been he I think I should have tied the royal hands."

Encouraged by Browning, who constantly expressed the hope that she had been able to go out, her walks and drives became much more frequent as the summer advanced. There was a never-to-be-forgotten day when she drove to Regent's Park with Arabel. She had, like Walt Whitman, " business with the grass," and to feel it under her feet was ecstasy to the released prisoner. " The sun was shining with that green light through the trees as if he carried with him the very essence of the leaves to the ground. . . . And I wished so much to walk through a half-open gate along a shaded path that we stopped the carriage and got out and walked, and I put both my feet on the grass . . . which was the strangest feeling, and gathered this laburnum for you." It was, she told him, like " a bit of that Dreamland which is your especial dominion. . . . Dearest, we shall walk together under the trees some day."

One recalls with something of dismay that they had never seen each other except in that gloomy back room at Wimpole Street, where the climbing ivy and etiolated convolvulus made a poor travesty of summer against the window-pane.

One night her father brought her some flowers. She put them into a vase near to those Robert had given her, but in the morning they looked faded, while his roses were as fresh as ever. She looked from one to the other and wished Mr. Barrett had not given them to her ; she could draw no glad omen from them.

" If he had let me I should have loved him out of a heart altogether open to him. It is not my fault that he would not let me. Now it is too late. I am not his nor my own any more."

Meanwhile they continued to make perfunctory inquiries about the various places in Italy which had been recommended as suitable health resorts for Elizabeth. The pursuit of such investigations invariably resulted in their hearing some adverse opinion which caused them to change their mind. Florence then, even as now, the place most frequented by the English in Italy, was too crowded with their compatriots, added to which the lead in the water was injurious to health. Ravenna—with its memories of Lord Byron—Pisa, La Cava, Salerno, were each in turn discussed and rejected. Amalfi was, however, described as " very habitable." Salerno was said to be " illuminated by fireflies," and I am sure the thought of those brilliant elusive insects, so beloved of poets, must have made a special appeal to Elizabeth. Moreover, it was also said of Salerno that the " chanting of the frogs covered the noises of the city," but that was before the days of strident Klaxons.

They listened, perhaps, too attentively to the voices that warned them on no account to go to this place and at all costs to avoid that one. It must surely be in the experience of us all that the moment we suggest visiting a particular spot we find people eager to entreat us not to do so. " Oh, don't go there—you'll find it is so hot, or so cold, or so unhealthy ! " as the case may be. I remember once being warned not to go to Florence, " because it has such a dreadful railway station." Now railway stations are venues of sheer utility ; one does not expect them to be otherwise than noisy, crowded and gritty, but it has always seemed to me that the one at Florence compares quite favourably with other places of the kind.

4

Elizabeth became more adventurous, as if with the endeavour to prepare herself for such journeys as might await her. She walked out almost regularly, sometimes going as far as the post-office, which was just below Hodgson's, the bookseller's, to post her letters to Browning. It will be remembered that on the day of their departure for France they met at the said Hodgson's, which was only a few minutes' walk from Wimpole Street. If she came back tired from these expeditions the faithful Stormie was always ready to carry her upstairs. Again, at the end of May she drove to the Botanical Gardens with Arabel and Flush, and disregarding all the by-laws gathered some flowers there for Browning. " What I most enjoy to see is the green under the green—where the grass stretches under trees."

There were visits to be paid. One of her first was to Miss Trepsack, otherwise Treppy, who always dined with the Barretts on Sundays. She was an aged Creole, a contemporary of Mr. Barrett's mother, and her memory stretched back to the great-grand-father who flogged his slaves with a long whip and was regarded by them in the light of a divinity. Treppy adored Elizabeth and regaled her—or tried to do so—with all kinds of ice-creams and cakes. Flush enjoyed these delicacies more than did his mistress.

Visitors still flocked to the upper room. Mrs. Jameson, Miss Mitford, Lady Margaret Cocks—a friend of the old Hope End days who considered *Pippa Passes* " pretty and odd "—Miss Bayley who offered to accompany her to Italy should she ever go there, and Miss Heaton, who, as we have seen, stayed three hours and gossiped about Browning's past, so that afterwards Wilson told Elizabeth she looked like a ghost. Then there were letters to be written, to Mr. Boyd, Mrs. Martin, Miss Martineau and a host of others. She was finding it less easy to write to her old friends since the one subject that was uppermost in her mind must never be mentioned.

The wedding of her cousin, Miss Arabella Hedley, to Mr. Bevan of Barclay and Bevan's brewery, brought an unusual influx of relations to London that summer. During their visit Mr. Barrett was constantly in the house. He had that clannish feeling often discernible in otherwise unsociable and inhospitable men. One hears nothing of the effect Miss Hedley's wedding produced upon him, but no doubt he deplored it and must have hoped, too, that it would not put ideas into Henrietta's foolish head. Of Elizabeth he had no fear. Was she not, as he had once said, the purest woman he knew ? She had never approached him on the subject of marriage even in her youth.

While they were in London it was more than ever difficult for her to receive Browning. They had a narrow escape on one occasion, for Henrietta only just succeeded in deterring Mr. Hedley from " going up to see Elizabeth " when he was there.

On June 4th Elizabeth wrote :

" We are standing on hot scythes, and because we do not burn our feet by a miracle we have no right to count on the miracle's prolongation. . . . I shudder to look back to the days when you were not for me. Was ever life so like death before ? My face was so close against the tombstones that there seemed no room even for the tears."

Yet so well was the secret kept that Mrs. Jameson remarked one day to Browning : " How I should like to introduce you to Miss Barrett ! Did you ever see her ? "

Browning was equal to the difficult occasion. " Nobody, as you know, sees her," was his evasive reply.

But the secret, as he constantly reminded Elizabeth, was not his but hers. He only kept it at her wish, and for himself was desirous, even anxious, to take both Kenyon and Mrs. Jameson into their confidence. It may be that he felt, too, that Elizabeth would need further and even outside help when the crucial moment for putting dreams into action arrived.

And then once more he expressed his earnest wish to go through the form of marriage with her so as to enable him, if difficulties arose, to have the right at least to be by her bedside. He reminded her that in his very first letter he had told her that he loved her.

" It was so, could not but be so, and I always loved you as I shall always. . . . To the end, the very end, I am yours. . . .

It was evident that he feared a renewed breakdown in her health and saw himself separated completely from her, with no right or claim to approach

her. His position was indeed an increasingly difficult and anomalous one. He hated the secrecy,
the prevarications that were so necessary ; he only
wanted to proclaim their engagement to the whole
world and to marry her as soon as possible.

He was anxious to bring his sister Sarianna to
see her, but this Elizabeth firmly declined, declaring
she would rather meet Queen Victoria and all her
Court.

Mr. Kenyon took her to see the Great-Western
train come in one day that June. "The earth-thunder
of the train " almost overcame her, she told Robert.

Then one evening Mrs. Jameson came, and drove
out with her in the carriage, and in the gathering dusk
Elizabeth told her a little—just " what might be
told." Browning was delighted when he heard this,
feeling that at last the ice had been broken and
that she had enlisted the sympathy of a friend who
would certainly help her when the hour struck.

She drove to Harrow with Arabel, refusing, however, to go into the cemetery—she always hated
cemeteries—and once, too, they went to see Mr.
Boyd, though the thought of the visit made her so
nervous she longed to turn back. " Oh, Ba—such a
coward as you are will never be married ! " Arabel
told her, laughing.

One night, when all the rest of the family were
assembled at dinner, Elizabeth walked out alone
with Flush. Wilson was taking a holiday and no
other companion was available. Her little gesture of
independence was rather spoilt by Flush's conduct ;
he insisted upon walking on the other side of the
street, and she trembled lest he should be once more
snatched by the dog-stealers.

Mrs. Jameson took her to see Rogers' collection
of pictures. The fear of exertion, of going to fresh
places or of meeting strangers, was beginning to
wear off. Gradually she was preparing for that
day—now not so far distant—when she would
gather up courage to throw in her lot with Browning's
for ever. There was little talk of poetry, either his

or hers, that summer. But the *Sonnets from the Portuguese* must have been nearing completion.

No longer did she try to cure him of his love for herself. On the contrary, the thought of his love possessed, absorbed and sustained her as it had never done before. She felt that she owed everything to him, her restored health, her recovered happiness, all the beautiful moments she now enjoyed. His love had called her back to life just when she seemed, not only to herself but to others, to be slipping into the grave.

" For I have none in the world who will hold me to make me live in it except only you. I have come back for you alone . . . at your voice, and because you have use for me. I have come back to live a little for you. My fault is not that I think too much of what people will say. ' People ' did not make me alive for them. I am not theirs but yours. I deserve that you should believe in me because my love for you is ME. . . ."

5

The suicide of Haydon, the artist, that summer, was a grief to both Miss Barrett and Robert Browning. Elizabeth had never met him, but they corresponded, and he was in the habit sometimes of consigning certain pictures and boxes to her care, lest—as it afterwards transpired—they should fall into the hands of his creditors. His chagrin had been deep because his cartoons for the decoration of the Houses of Parliament had been rejected, and when his two pictures, " Aristides " and " Nero," were being exhibited at the same time as General Tom Thumb in adjoining rooms at the Egyptian Hall, the public flocked to see the dwarf to the complete neglect of his paintings. This mortification, combined with an almost chronic pecuniary embarrassment, had temporarily unhinged his mind.

Elizabeth blamed herself bitterly for not having offered him some help, since the arrival of his pictures and boxes at Wimpole Street invariably signified with him a period of acute financial straits.

Browning was now becoming impatient for her to fix the month, if not the day, of their wedding. He suggested September, for he could not be blind to the risk of her embarking upon the long journey to Italy after the cold weather had set in. She was a little hesitating :

" Still, seriously there is time for deciding, is there not ? . . . even if I grant to you at once that the road does not grow smoother for prolonged delays."

But she had been to Highgate that day and felt all the better for it. *" How strong you make me, you who make me happy. . . . "*

On one occasion they had planned to meet at Mrs. Jameson's. Elizabeth had promised to go and see her one day, and meeting Robert, Mrs. Jameson had invited him to come, without apparently mentioning that Miss Barrett would be there. However, the uncles and aunts prevented it. They had announced their arrival for such a late hour that it would be impossible for Elizabeth to see them that same night, and her sisters assured her that she could hardly go out at twelve o'clock on the following morning, an hour at which they might reasonably expect to be admitted to her room. " " Just see how it becomes possible and impossible for us to touch hands ! "

But the visitors did not come ; instead they sent word to say they would arrive on the Saturday, leaving the Barretts to calculate the hour—probably somewhere between one o'clock and six. This rendered any meeting impossible for that day, since Mr. Barrett would certainly be in the house to await their arrival, " which would be a complication of disadvantages to us." It meant, too, that they would have been separated for a whole week, if not longer, for she dared not promise to be able to receive him on the following Monday. "What will keep me, I wonder, from being sullen to my aunt and sulky to my cousin ? "

And after all it would have been difficult to meet him at Mrs. Jameson's. She was subject, she told him, to the madness of saying Robert without knowing it. . . .

When her aunt arrived, Elizabeth had the feeling that her presence threw her back, out of her dream-life, into the " old dreary flats of real life." Mrs. Hedley did not even know his name—she saw in her just the old Ba, who was not his Ba at all. She felt herself slipping back into the old melancholy. But her aunt asked her if the flowers on the table had come from Miss Mitford, and Arabel, who seemed to be on the point of offering information on the subject, was silenced by a look from her sister.

Their meeting did not take place until the following Wednesday, and then was marred by an unfortunate episode, inasmuch as Flush in an access of jealousy flew at Browning and bit him.

" Ah, Flush, Flush—he did not hurt you really ? You will forgive him for me ? The truth is that he hates all unpetticoated people, and that though he does not hate you, he has a certain distrust of you, which any outward sign such as the umbrella reawakens. But if you had seen how sorry and ashamed he was yesterday ! I slapped his ears and told him that he should never be loved again ; and he sat on the sofa (sitting, not lying) with his eyes fixed on me all the time I did the flowers with an expression of quite despair on his face. At last I said : ' If you are good, Flush, you may come and say you are sorry ! ' . . on which he dashed across the room and, trembling all over, kissed first one of my hands and then another, and put up his paws to be shaken, and looked into my face with such great beseeching eyes that you would certainly have forgiven him just as I did. . . ."

Robert was, of course, magnanimous :

" Oh, poor Flush—do you think I do not love and respect him for his jealous supervision ?—his slowness to know another, having once known you ? All my apprehension is that, in the imagination downstairs, he may very unconsciously play the part of the dog that is heard to bark violently while something dreadful takes place ; yet I do not sorrow over his slapped ears as if they ever pained him very much—you dear Ba."

A few days later Mrs. Hedley announced at dinner that she had not seen Ba all day, and that when she had gone to her room she had discovered, much to her astonishment, a gentleman sitting there.

" Who was *that* ? " said Papa's eyes to Arabel. " Mr. Browning called here to-day," she answered. " And Ba bowed her head," continued my aunt, " as if she meant to signify to me that I was not to come in——" " Oh," cried Henrietta, " that must have been a mistake of yours ! Perhaps she meant just the contrary." " You should have gone in," Papa said, " and seen the *poet*."
Stormie also volunteered the information that Mr. Browning was a great friend of Ba's, and that he came to see her twice a week. Mrs. Hedley, encouraged by this evidence of sociability, insisted that Ba should meet her future son-in-law, Mr. Bevan. The latter, an immensely tall young man, began immediately to discourse upon ecclesiastical architecture, which was his great subject. Elizabeth described him as a " clever third-class man—better than the mass for sense but commonplace essentially."
Mrs. Hedley flung her into incredible confusion by telling him as she introduced them that it was a great honour, inasmuch as Elizabeth never saw anyone except Mr. Kenyon and a few other gentlemen. Whereupon Mr. Barrett, who seems to have been in an almost dangerously genial humour during

the visit of these relations, observed ironically :
" Only *one* other gentleman indeed ! Only Mr.
Browning—the man of the Pomegranates."

Browning was, however, delighted with this unexpected display of goodwill towards him on the
part of Mr. Barrett.   It was always difficult to make
him believe that he was really such an ogre as Kenyon
and others were wont to depict.   And he considered
his words on that occasion very kind indeed.   He
felt confused, perhaps even a little humbled, by them.
. . . He was sure that at heart he was infinitely
kind—he was ready to see him with Elizabeth's
eyes.   He believed, too, that if Mr. Barrett could
know him and his purpose he would soon reconcile
himself to it all.

Mr. Barrett made things unusually difficult for
his daughter just then.   He became almost unbearably affectionate towards her, calling her " my love "
and " my puss "—terms of endearment which she
had not heard from him since their dispute about
Pisa during the previous year.   She quailed before
them, she confessed, " as if they were so many knife-
strokes."   She wanted Robert to understand " the
two ends of truth," that although Mr. Barrett was
not really made of stone he was as immovable as
stone.   Yet she herself had toyed with the thought
of approaching him, wondering whether it wouldn't
be better after all to make some appeal to him.   But
she hadn't the courage.   For from that hour she
was aware that she and Browning would be arbit-
rarily separated.   They would be prevented from
meeting or writing.   And the inevitable scenes, the
angry voice and recriminations, would induce those
fainting fits to which her " inconvenient nervous
system " predisposed her.

On another occasion they were interrupted by
Mrs. Hedley, who was turned somewhat cavalierly
from her niece's room by the watchful Arabel.
" Pray, which of Ba's lovers may this be ? " she
inquired, not, we think, without some acerbity.
Arabel was, of course, obliged to reveal that the man

was Mr. Browning, and on the following morning Elizabeth was subjected to considerable questioning as to whether it had been an agreeable visit and what he had written. Quite evidently they had never heard of him before. Mr. Hedley had no love for poetry. She believed that it was quite past his comprehension that anyone should wish to read her own verses.

They had three hours together on Monday, July 16th, and Robert wrote rather anxiously lest she should have had to pay any price for it. Flush in another access of jealous fury flew at him again and bit him, and was whipped by Wilson, who received no reprimand for such an unheard of act. Flush, no doubt, felt the tension, which was at its worst during those months of July and August. Elizabeth was really annoyed with him, and even spoke of muzzling him during Browning's visits. Still, she was able to assure him that no one had heard of his long visit or of Flush's misdoings. Wilson had shown her usual discretion. Of all those who had been told nothing, the maid had, Elizabeth averred, the most certain knowledge of the truth. Captain Surtees Cook had, however, been admitted by this time to the secret, for Henrietta had just had a letter from him in which he expressed the hope that Ba would have courage to the end.

Her letter ended with the significant words : " You shall see some day at Pisa what I will not show you now."

CHAPTER X

I

AT the end of July Mr. Kenyon paid a visit to Wimpole Street, and insisted upon interviewing Henrietta and Arabel before going up to see their sister. He wished to speak to them on the subject of her going to Italy with Mrs. Jameson, a plan which that lady had suggested. Mr. Kenyon was very strongly of opinion that Elizabeth ought to be accompanied by a relation, and that no one outside of her own family would be justified in accepting the responsibility. He alluded to the events of the preceding year, and warned them that if Elizabeth did insist upon going abroad such an act of disobedience would entail her being " cast off " as if for a crime. Mr. Barrett was not spared, either to the two sisters or apparently to Mrs. Jameson when the matter had been discussed with her. Kenyon added he had told Mrs. Jameson that it was impossible for her to " do any good."

He was anxious to know if Elizabeth ever spoke of going to Italy and whether they thought her mind still dwelt on it. They answered that they believed she intended to go.

" But *how* ? What is the practical side of the question ? " Kenyon asked. " She can't go alone —and which of you will go with her ? You know last year she very properly rejected the means which involved you in danger."

Henrietta very wisely advised that nothing should be said or done. " Ba must do everything for herself. Her friends cannot help her. She must help herself."

" But she must not go to Italy by herself. Then, how ? "

ELIZABETH BARRETT BROWNING

From a drawing by Field Talfourd
Rome 1859

p. 134

It was obvious that Kenyon, with the kindliest intentions, was trying to get to the bottom of the mystery.

"She has determination of character," was Henrietta's reply. "She will surprise everybody some day."

"But *how*?" Kenyon repeated.

Henrietta was subsequently scolded by Elizabeth for her imprudent speech.

Kenyon had discussed the matter also with Mr. Hedley, and now inquired whether Mrs. Hedley had no influence "with the highest authority." The sisters were able to assure him that she had none. Indeed, there did not exist a single living person who was capable of influencing that domestic autocrat.

Mr. Kenyon went up to see Elizabeth and found Browning on the stairs. In his subsequent letter Robert told Elizabeth that the ground was crumbling beneath their feet, and that he was in hourly expectation of Kenyon's approaching him on the subject, for he was certain now that he knew everything. "How else after such a speech from your sister?" And then instead of meeting Mr. Kenyon it might have been her father whom he had encountered on the stairs, or even in the room, when there would have followed a scene of passionate indignation. "I daresay we should have been married to-day," he added. Once more he suggested that he should tell Kenyon, but Elizabeth wrote reminding him of his promise not to do so.

"But you *promised*. I have your faithful promise, Robert. If ever you should be moved by a single one of those vain reasons it will be an unfaithful cruelty in you. You will have trusted *another* against *me*. You would not do it, my beloved."

He could always soothe her. "All this missing of instant understanding—for it does not amount to *mis*understanding—comes of letters and our being divided."

But early in August the danger of discovery became more acute, definite and proximate. There was a thunderstorm one afternoon, and its violence prevented Robert from leaving the house before six o'clock, when Mr. Barrett invariably returned home. All the time he was sitting there Elizabeth was uneasy, thinking she could see her father's face through the floor. But she was terrified of thunder, and Browning could not leave her. " I felt your dear hand press closer while the thunder sounded," he wrote afterwards.

At seven o'clock Mr. Barrett mounted to his daughter's room, and his face looked as if the thunder had passed into him. He found her lying on the sofa in a loose white dressing-gown, and eyed her with stern and angry disapproval.

" Has this been your costume since the morning, pray ? " he asked.

" Oh no—I have only just put it on because of the heat ! "

His face grew sterner. " It appears, Ba, that *that man* has spent the whole day with you ! "

" He tried to go several times but he was stopped by the rain," she assured him. But, as she afterwards confessed, the lightning that day had made the least terror.

Mr. Barrett had been afraid lest she should be ill with fear " and only Mr. Browning in the room." Yet he had not seen him go—he himself had left at five. But none the less he had made himself acquainted with the duration of Browning's stay. She wondered whether it would be safe for them to meet on the following Tuesday. Her father would certainly be out, but in any case she would write.

Even before the triple storms of that unfortunate Saturday, which must have shown them both how precarious was their position, Elizabeth confessed that she had had a presentiment which had oppressed her for two days—a presentiment that it would all end ill, through some sudden accident or misery.

" What is the use of my telling you this ?   I do
not know.   I will tell you besides that it cannot . . .
shall not be . . . by my own fault or failing.   I may
be broken indeed, but never bent."

Even while she was writing Mr. Kenyon appeared,
but fortunately without the spectacles, which he
carried broken in his hand.   Elizabeth at once
said that she sincerely hoped they would never be
mended, and told him they were the most unbecoming things in the world.   But he was not deterred
from his purpose by these irrelevant pleasantries.
" Did you see Browning yesterday ? " he asked.
" Yes."
" I thought so.   I intended to come myself,
but I thought it probable that he would be here and
so I stayed away."
He talked a little of Browning, praising him,
alluding, too, to his inexhaustible knowledge and
general reasonableness.   Then suddenly she had
to listen aghast to the following question.
" Is there an attachment between your sister
Henrietta and Captain Cook ? "
" Why, Mr. Kenyon, what extraordinary questions,
opening into unspeakable secrets, you do ask ! "
" But I didn't know it was a secret.   How was
I to know ?   I have seen him here very often, and
it is a natural inquiry which I might have put to
anybody in the house touching a matter open to
general observation.   I thought the affair might be
an arranged one by anybody's consent."
" But you ought to know that such things are
never permitted in this house.   So much for the
consent.   As for the matter itself, you are right in
your supposition—but it is a great secret—and I
entreat you not to put questions about it to anybody
in or out of the house."
She was frightened . . . frightened, she told
Robert, and not exactly for Henrietta.   What had
he meant by those words ?   What had he in his
mind ? . . .

Kenyon then advised her to write and thank Mrs. Jameson for her kindness in offering to accompany her to Italy. He had told her that Miss Barrett, if she went to Italy, could only go by sea, which for some reason or other would be impossible for Mrs. Jameson.

And it would not be safe for them to meet again just yet because Mrs. Hedley was still in London and had said she meant to see a great deal of her. . . .

2

Browning was more certain than ever after this episode that Mr. Kenyon knew.

" This is the beginning of his considerate cautious kindness—he has determined to hurry nothing, interfere abruptly in no case, to make you *infer* rather than pretend to instruct you—as you must —for if the visits of Captain Cook *have* that appearance, etc., must not those of R.B., etc. . . . So this is not from Chorley's information, mind, but from his own spectacled acumen. . . . "

But an increased caution was necessary. When he came, if her father were in the house, he would receive a note instead of admittance, and by this sign he would know it would be unwise for them to meet. But she was not afraid that he would be forbidden the house, or that the servants would receive orders not to admit him.

He said that for himself there was no unstable footing in the whole world save only in her house. It was the one place where he ought not to be and where, if he were discovered, everything he could do or say would inevitably be wrong. With Mr. Kenyon it would be different. If he broached the subject to him he felt that he could justify himself even if he failed to convince him.

Browning again inquired about this time exactly

how she stood financially, and she applied for exact information to Stormie, who told her that she had eight thousand pounds in the funds, of which the interest was paid quarterly.   Her father, first deducting the income-tax, gave her from forty to forty-five pounds every three months.   Besides this there was the ship money, which amounted to about two hundred a year.   So far she had not used this at all, and the annual amount had therefore been added to the Fund money until recently, when it had been invested in the Eastern Railroad.   This paid so well that Stormie was anxious that all her money should be similarly invested.   Her father had agreed to this being done, since it would nearly double her available income without running the slightest risk. But she did not like to remind him just now to take the necessary steps—it would inevitably arouse his suspicions if she were to show any wish to touch " such matters with her finger."   She had besides ten shares in Drury Lane Theatre which paid nothing at all.

She confessed that she spent the whole of the forty pounds she received every quarter, although she had never expended more than twenty pounds a year on her own dress.   The morphine was, of course, her greatest expense.   But she promised him that he would not find her extravagant.

Still, there would be some difficulty, although the money was incontestably hers, in putting her hand on any large sum such as for instance they would require for the journey.   The next quarter would not be due till October, which was quite a month later than Browning had proposed to leave England. There would be something, but not enough.   She suggested waiting somewhere on the way to Italy until the money could be sent, or even borrowing a hundred pounds for a few weeks.   She was aware that her father's first action would be to abandon the management of her affairs.

In the end, Browning borrowed a hundred pounds from his parents to pay their expenses until Elizabeth could take the control of her money into her own hands.

Mrs. Jameson was the next to approach her on the subject of the proposed Italian journey. She came to see her during the first week of August and asked her if she had given up the idea. Elizabeth assured her that she had not, but that she could not be frank with her at present ; there were reasons that prevented it. And she begged her not to mention the matter again to Mr. Kenyon.

" She promised. She was kind beyond imagination—at least far beyond expectation. She looked at me a little curiously but asked no more questions until she rose to go away. And then—' But you will go ? ' ' Perhaps if something unforeseen does not happen.' ' And you will let me know when you can—when everything is settled ? ' ' Yes.' ' And with efficient companionship ? ' ' Yes.' ' And happily and quietly ? ' ' "

But to that Elizabeth was unable to say yes. She knew that in any case it could not be done quietly.

At the end of the letter there were further explanations about her money. The ship shares were in the *David Lyon*, a vessel engaged in the West Indian trade and in which her father also held shares. Stormie had told her that she certainly did not receive the entire dividends of the money she held in the Funds—there should have been at least three hundred a year from that alone, even allowing for the low interest and the income-tax. It would be easy enough to borrow money on these securities, but she was afraid of the transaction reaching her father's ears. At this stage a single false move would have been their undoing. One is apt to forget, in reading thus of the straits to which the lovers were reduced, that Elizabeth Barrett was now over forty years of age and one of the most celebrated women in England, possessing, too, what was in those days a very adequate fortune of her own. Yet all this secrecy, these perpetual contrivings to meet, were imperatively necessary. One simply had to take Mr. Barrett seriously, and as his daughter had not the physical strength to face a scene she was obliged to make all her plans and preparations without his knowledge.

And lately he had become more terrible, as if he were reacting in some sense to the atmosphere of mystery and emotion that pervaded his house. There were other unfavourable signs which Elizabeth mentioned in her reply to a letter which Browning had written, asking who it was that had followed him up the stairs one night. There was, she said, a kind of throwing off of moral restraint, he was " a dumb Rousseau with the Confessions repressed within him." What precisely she meant by that it would be idle to conjecture. He was only happy when he was angrily abusing something or someone. He was, in fact, what in modern parlance we should call an " Anti."

" Oh yes, it was he who followed you up the stairs! There was an explosion that day among the many— and I had to tell him as a consequence that if he chose to make himself the fable and jest of the whole house he was the master, but that I should insist upon his not involving my name in the discussion of his violences."

Wilson had told her that Mr. Barrett was white with passion as he followed Browning up the stairs, and she herself was so frightened she could hardly open the door. But he was a little ashamed after-wards and made some sort of apology.

His suspicions were now definitely aroused. He had become aware of Browning, jealous of him, of the long hours he spent with his daughter. He no longer laughed at the Poet, the man of the Pome-granates. He was not deceived by the literary friendship. And he could see what they all saw, the immense and arresting change that had taken place in Elizabeth. The rhythm of her life was altered. She walked and drove out regularly; she was no longer lying eternally upon her sofa in that darkened upper room. She looked younger and better than she had done for years, and was happier than she had been since Edward's death. She no longer expressed a wish to die at his feet. It is said that love cannot be hidden, and Elizabeth's bright face and shining dark eyes, her renewed physical vigour, must have alarmed as well as astonished him.

" The household," wrote Professor Dowden, " was honeycombed with treasons." And Mr. Barrett, completely in the dark though he was as to the progress of affairs under his own roof, did react to that conspiracy of silence. His genial mood, so observable during the Hedleys' visit to London, had vanished, and had given place to a morose ill-humour which might at any moment break out into a transcendent fury. . . .

3

Miss Trepsack, with a strange perspicuity considering that she was not living in the house and only dined there on Sundays, was keenly alive to the atmosphere that pervaded it. She told Arabel that she preferred not to go to Wimpole Street just then, " when there were so many secrets. You think," she added, " that nobody can see and hear except yourselves, I suppose, and there are two circumstances going on in this house plain for any eyes to see."

" Oh, Treppy," Arabel interrupted, " you're always fancying secrets where there are none."

" Well, I don't fancy anything now. I *know*— just as *you* do." She went on to say something about " Ba's going to Italy," to which Arabel said : " And Treppy, do you think she will go to Italy ? "

" Why, there is only one way for her to go—but she may go that way.   If she marries she may go."

" And you wouldn't be surprised ? "

" I ?   Not in the least—*I* am never surprised, because I always see things from the beginning ! Nobody can hide anything from me."

Elizabeth was not afraid of Treppy, who adored her, but the episode was alarming because it showed her so clearly that people were gossiping and inferring.   And, of course, Treppy must not be told. She mustn't run the risk of Mr. Barrett's displeasure. " To occasion a schism between her and this house would be to embitter the remainder of her days."

She must have been a curious little creature, this Creole, transplanted from the tropical heats of Jamaica to the bleak gloom of the London streets. She was old, too, for had she not been a contemporary of Mr. Barrett's mother ? and Mr. Barrett was at this time nearly sixty years old.

Her devotion to the three girls, and especially to Elizabeth, was a touching trait in her character.

But if the change in Elizabeth was apparent to these other eyes, to herself it was no less great.   She could hardly believe in the reality of it all.

" Dearest—I feel to myself sometimes, ' Do not move, do not speak—or the dream will vanish.'   So fearfully like a dream it is !   Like a reflection in the water of an actual old, old dream of my own, too . . . touching which . . . now silent voices used to say ' That romantic child.' "

And at any moment she felt that the dream might be even cruelly killed.   There was hardly a person in the house devoid of suspicion, or at least of curiosity.   And even outsiders—intimate friends such as Mr. Kenyon, Mrs. Jameson and Treppy— were all, as we have seen, on the *qui vive*.   Was Ba still thinking of going to Italy ?   And if so when and how, and who was to accompany her ?   Or had she perhaps given up the idea ?   Her father had vetoed the project last year—would he be any more likely to give his consent now ?

Although it was August, a month when even then most people left London, few of their immediate circle went away that year. Mr. Kenyon hovered about, with his piercing eyes magnified by the enormous spectacles, and his constantly reiterated phrase : " Has Mr. Browning been to see you lately ? " Elizabeth wished heartily that he would go away, but he was never absent for long, and he seemed to haunt Wimpole Street just then—one may be sure with the friendliest and most helpful intentions—like an inquisitive ghost.

George returned from Sessions about the middle of the month. His first question was whether she were still thinking of Italy. She answered in the affirmative, but something in his manner made her feel afraid. " I am a little uneasy under George's eyes."

Even Mr. Boyd in his blindness discerned that changes were contemplated. Thus he inquired one day when she went to visit him whether she were thinking of becoming a nun. On the occasion of her next visit he asked her point-blank if she were going to be married, and Elizabeth permitted him to know the truth when she had elicited a solemn vow of secrecy from him. He had been one of her earliest friends, and there was no fear of his divulging anything.

" Is there harm in his knowing ? He knows nobody, talks to nobody, and is very faithful to his word."

Mr. Boyd had heard Browning's name but did not know his poetry at all. He was blind and deaf to modern literature, only caring for the classics. He asked Arabel if she thought " Ba " and Browning cared enough for each other. Elizabeth believed that his " unqualified adhesion " was less the result of his love for her than of his bitter feeling towards her father. " I am sure he triumphs inwardly in the idea of a chain being broken, which he has so often denounced in words that pained and vexed me."

4

Browning's letters at this time held many allusions to the probable dates of the sailing of ships, combined with doubts as to the best route to take. And in all these discussions it is remarkable to notice that Elizabeth, untravelled as she was, was far the more practical and accurate of the two.

Her fancy roamed far beyond Italy, which was their immediate objective :

" Shall we go to Greece then, Robert ? . . . I should like to see Athens with my living eyes. Athens was in all the dreams I dreamed before I knew you. Why should we not see Athens and Egypt too, and float down the mystical Nile, and stand in the shadow of the Pyramids ? *All* of it is more possible now than walking up this street seemed last year.

" Indeed there is only one miracle for *me*, my beloved—and that is your loving me. . . ."

It was chilly that August, which was perhaps the reason people preferred to remain in London. Mr. Kenyon gave up an expedition to the Quantock Hills because one of the party elected to go to the seaside instead. He intended, however, to spend a night at Richmond. He told Elizabeth that Miss Martineau was leaving Ambleside—which she always did in August to avoid the influx of visitors—and would probably come to London. " There are nets on all sides of us," she wrote. " Those are coming, and these are not going away. The hunters are upon us."

In the same letter she consulted Browning about the number of books she might take to Italy. They

K

could arrange not to take duplicates, and she would choose the smaller-sized ones and perhaps send them to him beforehand, as it would arouse suspicion were anyone to observe their removal.

" *My sisters must not observe.* The consequences would be frightful if they were suspected of knowing ; and, poor things, I could not drive them into acting a part."

Mrs. Jameson, who for some nòt quite comprehensible reason had rather avoided her of late, paid her a visit towards the end of August. Her first question was about her plans for going to Italy. Elizabeth answered that she was still unable to tell her anything, but in any case her departure could not take place till the end of September so that she did not wish to make any premature fuss.

" Very sudden then it is to be," said Mrs. Jameson, laughing. " In fact there is only an *elopement* for you ! "

The word aroused in Elizabeth something that was definitely Victorian. She was in a word shocked. " Dearest, no one will use such a word surely to the event ? " she wrote rather piteously.

She changed the subject rather hastily and began to talk of Mr. Kenyon. Mrs. Jameson was eager to know what he thought about her going to Italy.

" He thinks I shall not. In his opinion my case is desperate."

" But I tell you that it is not. Nobody's case is desperate when the will is not at fault. And a woman's will, when she wills thoroughly, as I hope you do, is strong enough to overcome. When I hear people say that circumstances are against them I always retort : ' You mean that your will is not with you.' I believe in the will—I have faith in it."

Thus spoke one of the pioneers of the emancipation of women. Anna Jameson was a disillusioned woman who had early embarked upon a literary career and made a success, both pecuniary and otherwise, of it. She was then about fifty-two years old, being twelve years older than Elizabeth. Her married life was not happy, and she lived chiefly apart from her husband. When she spoke thus of the triumph of the will she knew what she was talking about. Hers were strange, bracing counsels for the invalid of Wimpole Street. All the time she was talking she looked at Elizabeth with her pale, penetrating eyes . . . those " resolute, inquiring eyes. . . ."

That final month before her marriage must have taxed Elizabeth's courage to an almost incredible degree. One day towards the end of August, Arabel came into her room " with such a face." Stormie had suddenly asked her if it were true that there was an engagement between Mr. Browning and Ba ? Arabel was astonished and alarmed, but had the presence of mind to say : " If you want to know you'd better ask them. What nonsense, Storm ! "

He announced his intention of asking Ba when he went upstairs. George was present, grave and somewhat disapproving. No man in those days liked to see a woman exerting her own will, taking the bit between her teeth, no matter how severe the provocation. Still, when they did appear in her room not a word was said to the terrified Elizabeth, who had been warned of what she might expect by Arabel.

Of all her friends Hugh Boyd was the kindliest and most sympathetic. She went to see him, stayed two hours, and talked of nothing else. It must have been a relief to her to be able to speak of it so freely. He told her in return that nothing would make him gladder than the news that she had gone and escaped the storms.

This information about her brothers definitely alarmed Robert Browning. He thought it would perhaps be more prudent for them not to risk seeing each other as usual during the ensuing weeks. " We risk everything—and what do we gain in the face of that ?   I can learn no more about you, be

taught no new belief in your absolute peerlessness——
I have taken my place at your feet for ever ; all my
use of the visits is therefore the perfect delight of
them . . . and to hazard a whole life of such delight
for the want of self-denial during a little month—
that would be horrible ! "

She thought such a precaution unnecessary, and
said so. The crisis had passed, nothing more had
been said. Still, it would be wiser for him to come
on Wednesday because Mr. Kenyon would be at
Richmond on that day, and then they could wait
until the following week for their next meeting.
She subsequently changed the day to Friday because
Mr. Kenyon wrote to say he would come on the
Thursday afternoon, and she wanted to be able to
say, in reply to his inevitable question : " No, he
hasn't been here since I saw .you."

It would be safer, too, because during their vaca-
tions her brothers had nothing else to do but to
watch her. " I am so nervous that my own footsteps
startle me." But in the end, Friday seemed equally
imprudent, and she wrote in great haste on Thursday
evening to tell him so. Mr. Kenyon had not appeared
that afternoon, and thus would be certain to come on
the morrow, and the Hedleys were in town for a
couple of days, which put even all thought of Saturday
out of the question. " Shall I not really see you
before Monday ? It seems impossible to bear."

The letter found him beginning to dress for the
visit long before there was any necessity. But he
was now thoroughly alive to the need of prudence.
He did not want, as he had once told her, to receive
into his arms a lacerated creature who would only
reach them to sink there. " I am prepared for
difficulties enough without needing to cause them by
any rashness or wilfulness of my own."

The Hedleys unexpectedly left London on the
Saturday. They dined at Wimpole Street on Friday
night for a farewell visit. And although Mr. Kenyon
had not yet been, was it worth while being afraid of
him ? She left it to his " wisdom which was greatest."

But in reply to his suggestion that her father might suddenly take it into his head to send her to Madeira or Palermo she said that he had no more idea of her leaving home than he had of a journey to Lapland. Her brothers " wished that something could be arranged "—a wish that she put quietly aside when they suggested it. Mrs. Hedley was not, however, so easily deceived. " Ah Ba, you have arranged your plans more than you would have us believe ! But you are right not to tell us—indeed, I would rather not hear. Only *don't be rash*—that is my only advice to you." Her uncle, too, urged her to keep firm and go to Italy. They thought that for her to live on in that fashion in that room was lamentable to contemplate. With regard to the affair between Henrietta and Captain Cook, they considered that Mr. Barrett's consent should be asked as a matter of respect.

During this conversation " Papa " himself came into the room.

"How well Ba's looking," Mrs. Hedley volunteered.
" Do you think so ? "

" Why, don't you think so ? Do you pretend to say that you see no surprising difference in her ? "

" Oh, I don't know ! She is mumpish, I think ! " Then after a pause : " She doesn't talk."

" Perhaps she is nervous," said Mrs. Hedley, adding with what we can only characterise as surprising temerity. " When birds have their eyes out they are apt to be mumpish."

But the word " mumpish " was proof to Elizabeth of his displeasure. She assured Browning that she had shown as little sullenness as was possible, although it had not been within her power to be talkative and vivacious. Throughout the conversation she held her peace, but afterwards she told Mrs. Hedley she had been wrong to speak of her—a wrong with a right intention. She was very sorry that she had done so, she said.

" Poor Papa ! Presently I shall be worse to

him than mumpish. But *then* I hope he will try to forgive me, as I have forgiven him long ago."

But the episode put her more than ever on her guard. She was beginning to wish for no unnecessary delays. She shrank from her father's voice and look and trembled when she talked to her brothers. Even her sisters' sympathy filled her with sorrow and fear because she was afraid of their being made to suffer through their affection for her.

"How I can look and sleep as well as I do is a miracle exactly like the rest—or would be if the love were not the deepest and strongest thing of all and did not hold and possess me overcomingly."

This letter made him more passionately desirous than ever of putting an end to the odious and ambiguous situation.

"Show me one good reason or show of reason why we gain anything by deferring our departure till next week instead of to-morrow, and I will bear to perform yesterday's part for the amusement of Mr. Kenyon a dozen times over without complaint. But if the cold plunge must be taken all this shivering delay on the bank is hurtful as well as fruitless."

This letter hurt her. Hadn't he said, when she suggested September, that October or November would do as well? She had warned him, too, that the circumstances might prove painful, only he had not believed her until he began to feel the pricks. She felt that he had been a little hard on her. And she showed him that she could not possibly sail from the Thames as he suggested. The hours of departure were very early, and Arabel, who slept on the sofa in her room, seldom left it before nine o'clock. She was still quite resolute about not implicating her sisters. On certain points she was as obstinate as Mr. Barrett himself. And Browning, despite his urgent plea for an immediate departure, never made it

easier for her by forming precise and practical plans
for their journey.   One day he was all for going by
sea, on another for travelling across France by the
river route ; sometimes he suggested sailing from
Shoreham, sometimes from Southampton, and sometimes, again from the London docks.   If he had made
definite plans and invited her to fall in with them,
their departure might certainly have been accelerated
by some weeks.   Even towards the end an earth-
quake that shook Tuscany severely made him a little
tremulous about going to Pisa ! . . .

<h2 style="text-align:center">5</h2>

All the petty differences that must have made
those last weeks so unbearable to them both, when
meetings were rare and necessarily shortened, were
thrust suddenly into the background by a new and
unforeseen   disaster.   Flush   was   stolen.   Robert
Browning must have felt something akin to despair
when he heard the news, for hadn't she told him that
she couldn't possibly leave Flush behind, since if
he did not accompany her to Italy his heart would
break ?   Until Flush was found there was no prospect of inducing her to make further plans for escape.
Elizabeth, with Arabel and Flush, had gone to
Vere Street on the morning of September 2nd.
The little dog followed them into the shop and out
of it again, and was close to Elizabeth when she got
into the cab.   She turned round, called to him, but
no Flush was visible—he had been caught up in
that moment almost from under the very wheels.
Arabel, noticing how white she had become, tried
to comfort her by telling her she would be certain to
get him back if she paid ten pounds.   But Elizabeth
refused to be comforted.   She was thinking of poor
Flush's blank misery at finding himself separated
from her.
Henry Barrett went immediately to seek out the
" captain of the banditti," who appeared to be

perfectly acquainted with the incident and promised to let them hear something that same evening. Henry had assured the thieves that his sister would not give a fantastic reward, but they must have known perfectly well that she would give them whatever they demanded. On the following day one of the gang called upon Henry and admitted that Flush was in Whitechapel, and that he himself was going down there that evening to confer with the thieves and decide upon the ransom. But even if they asked ten pounds she would give it to them— she couldn't run any risk, or bargain or haggle where Flush was at stake. There was a dreadful story of a lady who, having refused to pay the sum demanded, received a parcel containing her dog's head. . . .

Browning was a little unsympathetic about the matter ; he himself would not have paid the man five shillings, but would have done all he could to put down the intolerable traffic, even, so it would seem, at the expense of Flush's head. But he was ill when he wrote, for he sent another letter almost immediately to say that he would have given all that he was ever worth in the world to get Flush back for her.

But even then Flush had not returned to Wimpole Street. Mr. Barrett had desired Henry to refuse to pay the six guineas demanded, and Henry apparently did not dare to disobey. He said he was sure the man would come back that evening and ask for a lesser sum. Elizabeth was almost distraught with terror, and everyone was a little against her. Even Mr. Boyd called it an " awful sin " to encourage dog-stealing by paying such a reward. On the 5th of September Elizabeth went down to Whitechapel herself, as " Henry was far too lukewarm " and only warned her that she would probably be robbed or murdered. She added a postscript to say that she had come back safely, though without Flush. But she was to have him the next day.

She went with Wilson in a cab, driving through obscure streets. Wilson seemed to think as they drove home they had only escaped with their lives. They had not long been back at Wimpole Street when Mr. Taylor, with whom all the intermediary conversations had taken place, called there and received the six guineas from Elizabeth, who had to trust to his honour to restore Flush to her.   But in the midst of the bargaining Alfred appeared and called Taylor a swindler, a liar and a thief.   The man left in a passion, swearing they should never see their dog again.   There was a fierce dispute.   Elizabeth was furious with her brother and still more terrified for Flush.   Her first impulse was to make a second expedition to Whitechapel, but it was evening, dusk was falling, and they all told her she was mad to think of such a thing.   At last Sette goodnaturedly offered to go, promising his sister to be civil, and thus induced her to retire quietly to her room.   These final negotiations proved successful, and Flush reappeared at eight o'clock that same night.   His first action was to drink " his purple cup full of water, filled three times over."   But he was less delighted to see her than she had expected ; he seemed to her both frightened and bewildered. When she said to him :   " Poor Flush, did the naughty men take you away ? " he put up his head and moaned and yelled.   He was very dirty and much thinner and appallingly thirsty.

Elizabeth confessed to Browning that Arabel had said he ought to have been there to " manage " her on the preceding day when she proposed to go down to Whitechapel so late in the evening.   " But now—*was* I to let them cut off Flush's head ? "

Browning did not see her during those hectic days.   At first there were reasons connected with Mr. Kenyon for his not venturing to go to Wimpole Street.   And then for several days he was seriously unwell, suffering from headache and giddiness, and was obliged to remain in bed.   The long period of suspense and anxiety had begun to tell even upon his vigorous constitution.

CHAPTER XI

I

Mr. Barrett's own action precipitated the secret marriage. On the 10th of September the edict went forth that the house in Wimpole Street was to be repainted and decorated and that George was to seek for a furnished one in the country to which they could all migrate for a few weeks. Dover, Reigate and Tonbridge were suggested, but in the end a house was taken at Little Bookham. This bombshell was flung on the Wednesday, and they were told that on the following Monday they must all be ready to depart. There was no question about Elizabeth's remaining at home ; she was so well now that it was improbable the short journey would affect her. Nor was it in the least for her sake that they were going. If that had been the case Mr. Barrett would hardly have waited until the summer was over before making this sudden plan.

It may well be that he suspected something and thought that it would be better to get Elizabeth out of the way for a short time. Mr. Browning's visits, though much less frequent than formerly, had not been entirely relinquished.

Robert Browning was aghast when the news reached him. If she were to leave London on the following Monday their marriage would be impossible for another year. He had always dreaded the thought of taking her on that long journey to Italy after the cold weather had set in. And lately there had been so many trivial obstacles in their path. They had hardly even been able to meet to discuss plans. There was the loss of Flush, then his own indisposition, and now this final calamity.

" You see what we have gained by waiting," he wrote on the following morning. " We must be *married directly* and go to Italy. I will call for a licence to-day and we can be married on Saturday. I will call to-morrow at three and arrange everything with you. We can leave for Dover, etc., *after* that, but otherwise, impossible. Inclose the ring or a substitute—I have not a minute to spare for the post."

But it seemed there was no need for such untoward haste. George had only so far gone to look at houses, thus it would be impossible for them all to move as soon as Monday. But Robert could come to-morrow and she would give him the ring (which seems already to have been bought in readiness)—that would be better than sending it by post. It would be perfectly safe for him to come, as all the others were going for a picnic to Richmond.

" Will not this dream break on a sudden? Now is the moment for the breaking of it, surely ? "

Robert Browning wrote on the envelope of this letter the following significant date : " Saturday, September 12, 1846, ¼11—11¼ a.m. (91)." It was the record of his marriage in St. Marylebone Church, and the number 91 indicated that it was their ninety-first meeting.

When he thus came forward with a definite authoritative plan—which he ought to have done long before—Elizabeth was perfectly ready to acquiesce. At the hour appointed on that fateful Saturday morning she drove in a cab to the church, accompanied by the faithful Wilson, who alone had been admitted to the secret of these final arrangements. She was to accompany them abroad, and thus could in no way be made to suffer for acting as an accessory. Elizabeth Barrett was so faint during that short journey that she had to stop at a chemist's on the way and take a dose of sal-volatile, that infallible if nauseating remedy for the indisposition of Victorian ladies.

The marriage took place in the presence of two witnesses, of whom one was Wilson and the other was a cousin of Browning's. But as he looked down upon his pale, trembling little bride, her white face overshadowed by the long dark curls, Browning must have felt that yet another of his heart's wishes—the dearest and most important of all—had been almost miraculously fulfilled. For a year and four months he had pursued his suit with a persistence, a tenacity which had stormed one by one all the defences and demolished all the barriers that had stood so formidably between them. And when they parted at the church door he knew—and perhaps exulted in the knowledge—that even Mr. Barrett was powerless to separate them now. . . .

It is said that never on his subsequent visits to London did he fail to visit the church and, kneeling, kiss the spot where she must have stood during the ceremony.

Elizabeth did not immediately return to Wimpole Street after the wedding. Instead she drove to Mr. Boyd's—perhaps to establish an alibi should she be questioned—and feeling too the necessity of revealing her secret to someone, and especially to this old and sympathetic friend. She lay quietly on the sofa downstairs till he was ready to receive her. Then she was given a glass of Cyprus wine and some bread-and-butter, so that she might not look too pale when her sisters came. They were delayed, and when they did appear it was with such grave, anxious faces she half feared they must suspect the truth. Arabel had apparently forgotten what Elizabeth had told her on the previous evening, of her intention to go out that morning, thus they had taken alarm at her prolonged absence. It was only by consenting to accompany them to Hampstead that she was able to allay their fears. But when on their drive home they passed the church, she confessed there was a cloud before her eyes.

Naturally she suffered from a nervous crisis, although of a less violent kind than might have been anticipated. What if someone should examine the church register and discover the indubitable proof of their marriage ? But this was before the time when Press representatives made a daily diligent search of such documents for the purpose of discovering any tit-bit of the kind, and there was little danger of such an untoward revelation.

On the following day she wrote :

" Dearest, in the emotion and confusion of yesterday morning there was yet room in me for one thought which was not a feeling—for I thought that of the many, many women who have stood where I stood and to the same end, not one of them all perhaps, not one perhaps since that building was a church, has had reasons strong as mine for an absolute trust and devotion towards the man she married—not one.',

It was one of the most perfect and perhaps one of the simplest of all her expressions of love for him.

2

There was the usual gathering of the whole clan on the Sunday—the day that followed their wedding. Her brothers and sisters were all in her room, discussing their plans for migrating to the country. Treppy was there, and some old Herefordshire friends, and Elizabeth did not dare protest against the noise of talk and laughter because she was so afraid of attracting attention to herself. But in the midst of it all they heard the sound of church bells, and one of the country friends asked what they were. The unsuspicious Henrietta answered, " Marylebone Church bells."

She escaped at last from the din, and was sitting writing to Robert when Mr. Kenyon came in, " with his spectacles looking as if his eyes reached to their rim all the way round." These eyes he fixed upon her with their usual piercing gaze. "When did you last see Browning?" he inquired.

"He was here on Friday," she answered, changing colour.

Before he left he asked : "When do you see Browning again?"

She was only able to tell him that she didn't know. But she had so hated taking off the ring. Some day he would have to take the trouble ·of putting it on again. . . .

For a whole week they remained apart, for Browning had a scruple about going to the house and asking for Miss Barrett when she had no further right to that name. And on the whole, Elizabeth bore the interval with remarkable courage. Perhaps the feeling that come what might she was his wife sustained her.

She did not see her father again until the Monday after her marriage. Then he came up to her room about seven o'clock and spoke to her kindly, asking her how she was. But she loved him. She was ready to put herself under his feet to be forgiven a little. She would tell him that but for this one act she had submitted to his wishes all her life long. She would remind him of the long suffering she had endured, and entreat him to pardon the happiness which had come to her at last. "And he will wish in return that I had died years ago. For the storm will come and endure. And at last perhaps he will forgive us—it is my hope."

A hope, however, that to her eternal grief was destined never to be fulfilled. . . .

3

George had not as yet succeeded in finding a suitable house, though one at Watford was in contemplation. Thus the departure of the family was still of uncertain date, and they could well wait till the end of the week before accomplishing their final flight from England.

" I sit in a dream when left to myself.   I cannot believe or understand.   Oh, but in all this difficult and painful situation I look over the palms to Troy— I feel happy and exulting to belong to you past every opposition, out of sight of every will of man—none can put us asunder, now at least.   I have a right now openly to love you. . . . "

Browning realised, he told her in reply, the effort she had made, the pain she had endured, for his sake.   For ever her proof of love for him was made, and in return he would spend all his life in trying to furnish as deep a proof of his own love for her. *"My own eyes have seen—my heart will remember. . . ."*

His preparations were completed ; she had only to make her wishes known to him.   He advised her not to take more luggage than was absolutely necessary—she could supply all wants either at Leghorn or Pisa.   He had always travelled economically himself, and it was natural for him to remind her that every " ounce " had to be paid for.

He told her he had awakened that morning feeling perfectly well and quite free from all the old unpleasant sensations in his head.   The fact was that a burden of suspense and apprehension had been lifted from his mind.   He could awake to the thought that " Ba " was his wife from whom no earthly power could now separate him.

The news of this change in him filled her with joy.   " It is a joy that floats over all the other emotions."   She had feared the excitement might have been too much for him—so anxious was she always about the health of that vigorous man. But undoubtedly the strain of those long months of waiting, the increasing uncertainty of the issue, had told upon him.

A house at Little Bookham had been taken, and it was arranged that the family should migrate thither on Monday, the 21st of September.   Robert didn't know where Bookham was.   Even then he had not made any definite arrangements for their journey; he still suggested various routes with comments as to their respective disadvantages.

Little Bookham, she informed him, was six miles from the nearest railroad, and a mile and a half from Leatherhead, from which town a coach ran. It offered, therefore, few facilities as a starting-point from which they could effect their ultimate escape. And yet if she were to go away with him on the following Saturday, none of the necessary letters would be written, there would not be time, and in addition she was far too much agitated. She had begun a letter to her father but could not proceed with it for crying, and afterwards she had looked so pale that they had asked what was the matter with her. She submitted to his wishes about the luggage. She and Wilson would only have a box and carpet-bag between them, and she promised to be " docile about the books."

Again he made a quite unpardonable mistake by writing to say that Saturday would be impossible because the boats only left Southampton for Havre on Tuesdays and Fridays. In his haste he had noted down the departures from Havre, whereas the boat left Southampton at half-past eight on Friday night. She must thus be at Vauxhall Station by four o'clock on Friday afternoon. This letter was immediately followed by another. The Tuesday and Friday boats were those of the South of England Steam Company, whereas the Wednesday and Saturday ones were those of the South Western. She was quite naturally a little depressed and con-fused by his ambiguous, inaccurate instructions, and it was not until Friday morning that he was able to furnish her with a precise statement copied from the railway time-table. The packet was due to sail from Southampton Pier at nine on Saturday night, and their train left Vauxhall at five o'clock. He would meet her at Hodgson's—the bookseller's—would be there between half-past three and four on Saturday afternoon. From thence they would take a cab. . . .

She wrote in answer, a wistful little note—the last she was ever destined to send him, since from the morrow they were never again to be separated till her death ended one of the most perfect marriages the world has ever seen.

" At from half-past three to four, then—four will not, I suppose, be too late ?   I will not write more—I cannot.   By to-morrow at this time I shall have you only to love me—my beloved !

" You *only*.   As if one said *God only*.   And we shall have Him beside, I pray of Him.

". . .Your letters to me I take with me, let the ' ounces ' cry out aloud ever so.   I *tried* to leave them and I could not.   That is, they would not be left : it was not my fault—I will not be scolded.

" Is this my last letter to you, ever dearest ?   Oh, if I loved you less . . . a little, little less."

Her courage did not fail her.   Between half-past three and four o'clock on September 19th, 1846, Elizabeth Browning slipped out of her father's house in Wimpole Street with Flush under her arm and the faithful Wilson at her side.   Her relations were assembled at dinner, so that the hour was fairly propitious.   The only danger was from Flush.   She cuddled him close to her, whispering : " Flush, if you bark now I am lost ! "   Flush was silent as if aware that great events were in progress, and the little walk to Hodgson's was safely accomplished. Robert Browning was already there awaiting her, and they drove without delay to Vauxhall, *en route* for Southampton and their destination beyond the seas.

Elizabeth Browning never entered the house at Wimpole Street again.   She was made to pay the full price of her action, but even she could not know that never, never in this world was she to receive her father's forgiveness or look upon his face again.

From the hour of her ultimate rebellion she was dead to him.

L

CHAPTER XII

I

To many people it must seem that the most dramatic part of the story ended with that flight from Wimpole Street. But even if this be true it is certain that the greatest happiness of Mrs. Browning's life was still in store for her. With Rabbi Ben Ezra she could have said : *The best is yet to be.* Writing many years later of Shelley's second marriage, Francis Thompson said : " Few poets were so mated before, and no poet was so mated afterwards until Browning stooped and picked up a fair-coined soul that lay rusting in a pool of tears."

Whether from genuine anger or from policy or from that keen sense of freemasonry which exists among men, it would be idle to conjecture, but the fact emerges that Mrs. Browning's brothers unexpectedly sided with Mr. Barrett. Even the one who had most eagerly urged her departure for Pisa in the previous year, and had even told her, " He does not love you—do not think it "—reproached her now for her want of affection towards her father. Fortunately this estrangement was only temporary, for *au fond* the Barretts were a thoroughly devoted and united family. Her sisters remained then and always perfect in their love and devotion and loyalty.

With the exception of Mr. Barrett and his sons everyone was, as we should say now, " terribly " kind. Mr. Kenyon—who surely must have smiled at the remembrance of his own perspicuity—sent not his forgiveness, but his sympathy and affection, justifying them to the uttermost. I am quite sure that had they appealed to him long ago he would have proved ready and eager to help them, both financially and otherwise. " I considered that you had perilled your life," he wrote to Elizabeth, " upon this undertaking, and reflecting upon your last position, I thought that *you had done well*." Mr. Chorley had tears in his eyes when he heard of it, and the kindliest messages reached them from Monckton Milnes, Mr. Procter, and other members of that literary circle which Robert had for so long frequented. Mr. Horne, too, signified his approbation with unfailing kindness.

In Paris they accidentally came upon Mrs. Jameson, who was on her way to Italy with her niece, Gerardine Bate. She took them both into her arms and called them children of light, telling them that she would have been proud to have had anything to do with their marriage. " I have here a poet and a poetess," she wrote to a friend, soon after that meeting in Paris—" two celebrities who have run away and married under circumstances peculiarly interesting and such as to render imprudence the height of prudence. Both excellent ; but I know not how the two poet heads and poet hearts will get on through this prosaic world."

Browning, who had always dreaded that long journey for his wife, even though Wilson was there to share the responsibility with him, welcomed Mrs. Jameson's suggestion that they should all travel to Italy together. Mrs. Jameson, in writing to her friend Charlotte Murphy, described the journey as very tedious and very anxious, although she said she would not have forgone it for the world. The poor invalid, she affirmed, suffered greatly, often fainting, and often so exhausted that she could go no further, and they had to halt perhaps for a whole day at some wretched place. The weather, too, was terrible, and they encountered incessant rain all the way down the Rhône from Lyons to Avignon, so that they had to take refuge in the hot, crowded cabin of the daily steamboat. Yet, in spite of these uncomfortable experiences, she declared that she had enjoyed the journey and did not in the least regret it. Her niece, Gerardine Bate, had been very good and very efficient . . . considering. . . .

At Avignon, Elizabeth stayed in bed while the rest of the party visited the Palace of the Popes. She was full of sweetness and good-humour, Mrs. Jameson reported, and was only too glad that Robert should be amused.

They stayed two days at Avignon and from thence made a pilgrimage to Vaucluse, in honour of Petrarch and Laura. " I and my husband sate upon two stones in the midst of the fountain," Mrs. Browning wrote, describing the charming little scene to Mr. Westwood, an American correspondent, " which in its dark prison of rocks flashes and roars and testifies to the memory of Petrarch. It was louder and fuller than usual when we were there, on account of the rains ; and Flush, though by no means born to be a hero, considered my position so outrageous that he dashed through the water to me, splashing me all over, so he is baptized in Petrarch's name. . . . The fountain works out its soul in its stony prison, and runs away in a green, rapid stream."

It was at Avignon, too, that she was singled out among all the little company for a present of pomegranates—a " significant gift," she called it. She had never seen such a thing before, and naturally proceeded to cut one " deep down the middle " !

During the voyage from Marseilles to Genoa she was able to sit on deck and let her eyes feast upon a " vision of mountains, six or seven deep, one behind another." The freed prisoner from Wimpole Street must have gazed almost incredulously upon that lovely landscape so familiar to all travellers to the South—the dazzling peaks of the Alpes Maritimes outlined in almost spectacular splendour against the blue sky.

2

They reached Pisa in safety and took rooms near the Campo Santo in the Collegio Ferdinando built by Vasari. Their apartment consisted of three excellent bedrooms and a sitting-room, all comfortably carpeted and matted, with windows looking out upon the Leaning Tower.

Mrs. Browning revived in the warm southern air. Mrs. Jameson, who stayed there for a few weeks before going on to Florence and Rome in order to collect material for her book *Sacred and Legendary Art*, pronounced that she was not only improved but transformed. Perhaps the reason was that for the first time in her life she was perfectly happy and perfectly free. In one of her letters to her old Malvern friend, Mrs. Martin, she wrote :

" Every day I am walking out while the golden oranges look at me over the walls, and when I am tired Robert and I sit down on a stone to watch the lizards. We have been to your seashore too, and seen your island, only he insists on it (Robert does) that it is not Corsica but Gorgona, and that Corsica is not in sight. . . . Also we have driven up to the foot of mountains and seen them reflected down in the pure lake of Ascuno, and we have seen the pine-woods, and met the camels laden with faggots all in a line. So now ask me again if I enjoy my liberty as you expect. My head goes round sometimes, that is all. I never was happy before in my life."

Their rooms were chilly enough that November to make it necessary for them to have a little wood fire. They lived very cheaply and simply. Eggs for breakfast ; dinner sent in from a *trattoria* at two o'clock ; coffee with milk rolls at six, and roast chestnuts (which Flush also enjoyed) at nine. " No trouble, no cook, no kitchen ; the prophet Elijah or the lilies of the field took as little thought for their dining. . . ."

It was all very well for Mrs. Browning to make her principal meal of the day off thrushes and Chianti "with miraculous cheapness," but one is forced to wonder how such a diet could sustain the more robust frame of her husband. He, however, ordered the dinner and divided with her the task of pouring out the coffee, so it must be presumed that he was satisfied. His one fear was of running into debt, so perhaps he was consoled by the thought of the miraculous cheapness.

In December she was able to write that they were now in the fourth month of wedlock and there had never been a shadow between them—not a word. The only change she could and did perceive in him was an increase in his love for her. Their happiness was then, as it always remained, quite flawless. Two years of steadfast affection from such a man would, she told Miss Mitford (who was never very sympathetic upon the subject of marriage) have overcome any woman's heart. She was often to be reminded in those days of Mr. Kenyon's words : *Robert Browning is great in everything.*

Mrs. Browning received good news from Wimpole Street. Her sisters wrote that Mr. Barrett was in high spirits and had people to dine with him every day. So that after all, as she rather wistfully said, she had done nobody any harm by doing herself so much good. Her father had, of course, renounced the administration of her affairs, but Mr. Kenyon had accepted the task. He actually wrote to Mr. Barrett justifying them with the whole weight of his personal influence, and took charge of her finances "when nearer hands let them drop." Indeed, to the very end Mr. Kenyon proved a kind and generous benefactor. After the birth of their son he allowed them £100 a year and at his death bequeathed £11,000 between them, thus putting them beyond all possibility of financial anxiety.

Early in February, Wilson was taken ill, and she who had so long nursed and tended her mistress was now to be nursed in her turn. Mrs. Browning confessed that she learned during those anxious days to comb and " do " her own hair, lace her stays, and fasten hooks at the back of her dress, to say nothing of making toast-and-water for the invalid. But, of course, she wasn't allowed to perform these strenuous tasks quite unaided, for Robert was there to lift the kettle for her and to see that she didn't burn the bread when making toast.

Flush was happy at Pisa ; he went for daily walks and talked Italian to the other little dogs. But he became more autocratic than ever, as if he discerned with swift canine instinct that his place was less assured than it used to be. He barked to distraction when he wanted a door opened, and appeared to think that Robert Browning was there for the sole purpose of waiting on him.

But the principal incident of their sojourn at Pisa was not Wilson's illness, nor their expedition to the seashore and the pinewoods, nor the proved simplicity and economy of their ménage. For it was here that Mrs. Browning fulfilled a promise she had made many months before in London, that at Pisa she would show Robert what she had been writing.

Early in the year 1847, according to the account Browning gave to the late Sir Edmund Gosse, Mrs. Browning went upstairs immediately after breakfast one morning, leaving her husband standing by the window until the servant had cleared away the meal. This task was finished, and he heard someone enter the room after the maid had left it. It was his wife. She just thrust some papers into the pocket of his coat, holding him while she did so by the shoulder to prevent him from turning to look at her, and, begging him to read what she had given him and burn it if he didn't like it, escaped from the room.

In later years Mr. Pen Browning gave a perfectly different version to Miss Whiteing, who visited him some little time before his death. He said that his father had told him she had given him the poems at Bagni di Lucca in 1849, shortly after his own birth, and thus dating the episode quite two years later. This version is, however, disproved by the fact that the Sonnets were first privately printed at Reading under the ægis of Miss Mitford in 1847. Mrs. Browning's old promise to show Robert at Pisa what she would not show him in London was thus scrupulously fulfilled. She had then been married about five months, had found him, to use her own word, "flawless," and it was in any case unlikely that she would have kept them from him any longer.

Robert Browning was astonished. Knowing and loving and admiring her poetry wholeheartedly as he did, he could not but be conscious, and critically conscious, of those very faults that seemed to mar in ever so slight a degree the perfection of her thought and vision. But when he took the careful transcript from his pocket and read those very first words, what must his own thoughts have been ? They were for him alone, and in those pages the fullness of her genius and the profundity of her love were alike passionately revealed.

I thought once how Theocritus had sung
Of the sweet years, the dear and wished-for years,
Who each one in a gracious hand appears
To bear a gift for mortals, old or young ;
And, as I mused it in his antique tongue,
I saw, in gradual vision through my tears,
The sweet sad years, the melancholy years,
Those of my own life, who by turns had flung
A shadow across me. Straightway I was 'ware,
So weeping, how a mystic Shape did move
Behind me, and drew me backward by the hair,
And a voice said in mastery while I strove . . .
' Guess now who holds thee ? ' ' Death,' I said. But, there,
The silver answer rang . . . ' Not Death, but Love.'

They were beautiful—beautiful as even her letters had never been. No Englishwoman had ever written anything to equal them before, and had he been alive to-day Browning could confidently have told himself that no Englishwoman had written anything to equal them since. Not Alice Meynell with her exquisite *Renouncement*, which told of an experience no less passionate because it was so sternly repressed.   Not Christina Rossetti with her fluent music.   Not even Emily Brontë with the splendid cadences of her magnificent *Remembrance*, in which she sang as few women have dared to sing of an enduring if frustrated love.   It is by her sonnets that Elizabeth Browning claims her place among the women-poets of England, and what a high place that is we may learn by quoting her husband's own words.   He pronounced the *Sonnets from the Portuguese* to be the finest sonnet-sequence since Shakespeare.   And like Shakespeare's they carry no date.   They belong to all time, for they possess no quality which proclaims them to belong to this period or to that.   They are the perfect expression of a pure and passionate love, the story day by day of a woman's unique experience—that of being called back to life by the voice of love.   More graphically than even her letters do they relate the history of her gradual resurrection from that mattress-grave at the call of love.   You see in them her inability at first to believe that voice ; her conviction that for her there was nothing but death ; her initial rejection of the beautiful gift thus proffered.

> What hast *thou* to do
> With looking from the lattice-lights at me,
> A poor tired wandering singer—singing through
> The dark, and leaning up a cypress tree ?
> The chrism is on thy head—on mine the dew——

She makes an effort to send him away, as we know that she did most loyally and faithfully in the beginning :

> Go from me.   Yet I feel that I shall stand
> Henceforward in thy shadow.   Nevermore
> Alone upon the threshold of my door
> Of individual life, I shall command
> The uses of my soul, nor lift my hand
> Serenely in the sunshine as before,
> Without the sense of that which I forbore . . .

> Thy touch upon the palm.   The widest land
> Doom takes to part us, leaves thy heart in mine
> With pulses that beat double. . . .
> .   And when I sue
> God for myself, He hears that name of thine
> And sees within my eyes the tears of two.

She looks unflinchingly into the heart of her own situation, even as she did when she was writing her beautiful letters to him.

> O Belovèd, it is plain
> I am not of thy worth nor for thy place !
> And yet, because I love thee, I obtain
> From that same love this vindicating grace,
> To live on still in love, and yet in vain . . .
> To bless thee, yet renounce thee to thy face.

And again more poignantly because as it were with a new wisdom, a clearer vision :

> Nay, let the silence of my womanhood
> Commend my woman-love to thy belief—
> Seeing that I stand unwon, however wooed,
> And rend the garment of my life, in brief,
> By a most dauntless, voiceless fortitude,
> Lest one touch of this heart convey its grief.

She makes it clear that his love brought her at first only a new grief because she dared not accept what he offered.

> But I look on thee . . . on thee . . .
> Beholding, besides love, the end of love,
> Hearing oblivion beyond memory !
> As one who sits and gazes from above,
> Over the rivers to the bitter sea.

Little by little, even as in the letters, conviction comes upon her that he needs her too, cannot live without the love she is able to give.   A new note appears in the sonnets—a note of hope.

> Belovèd, my Belovèd, when I think
> That thou wast in the world a year ago,

What time I sate alone here in the snow
And saw no footprint, heard the silence sink
No moment at thy voice . . . but link by link
Went counting all my chains . . .
           . . . why, thus I drink
Of life's great cup of wonder !

Perhaps then for the first time Browning learned what his letters had really meant to her :

My letters !—all dead paper, mute and white—
And yet they seem alive and quivering
Against my tremulous hands which loose the strings
And let them drop down on my knee to-night.
This said . . . he wished to have me in his sight
Once, as a friend : this fixed a day in spring
To come and touch my hand . . . a simple thing,
Yet I wept for it !—this . . . the paper's light . . .
Said, *Dear, I love thee ;* and I sank and quailed
As if God's future thundered on my past.
This said, *I am thine*—and so its ink has paled
With lying at my heart that beat too fast.
And this . . . O Love, thy words have ill availed
If what this said I dared repeat at last ! . . .

There were moments when even the prisoner shrank from that new life that awaited her beyond her four walls :

If I leave all for thee, wilt thou exchange
And be all to me ?   Shall I never miss
Home-talk and blessing and the common kiss
That comes to each in turn, nor count it strange
When I look up, to drop on a new range
Of walls and floors . . . another home than this ?
Nay, wilt thou fill that place by me which is
Filled by dead eyes too tender to know change ?

We may wish perhaps that the magnificent sonnet, *How do I love thee ?   Let me count the ways*, which sums up all that has gone before, had been placed at the end of the sequence instead of being, as it is now, the penultimate one.   Its natural place is at the end, and anything that follows must necessarily be in the nature of an anti-climax.   The very charming

sonnet, *Beloved, thou hast brought me many flowers,*
could perfectly well have been relegated to a much
earlier place in the group.

Browning, as he read, saw that these poems were
not for himself alone, deeply intimate though they
were, and touching as they did on the secret life of
their long engagement and upon her love for him
which he could see now had existed, like his own for
her, almost from the very beginning. But they
were something more than the history of that
passionate experience. As poems, they were of the
highest order. The arbitrary pattern of the sonnet
had, so to speak, controlled and disciplined her fluent
pen. Browning, as a poet, could not but recognise
their literary quality, their perfect artistry, quite
apart from their content. But knowing they had
been written for himself and for himself alone I cannot but believe that his first sensation on reading
them was less of triumph than of humility. Her
final action of putting them into his keeping showed
too the measure of her trust, and her recognition
of the fact that never by word or deed had he
failed her.

His determination to give them to the world was
carried out despite any objection there might have
been to reveal to that world this intimate and almost
sacred glimpse of their love for each other. Mrs.
Browning, with the reticent modesty which characterised the women of her epoch, permitted herself a
slight camouflage, calling them at his suggestion,
Sonnets from the Portuguese. This could have deceived no one, the more so as they were first privately
printed at Reading in 1847—the year following her
marriage—under the simpler title of *Sonnets by
E.B.B.* This successfully proves the date and venue
of Robert Browning's admittance to the secret.
They had been produced and even printed for private
circulation within the first year of their marriage,
long before Penini was born or even—as nursery
parlance has it—thought of, thus refuting Miss
Whiteing's theory that Elizabeth did not show them

to her husband until after the birth of their son in 1849.

Mrs. Browning's first idea had been to entitle them *Sonnets from the Bosnian*, but Robert had always had an especial admiration for her poem *Catarina to Camoens*, and declared they were Catarina's sonnets and therefore must be from the Portuguese. After that he used sometimes to call his wife in jest, " My little Portuguese ! "

3

The six months' sojourn at Pisa almost completely re-established Mrs. Browning's health. It proved too—if such proof were indeed necessary—their absolute all-sufficiency for each other. They knew nobody except Professor Ferucci; who admitted them to a sight of the University Library, and Dr. Cook, who attended them in illness. They had few books, and for three months hardly saw a paper. Afterwards they subscribed to a French and Italian library and saw a French paper *Le Siècle* every evening, thus looking, as she called it, through a loophole at the world. For all society they had they might almost as well have spent those first six months of their wedded life on a desert island.

They left Pisa for Florence in April to join Mrs. Jameson, whose visit to Rome had not been an altogether successful or agreeable one owing to her niece, Gerardine Bate, having become engaged to the artist, Mr. Macpherson, whom she subsequently married. " Geddie " was therefore in deep disgrace, Mrs. Jameson for some reason or other disapproving of the marriage. However, their friend, who had now become Aunt Nina to them, spent Shakespeare's birthday with them in Florence, bringing a bottle of Arezzo wine with which to drink to his memory in company with two other poets. She brought them, too, news from Rome, then on the eve—as many think—of disastrous happenings. " The Pope was *doing what he could,*"but unfortunately, in her opinion, he lived in an atmosphere of love and admiration which Browning characterised as a dreadful situation for a man of understanding and honesty. " I pity him from my soul," he said, " for at best he can only temporise with truth ! " But in this regard we must remember that the Brownings were not only convinced Protestants but also Dissenters by birth and upbringing ; they lived in an age which was peculiarly intolerant of " Popery," and their long years' residence in Italy never afforded them the least glimpse into the reality and truth of the Catholic Faith, nor into the historical claims of the Catholic Church.

Elizabeth was delighted with Florence, " the most beautiful of the cities devised by man." She was able to do some sight-seeing, and duly admired the Venus and the " divine Raphaels." She stood by the tomb of Michelangelo in the Church of Santa Croce. She visited the Duomo, and went for walks along the Arno, although we must allow something for poetic exaggeration when she described it as " rushing through the midst of its palaces like a crystal arrow."

Their first abode was in the Via delle Belle Donne, but later, after a brief and somewhat disastrous expedition to Vallombrosa they took another suite of rooms in Palazzo Guidi which is now for ever tenderly associated with their names. Few English-speaking visitors can surely visit the City of Flowers without turning into the Via Maggio and pausing to read the inscription that commemorates Elizabeth Barrett Browning and her enduring love for Italy.

For the next three months they had both apartments on their hands, but the rooms in Via delle Belle Donne were so suffocatingly hot in summer that it was impossible for them to remain there. Mrs. Browning was beginning, as English people often do, to dread the tropical summer heat of Italy even more than its winter cold.

Their new rooms were but a few steps from Palazzo Pitti—then the residence of the Grand Duke

—and they had the right of entry to the Boboli Gardens, that delicious refuge of singing fountains and shady cypresses and ilex trees, with its incomparable views of the hills that girdle Florence.

" For me I take it for pure magic, this life of mine. Surely nobody was ever so happy before. . . . This Florence is unspeakably beautiful by grace both of nature and art, and the wheels of life slide on upon the grass (according to Continental ways) with little trouble and less expense. Dinner comes ' unordered ' through the streets and spreads itself upon your table as hot as if we had smelt cutlets hours before."

Mrs. Browning had always disliked the task of housekeeping, and long before her illness had relegated it to Henrietta. Italy therefore suited her perfectly in this respect, for even to this day—and without the necessity of ordering one's meals from a *trattoria*—the wheels of domestic life run more smoothly than in the majority of countries. And the Brownings had not been many months in Florence before they abandoned this line of least resistance, and installed a cook of their own whose manner of dealing with mutton cutlets was beyond praise. This has always astonished me, knowing the prejudice entertained towards mutton in any shape or form by the Italian servant, who can seldom be persuaded to cook it, far less to eat it. Still, cook or no cook, they were living on less than three hundred a year, and she had all the luxury she had ever had, including the port wine with which Robert dosed her twice daily.

Except for her preoccupation about Henrietta she would have been perfectly happy. Her father was said to be well and in good spirits, but Henrietta's engagement to Surtees Cook still hung fire, and there seemed to be no possible solution of the difficulty. The Barrett brothers were definitely opposed to the marriage on account of the lack of means ; they believed that no one should marry on less than two

thousand a year.   Mr. Barrett was further opposed
to it on account of the High Church views of the
prospective bridegroom.

In Florence the Brownings soon formed part of
an English and American literary and artistic circle.
The American sculptor Mr. Powers was living there
with his large family; the Hoppners, who had been
Byron's friends in Venice, opened their arms to these
latter-day poets; Miss Boyle, " a very vivacious little
person " with literary ambitions, who was then living
with her mother at the beautiful Medici villa at
Careggi, used frequently to join them in the evening
over their roast chestnuts and mulled wine.   The
Trollopes were among the older members of the
English colony, and Adolphus Trollope had married
en secondes noces a Miss Theodosia Garrow, whom
Elizabeth had known slightly at Torquay.   Browning was at first reluctant to meet Frances Trollope,
the writer, on account of a difference in political
opinions, combined with her avowed distaste for the
writings of Victor Hugo.   But he subsequently
conquered these prejudices, and in time even came to
like her.   Later on, their list of friends was augmented
by the addition of Isa Blagden, whose villa on Bellosguardo was the haunt of two generations of English
people, Frederic Tennyson, and young Mr. Robert
Lytton, afterwards Lord Lytton.

It was during this year that Robert unsuccessfully
tried to obtain a diplomatic post—that of secretary
to the British Mission to the Vatican, an appointment
for which his avowed religious prejudices made him
seem peculiarly unfitted.

Although Elizabeth was now at work on *Casa
Guidi Windows*, she admitted that happiness was not
conducive to literary activity.

" I cannot believe," she wrote to Miss Mitford,
about a lady who was said to be " pining in an access
of literary despondency," " I cannot believe of any
woman that she can think of *fame first*.   A woman
of genius may be absorbed indeed in the exercise
of an active power, engrossed in the charges of the

course and the combat, but this is altogether different to a vain and bitter longing for prizes . . . and what prizes, oh gracious heavens! The empty cup of cold metal—so cold, so empty to a woman with a heart."

Relations from England halted at Florence to visit them, no doubt urged by a little curiosity to see for themselves how " Ba's " wonderful and romantic marriage was turning out. Arlette Butler, now Mrs. Reynolds, was among the first to penetrate to Casa Guidi. " Oh, Ba, it is quite wonderful indeed ! " she exclaimed, astonished at the transformation of her cousin. But the still more complete trans-formation of Flush, who had had to be shaved that summer on account of the plague of fleas and whose curls had not yet grown again, met with less approval, and Mrs. Reynolds mourned aloud over the loss of his beauty. Flush had indeed never been in such spirits nor looked so ugly. He ran out into the Piazza when-ever he chose, without any peril from professional dog-thieves ; he played with the other little dogs whom he met there, wagged his tail at the sentinels and civic guard, and regarded the Grand Duke of Tuscany as a sort of neighbour whom it was proper for him to patronise. He ate enormous bunches of grapes when they were in season, and had certainly lost whatever grace of aspect that still remained to him.

4

Elizabeth loved Florence, " with all its dust, cobwebs, spiders even," and " with something of the blind, stupid, respectable, obstinate love which people feel when they talk of beloved native lands." Robert, too, was happy there, for he wrote to Mrs. Jameson at Christmas that year : " We are as happy as two owls in a hole, two toads under a tree stump, or any other queer two poking creatures that we let live after the fashion of their black hearts, only Ba is fat and rosy."

M

When spring came they drove in the Cascine and through the city streets, passing sometimes the window where Bianca Capello gazed down at the Grand Duke as he rode by, commemorated for ever in the *Statue and the Bust*. They saw, too, the famous stone upon which tradition said that Dante used to sit. Rumours of revolution were in the air, and the English were flying from Florence, but these things did not disturb the lovers of Casa Guidi. Mrs. Browning averred she would rather face two or three revolutions than an English winter. But Italy was dreaming of a final emancipation from the Austrian yoke, and there were sometimes stirring scenes to be witnessed in Piazza Pitti.

The comparative emptiness of Florence was in their favour when in May they resolved to rent an unfurnished apartment in Casa Guidi. They paid only twelve guineas a year for it. It had been the favourite suite of the last Conte Guidi, and his arms in *scagliola* were emblazoned on her bedroom floor. There were six large rooms and a kitchen, and three of the rooms opened upon a terrace. They bought furniture by degrees, an original outlay of fifty pounds supplying them with all necessities. Mrs. Browning's own tastes were simple. She stipulated only for a sofa to loll upon, and a supply of rain water in which to wash, the latter being kept in an immense Tuscan oil jar.

As summer advanced they took drives and walks daily. They liked to stroll as far as the Trinità Bridge and watch the sunset turning Arno to gold ; sometimes, too, they walked out in the breathless warmth of the June night, when the scene was flooded with moonlight and the corn under the olive trees was tangled with fireflies. That brilliant southern moon must have been in Browning's mind when he wrote :

> Still we find her face, the thrice-transfigured,
> Curving on a sky imbrued with colour,
> Drifted over Fiesole by twilight,

CASA GUIDI (interior)

p. 178

Came she, our new crescent of a hair's-breadth.
Full she flared it, lamping Samminiato
Rounder 'twixt the cypresses and rounder,
Perfect till the nightingales applauded. . . .

In August they planned a little journey to Arezzo,
Urbino and Fano, and thence to Loreto and Ancona,
but they found Fano so unbearably hot that they fled
from it after three days.   Cardinal Wiseman's mother
was living there, as she had done for the past seven
years, in a state of permanent moaning, despite the
fact that she was near her daughter, Contessa Gabri-
elli, whose husband had property there.   Guercino's
picture evoked from Robert his beautiful poem
The Guardian Angel.   And they wondered—possibly
as many far more modern critics have wondered—
how such a great writer as Ruskin could blaspheme
so against so great an artist as Domenichino, when
they stood entranced before his " David " at Fano.

From Fano they went to Ancona—a " striking
sea-city holding up against the brown rocks and
elbowing out the purple tides."   They remained
there for a week, living upon fish and cold water,
a somewhat dangerous diet in such a place and at such
a time.   The heat was too much for Elizabeth, who
lay dishevelled upon the sofa in a white petticoat and
wrapper.   After spending a day at Loreto they
returned to Ancona and thence went to Sinigaglia,
Fano, Pesaro, Rimini, Ravenna, and back over the
Alps from Forli.   A " bel giro," she called it.   They
were back in Florence in three weeks, and it seemed
quite cool there in comparison.   Flush, of course,
had accompanied them.

It is interesting to know that about this time
gossip reached her concerning *Jane Eyre*, a book she
had not then read, but which she was informed had
been written by a governess in Thackeray's house.

CHAPTER XIII

I

Outside their Florentine terrace the world was in upheaval. The revolution in France had resulted in the exile of Louis Philippe and the establishment of another republic. In the autumn of 1848 Pope Pius IX had been forced to flee to Gaeta. Revolution was in the air, and her friends at home wondered how Mrs. Browning could have the temerity to talk of furnishing at such a time. " These things look worse at a distance than they do near," she wrote. But still, in view of the fact that she was expecting her child in a few months' time—a prospect fraught with more than its usual peril for a woman of her frail physique—it is astonishing that Browning did not take her to some more tranquil spot for the winter.

Robert himself was laid up for a month with fever and an ulcerated throat that autumn. She was anxious and unhappy about his burning hands and languid eyes—the only sadness, she declared, that they had ever given her. Father Prout, the famous Jesuit whom he had met years before at Emerson Tennent's, turned up in Florence just then, laughed at Mrs. Browning for a *bambina*, and administered a potion of eggs beaten up in port wine which induced sleep and quieted the pulse, despite the horror of their Italian servant, who could certainly never have heard of such a remedy before.

Few letters are available to cast any light upon the next few months. Miss Mitford mentions in one of her letters that Mrs. Browning was looking forward to the event with considerable courage, but those at home could hardly have been without keen anxiety for her.   However, all went well, and in March 1849, some two and a half years after their marriage, she gave birth to a son, Robert Wiedemann Barrett Browning, always in after-life to be known as Penini or Pen :

> To whom
> The earliest world-day light that ever flowed,
> Through Casa Guidi windows, chanced to come.

Mrs. Browning was then forty-three years old. She had suffered for many years from an obscure form of spinal complaint that condemned her for many of those years to a couch in a darkened London room, from which it was never imagined that she would again emerge alive ; she was undoubtedly tuberculous, and at one time there had been constant slight hæmorrhage from one of her lungs.   Yet her son was a perfectly normal child, if a little small ; he lived for sixty-three years, and there is no sign that he ever inherited anything of his mother's delicacy.

His birth filled her cup of happiness to the brim. She was in ecstasies over him.   He was " a lovely fat strong child with double chins and rosy cheeks, and a great wide chest and undeniable lungs."   " I never saw a child half so beautiful for my part. . . . He is so fat and rosy and strong that almost I am sceptical of his being my child."   And to Mrs. Martin she wrote :

> " My child you never would believe to be *my child* from the evidence of his immense cheeks and chins, for pray don't suppose that he has only one chin ! "

He was immensely admired in the Cascine when taken thither by his nurse and Wilson.   " *Che bel bambino!*" they used to hear people say as they passed.

The sparkling vivacity which in her former letters had been reserved for the recital of Flush's adventures and transgressions was now dedicated to her baby. Small wonder that poor Flush fell into deep depression after the appearance of this formidable rival. This phase lasted for a fortnight, after which, accepting the inevitable, the little dog began to show a certain interest in the cradle and its occupant.

The baby was baptised without sponsors in the French Lutheran Church at Florence. They tried at first to call him Wiedemann, but he disposed of this in childish fashion soon after he began to talk by alluding to himself as Penini, which was certainly more euphonious.

Robert's mother died rather suddenly of ossification of the heart a day or two after Penini's birth, and thus his first joy at his wife's safety, and the rapture of his own fatherhood, was changed to deepest sorrow. More than a common sympathy had endeared him to his mother, and his grief was so great that at first even the baby was powerless to comfort him. Still, his interest in the little creature did not flag, and he attended the nightly ceremony of the bath, and carried him in his arms up and down the terrace during the day.

Robert felt bitterly being parted from his father and sister at such a sad time, for they had always been a singularly united family. He could not, however, leave his wife and child, and it was impossible for either of them to travel to England so soon. Nor could he persuade his relations to come to Italy. Florence was in a highly disturbed state ; there was a renewal of street-fighting in April, and on one occasion Robert was hardly able to get across the bridge in safety on his way back to Casa Guidi. Small wonder, therefore, that the elder Browning and his daughter did not jump at Elizabeth's invitation to join them in Florence.

The baby continued to flourish.   At three months old he talked to himself ; he was put on the floor to kick, and, Wilson declared, would walk with the slightest encouragement.   In fact, his progress was that of all healthy, intelligent babies, the only wonder was that such a marvel of strength should indeed be, as she said, her own child.

Mrs. Browning had her own private grief at that time.   Shortly after Penini's birth she had written to her father, and when for some weeks the letter had not been returned to her she began to cherish the hope that at last he would write and forgive her.   But not even the birth of his first grandchild could touch that hard, autocratic, unforgiving heart, and years later all her letters were returned to Robert when they were in London, with their seals unbroken.

2

Partly for the baby's sake and partly in the hope that change of scene would relieve her husband's depression, Mrs. Browning seconded the suggestion that they should spend the summer at Bagni di Lucca, always a favourite summer refuge with the English exiles in Italy.

It was a stormy, eventful summer, and the trend of political happenings was not at all in accordance with Mrs. Browning's hopes.   The battle of Novara had ended in the abdication of the Piedmontese king, Charles Albert, and the Tuscan Republic was at an end, the Grand Duke having re-entered Florence under the protection of Austria.   Venice had fallen before the Austrian attack, and Sicily had submitted to the Bourbons of Naples.   Under the protection of French troops Pius IX had returned to Rome.

But Elizabeth was not as yet so passionate and prejudiced a politician as she afterwards became.   Three years later Mrs. Jameson declared that she never talked politics with Ba, considering her fine intellect demented on that point.   Few people in England, it must be said, shared indeed her impassioned enthusiasm for Louis Napoleon.

The Brownings were charmed with Bagni di Lucca. They paid twelve pounds for their apartment for the four months of their stay and found living even cheaper than in Florence. Their home was a sort of eagle's nest, " the highest house of the highest of the three villages," which constitute the little mountain town.

The place was very quiet and peaceful, particularly so after the recent street-fighting in Florence, and the only sounds they could hear were the murmur of the river and the ceaseless song of the *cicale*. No echo of Austrian guns penetrated to that remote spot.

Penini's cheeks grew rosier ; he spent all day out of doors like any modern baby. " He fixes his blue eyes on everything and smiles universal benevolence." He was devoted to Flush, pulling his ears and riding on his back ; and Flush, despite the outrage to his dignity, for never in his life before had such untoward things happened to him, made no protest except to turn his head and kiss the little bare toes.

" Is it not curious that *my* child should be remarkable for strength and fatness ? " Mrs. Browning wrote to Miss Mitford. " He has a beaming, thinking little face."

Her own health had improved so wonderfully that she was able to climb the steep hills with Robert and get lost in the chestnut woods. The mountain air, the tranquillity, the free outdoor life revived her to an extent that must always seem miraculous. Over and over again Robert must have looked at her half in amazement and half in triumph at his own achievement. He had run immense risks in taking her away from Wimpole Street ; people had not been slow to warn him that the long journey to Italy would probably kill her, yet here she was, nearly three years later, a miracle of eager energy and happy motherhood.

The starry nights, the fireflies tangling the trees with their wandering lights, the sound of the river, the glorious sunshine by day, must have seemed like a dream to the woman who had so long been immured. And part of the dream and hardest to be realised must have been the bright rosy face, the fair golden curls, the blue thinking eyes of her little son, Penini.

Wilson was devoted to him, declaring that he was prettier than any of the other babies at Bagni di Lucca. He was forward for his four months; people told his mother that babies of ten months or a year could hardly do as much. Day by day he grew " fuller of roses and understanding." Before he was six months old he would stretch out his little hands and feet when bidden to do so, and put up his little mouth for a kiss. He knew his parents well as Papa and Mamma, and greeted them with crows of joy when he met them out of doors. When they went for long excursions into the mountains the baby accompanied them, and while they " dined with the goats," lay upon a shawl, rolling and laughing. Elizabeth in her renewed health and vigour rode up those steep hills on a donkey and seemed to incur scarcely any fatigue.

The quiet outdoor life in that brilliant summer weather was not, however, conducive to the writing of much poetry. Elizabeth did a little, as she said, now and then, but Browning did nothing at all. She excused him because his nerves had been shaken by the sudden death of his mother. They saw few people, although for a time they struck up a friendship with Lever, who was spending the summer there with his numerous family. But no more than at Florence did they seek the diversions of society. Penini was the only popular one of the little group, because he did not " hide in the woods like his ancestors," but smiled at everyone. They did, however, attend some Shakespearean lectures given by a Mr. Stuart, and were amused to hear him quote Mrs.

Jameson, saying, " As Mrs. Jameson observes."
Otherwise their life was singularly uneventful in that
mountain fastness.   They were, however, perfectly
contented.

" Ba must have told you about our babe,"
Browning wrote to Mrs. Jameson, " and the little
there is else to tell—that is for *her* to tell, for she is
not likely to encroach upon *my* story which I could
tell of her entirely angel nature, as divine a heart as
God ever made.   I know more of her every day ;
I who thought I knew something of her five years
ago."

3

But the time was by no means wasted, even as
far as the dilatory Robert was concerned.   One of
the most beautiful of his poems, *By the Fireside*, was
inspired by those days at Bagni di Lucca.

> A turn, and we stand in the heart of things ;
>   The woods are round us, heaped and dim ;
> From slab to slab how it slips and springs,
>   The thread of water single and slim
> Through the ravage some torrent brings !
>
> Does it feed the little lake below ?
>   That speck of white just on its marge
> Is Pella ; see, in the evening glow
>   How sharp the silver spear-heads charge
> When Alp meets Heaven in snow !
>
> Oh, the sense of the yellow mountain flowers,
>   And thorny balls, each three in one,
> The chestnuts throw on our path in showers !
>   For the drop of the woodland fruit's begun
> These early November hours.
>
> And all day long a bird sings there,
>   And a stray sheep drinks at the pond at times ;
> The place is silent and aware ;
>   It has had its scenes, its joys and crimes,
> But that is its own affair.

And further on, to show how the very spirit of the place had entered into their life together and become in a sense incorporated with it :

> Come back with me to the first of all,
>   Let us lean and love it over again,
> Let us now forget and now recall,
>   Break the rosary in a pearly rain,
> And gather what we let fall !
>
> Oh moment, one and infinite !
>   The water slips o'er stock and stone ;
> The West is tender, hardly bright :
>   How grey at once is the evening grown—
> One star, its chrysolite !
>
> We two stood there with never a third,
>   And each by each, as each knew well :
> The sights we saw and the sounds we heard,
>   The lights and the shades made up a spell
> Till the trouble grew and stirred.
>
> Oh, the little more, and how much it is !
>   And the little less, and what worlds away !
> How a sound shall quicken content to bliss,
>   Or a breath suspend the blood's best play
> And life be a proof of this !
>
> Had she willed it, still had stood the screen
>   So slight, so sure, 'twixt my love and her :
> I could fix her face with a guard between,
>   And find her soul as when friends confer,
> Friends—lovers that might have been.
>
> .   .   .   .   .
>
> For a chance to make your little much,
>   To gain a lover and lose a friend,
> Venture the tree and a myriad such,
>   When nothing you mar but the year can mend :
> But a last leaf—fear to touch !

Something of autobiography had undoubtedly crept into those passionate stanzas, and the suspense of the days when he was on probation at Wimpole Street imbued his present happiness with a strange wistfulness.

Worth how well, those dark grey eyes,
　　That hair so dark and dear, how worth
That a man should strive and agonise,
　　And taste a veriest hell on earth
For the hope of such a prize !

You might have turned and tried a man,
　　Set him a space to weary and wear,
And prove which suited more your plan,
　　His best of hope or his worst despair,
Yet end as he began.

But you spared me this, like the heart you are,
　　And filled my empty heart at a word.
If two lives join, there is oft a scar,
　　They are one and one, with a shadowy third ;
One near one is too far.

I am named and known by that moment's feat ;
　　There took my station and degree ;
So grew my own small life complete,
　　As nature obtained her best of me—
One born to love you, sweet !

And to watch you sink by the fireside now
　　Back again, as you mutely sit
Musing by firelight, that great brow
　　And the spirit-small hand propping it,
Yonder, my heart knows how !

It would be safe to say that none of Browning's
poems is better known and more frequently quoted
than the beautiful *By the Fireside*. Such phrases
as :

Oh, the little more, and how much it is !
And the little less, and what worlds away !

(which Tennyson confessed to his son that he wished
he had written) and " A last leaf—fear to touch,"
as well as the expression " a shadowy third,"
have passed into our language like many of the
phrases in Shakespeare. The tender, flowing
melody makes it also one of the easiest of his poems
to memorise. And reading between the lines we
are aware of his intense happiness—the happiness

that came to him from wife and child, which he had so feared might be withheld, and which he had risked so much to obtain.

Although change of scene often with him induced idleness, a disinclination to work, his mind was always storing fresh impressions for future use.   And if he had only written *By the Fireside* those months spent at Bagni di Lucca must have seemed abundantly fruitful.

4

They remained there rather late, in order to see the vintage, but returned to Florence in October when Mrs. Browning was almost immediately taken ill. The " poor feet," as she called them, had fallen into their old evil ways again and she had to give up her long walks.

Soon after their return they met Margaret Fuller, now Marchesa Ossoli, with whom they had corresponded.   Apparently no one was aware of her marriage, and she took everyone by surprise by appearing suddenly in Florence with her husband, and a baby but little older than Penini.   Mrs. Browning found her interesting, thoughtful and spiritual, not only exalted but *exaltée* in her opinions, but calm in manner withal.   This casual acquaintance might have become a lasting friendship, but in the following year a tragic event occurred.   The Ossoli family, before leaving for America, spent their last evening in Florence with the Brownings, when the marchesa presented Penini with a Bible as a parting gift from her own child, Angelo.   Strange to say, the inscription she wrote on the fly-leaf ran as follows : " In memory of Angelo Eugène Ossoli."   And during that last evening they referred jestingly to a warning her husband had received, " that he should shun the sea, for it would be fatal to him."   She, however, turned to Mrs. Browning and said with a smile : " Our ship is called the *Elizabeth* and I accept the omen."

From Gibraltar she wrote to Mrs. Browning

telling her that the captain had died of smallpox. Afterwards they heard that both she and her child had taken the disease, and both lay for a long time between life and death. The ship was subsequently wrecked off the coast of America and the little party were all drowned. The disaster was not only affecting in itself, as Elizabeth wrote to Miss Mitford, but also on account of its association with that other shipwreck, "when the arrowhead of anguish was too deeply broken into my life ever to be quite drawn out." Robert had indeed wished to keep the news from her till she was stronger, but "we live too *close* for him to keep anything from me."

From November to January she never left the house. On Christmas Day, 1849, Penini, who was then little over nine months old, began to crawl. The admiring parents threw things across the room and he crawled after them on all fours like a little dog. He, too, suffered from a bad cold that winter, and naturally she was unduly anxious about him, as a very delicate woman was bound to be about her child. She was occupied at that time in preparing for the press a new edition of her poems, which was to include those published in 1838 as well as those of 1844 with the addition of a few new ones. Robert Browning was then at work on *Christmas Eve* and *Easter Day*.

Even at that early age little Penini was sensitive to rhythm. He was such a darling little creature, she wrote, who could help loving the child ? He was growing fatter and developing a spirit of mischief in which his mother delighted. And he still continued to smile at everyone, being as sociable as his parents were the reverse. The Brownings continued to resist all the advances made to them by the English colony in Florence. Not so their little son, who was ready to kiss anyone who smiled upon him ; and it is certain that a great many people must have smiled upon the laughing, rosy, blue-eyed baby whose parents were celebrated wherever the English language was spoken.

But Mrs. Browning was not without anxiety that winter. Hearing that her father was ill, she took the opportunity of writing to him again, "the humblest and most beseeching of letters." The letter, like all its predecessors was not then returned, a circumstance from which his daughter continued to derive a modicum of comfort and hope. It is a pity that none of these letters have been published ; they must surely have been among the most beautiful she ever wrote. "I have confined myself" (she told her old friend Mrs. Martin in a letter) "simply to a supplication for his forgiveness of what he called, in his own words, the only fault of my life towards him, and an expression of the love which even I must feel for him whether he forgives me or not." She had even begged him to exclude her from every future financial advantage he intended for his other children if he would only give her his pardon and affection. It was a generous impulse and it met with Robert's approval, but the letter elicited no reply. Neither then nor at any other time did Elizabeth soften that proud, obdurate heart.

Florence continued to be in a highly disturbed state. It " bristled with cannon on all sides," and a promise of bombardment threatened the first rebellious movement. " That the Papacy has for ever lost its prestige and power over souls is the only evident truth bright and strong enough to cling to." History does not endorse this dictum, but Mrs. Browning was not the first to be deceived by the violence of an anti-clerical movement.

The news of Mr. Barrett was satisfactory. He suddenly refused to take any more of the lowering remedies prescribed by his doctor, and from that hour recovered. In March, 1850, another blow was struck at his domestic peace, inasmuch as his second daughter, Henrietta, after a long and anxious engagement lasting five years, married her cousin, Captain Surtees Cook. Mr. Barrett forbade her name to be mentioned in his presence and, like Elizabeth, she never saw him again.

The news only reached Mrs. Browning three days before the wedding actually took place, and she was naturally very much upset by it. There were in fact grave objections, since neither Henrietta nor her husband had much money. The dreadful event passed off, however, better than anyone could have hoped, and Arabel reported that things were going on quietly at Wimpole Street. Henrietta was to live at Taunton, where her husband, who was in the Army, had an appointment. But this event reacted upon Mrs. Browning's own prospects of reconciliation. " All this, you see, will throw me back with Papa, even if I can be supposed to have gained half a step, and I doubt it. My heart sinks when I dwell upon peculiarities difficult to analyse. I love him very deeply. When I write to him I lay myself at his feet." Only he never opened or read the letters. . . .

Henrietta wrote a little wistfully : " I wonder if I shall be as happy as you, Ba ? " Her brothers had been kind and affectionate to her.

For this and many other reasons the Brownings had been especially anxious to visit England in the summer of 1850. Mrs. Browning in particular desired to show Penini to her friends and relations, and perhaps she cherished a secret hope that the child—his first grandchild—might make some appeal to Mr. Barrett. But the journey was not to be, on account of the expense, and they remained in Florence all through the hot weather until September, when they spent a few weeks at Siena.

She had been ill that summer and the change to Siena revived her. They took a villa nearly two miles from the town on the hill called Poggio al Vento. It was set among vineyards and olive-groves and orchards of apple and peach, and boasted a little flower garden of its own as well. There were seven rooms, and for this they paid a sum equivalent to eleven shillings and one penny farthing per week ! A trifling inconvenience was caused by the inability of the doors to shut ; thus, when Penini was asleep they had to speak in whispers for fear of awakening him.   But the air was cool—like English air—and they were supplied with excellent milk, butter, eggs and wine.   Daily, Penini's cheeks grew rosier, and he took a childish delight in the pigs, pigeons, donkey and great yellow dog.   Unfortunately he had a touch of the sun, and lay for twenty-four hours in a stupor, with burning head and glassy eyes. " Terrible the silence that fell upon the house without the small pattering feet and the singing voice."

Penini is revealed to us through his mother's letters, and by the descriptions of those who saw him, as a highly sensitive, elfin child, eager, intelligent, excitable, nervous and impressionable.   He cried when Flush was scolded, but he could be jealous of him too, when the dog's silky head lay on Mrs. Browning's lap and she stretched out her fragile little hand to caress him.   The boy was acutely sensitive to music, and would rush into church and kneel down at the sound of it.   From both father and mother he inherited the artistic temperament that led him to admire and appreciate beauty in every form of art, and though it did not in his case find expression in any outstanding talent, it at least provided him with a creditable and adequate career as a portrait painter.

In November they returned to Florence.   "We both of us grew rather pathetical on leaving our Sienese villa, and shrank from parting with the pig," Elizabeth wrote to Miss Mitford.

Their resources were severely taxed that year, despite the cheapness of their apartment in Florence and of the Sienese villa.   Neither she nor Robert made anything by their poetry, and although Mr. Kenyon allowed them a hundred a year from the time of Penini's birth, they could have only had a narrow margin with a child and nurse to keep.   Mrs. Browning still believed that poetry paid better than novel-writing.   In a letter to Miss Mitford she gave some interesting details about *Mary Barton*, which had been offered to most of the London publishers by Mrs. Gaskell without success.   Finally, Chapman

N

and Hall gave her one hundred pounds for the copyright, generously sending her a similar sum for the second edition. Two hundred pounds seemed to Mrs. Browning a good price for a novel. Tennyson was said to have received £500 from Moxon during the previous year, which had seen the publication of *In Memoriam*. These statistics must have cheered and encouraged the two impecunious poets living in their resolute retirement in Florence.

5

In 1851 the Brownings were in a position to give themselves their long-promised holiday. Mrs. Browning had now completed the second part of *Casa Guidi Windows*, which was published in June—the month after they left Florence for Venice. The book had less success than it merited. Interest in Italian politics had become slightly chilly in an England absorbed in the wonders of the Great Exhibition, which was called—according to Miss Mitford—Prince Albert's Folly. And the diatribes against the Papacy must assuredly have alienated many of Mrs. Browning's Catholic readers. Nevertheless, the poem contains passages of real beauty, although it is among the least successful of her writings. In her excuse it must be said that she was angry and disappointed at the trend of political events in Italy. She, who had for so long been immured and shut off from any close contact with the world of men and affairs, was perhaps unable to see those things that happened beneath that fruitful window of Casa Guidi in their rightful proportion. She was angry, and poetry is not the proper vehicle for the conveyance of political anger. She was angry with Italy, angry with England—though less so then than later—angry with the Pope, and even, so it would seem, with the Crystal Palace !

She had been too easily deluded, perhaps, by the street-fighting, the cries of *Evvivà*, the demonstrations that took place in Piazza Pitti, believing that they indicated a serious and concerted effort in the cause of liberty. And she, reared in seclusion, and ignorant of the horrors of war, desired war. . . .

In the previous year the Brownings had made the acquaintance of Miss Isa Blagden, who lived at the Villa Bricchieri on the heights of Bellosguardo. This acquaintance ripened into an intimate friendship that lasted till the end of Mrs. Browning's life ; indeed, she received Miss Blagden only a few hours before she died, when no one imagined the end was at all near.

Miss Blagden had written a couple of novels, and moved in an intellectual and literary set. She was small, dark, and vivacious, with sparkling black eyes and an olive-hued complexion which seemed to confirm the report that she had a " touch of the tar-brush."

From now onwards some of Mrs. Browning's most intimate and charming letters were addressed to " dearest Miss Blagden," so soon to become " dearest Isa," in an age when women did not habitually address each other by their Christian names as they do now.

The Brownings had planned an extensive trip starting with Rome and Naples that spring, but the apartment was being put in order, as they had decided to let it, and their departure was delayed until May. When everything was settled and their plans for the journey complete, they were suddenly seized with misgivings. It was far too late in the season for Rome. . . . (Someone in Florence must have suggested these objections to them !) The Festas would all be at an end. It would be far too hot for the baby (who was still incredibly alluded to as Wiedemann), and besides, it would be enormously expensive to go first to Rome and Naples and afterwards to France and England. The carriage was actually ordered, when they changed their plans and went to Venice. They were accompanied by

Wilson and some new friends—Mr. and Mrs. David Ogilvy. To the latter was sometimes relegated the distasteful task of administering Penini's medicine, his mother being too soft-hearted to do it herself.

Like all poets, Mrs. Browning was enchanted with Venice. "Never had I touched the skirts of so celestial a place. . . . Venice is quite exquisite ; it wrapt me round with a spell at first sight and I longed to live and die there—never to go away." Something in her frail, indolent nature responded to the silent charm, the enervating airs, the poetic but almost unreal beauty of the place. It soothed her nervous system. After the somewhat noisy Piazza Pitti its enchanting stillness must have fallen upon her like a benediction.

Robert, however, flagged visibly beneath the on-slaughts of the May sirocco ; his nerves were on edge ; he could neither eat nor sleep. Wilson was similarly affected, and Mrs. Browning was obliged to envisage the fact that while Venice suited her and the child admirably, it was making both Robert and her maid deplorably ill. Still, they stayed there for nearly a month, perhaps in the hope that the two might become acclimatised.

Little Penini's sense of beauty was even then so strong that when he first saw St. Mark's he flung his arms round Wilson's neck and kissed her in an ecstasy of joy.

They left in June and went to Padua, arriving there on the 12th, when the place was filled for the Feast of St. Antony on the following day, and lodgings were proportionately dear.

From thence they drove to Arqua—the second pilgrimage they had made in honour of Petrarch. "Did you ever see it—you ? " (Elizabeth wrote to Kenyon). "And didn't it move you, the sight of that little room where the great soul exhaled itself ? "

They passed through Brescia in a flood of brilliant moonlight. Few Browning lovers can, I think, visit that city without the stirring lines of *The Patriot* sounding in their ears.

Thus I entered Brescia[1], and thus I go !
  In triumphs people have dropped down dead.
" Paid by the world, what dost thou owe
  Me ? "—God might question ; now instead
'Tis God shall repay :   I am safer so. . . .

On the following morning they were in Milan, where they remained for two days, and where Mrs. Browning performed the—for her—astonishing feat of climbing to the topmost pinnacle of the Cathedral. Like Shelley, she admired it, and indeed, after years of adverse and disdainful criticism, people are beginning to trust to their own taste and to perceive its unique and arresting beauty.

" How glorious that Cathedral is—worthy almost of standing face to face with the snow Alps ; and itself a sort of snow-dream by an artist-architect taken asleep in a glacier."

Shelley's description, while quite as enthusiastic, is less fanciful :

" This Cathedral is a most astonishing work of art. It is built of white marble, and cut into pinnacles of immense height and the utmost delicacy of workmanship, and loaded with sculpture. The effect of it, piercing the solid blue with those groups of dazzling spires, relieved by the serene depth of this Italian heaven, or by moonlight when the stars seem gathered among those clustered shapes, is beyond anything I had imagined architecture capable of producing."

By this time Mrs. Browning had, alas, renounced her admiration for Guido and Guercino ; she stigmatised Caracci as " soulless," though she was enthusiastic about Correggio because, as she wrote, he had " the sense to make his little Christs and angels after the very likeness of my baby ! "

---

[1] The word " Brescia " is omitted in later editions.

Their homeward route lay across the St. Gothard, and they halted for a few days at Lucerne, which she considered, half reluctantly, to be finer than the Italian Lakes. Thence they proceeded to Paris by way of Strasburg. The baby was an excellent traveller—like his mother—and arrived in Paris " as fresh in spirits as if just alighted from the morning star." They stayed there a short time before going on to London.

It lacked but a few weeks of five years since their hurried escape from Wimpole Street. There was still no sign of relenting on the part of Mr. Barrett, whose paternal feelings had again been violently lacerated by the outrageous behaviour of yet another of his daughters. And none of the brothers had so far made any step towards a reconciliation. With Henrietta in exile from Wimpole Street there was only Arabel upon whose welcome Mrs. Browning could count. If it had not been for Arabel—always the sister who was closest and dearest to her—she would have hesitated before setting foot in England again.

CHAPTER XIV

I

THE visit, however, could not for many reasons be deferred. Robert was naturally anxious to see his father and sister again after such a long separation, and there was business to be accomplished with respect to their various publications.

August found them back in London and settled in Devonshire Street. Rain and fog prevailed, and the climate at once took its toll of Mrs. Browning. Her cough returned. She had not had such difficulty in breathing since she left England five years before.

She refused the Martins' invitation to stay with them at Colwall, shrinking even after twenty years from revisiting the spot that was so full of her childish memories of Edward. " The past would be too strong for me." Not that she regretted Hope End ; she had been far happier at Casa Guidi than she had ever been there—but it was the thought of Edward that deterred her. " You know a little if not entirely how we loved one another, how I was first with him and he with me." She seemed in a sense anxious to show her friend that she was still faithful to that love, and that other ties had not entirely dispossessed it from its once foremost place in her heart.

The Brownings were a good deal fêted on their arrival in London, and for the first time tasted the tangible sweets of their fame. Both were celebrities, and the romantic story of their courtship and marriage was well known. As " all the world loves a lover," this fact had imbued their figures with a kind of glamour. Had they chosen to do so they could have enjoyed endless hospitality. Nor was Mrs. Browning disappointed with the literary celebrities whom she met for the first time. They saw a great deal of Carlyle. Tennyson they had already met in Paris, when he had generously offered them his house at Twickenham for their use as long as they remained in England. Fanny Kemble called on them and left tickets for her Shakespearean readings.

They were invited to breakfast—as everyone with any claim to fashion or fame was in those days—with Rogers. Barry Cornwall paid them a daily visit while they were in London. Their older and more intimate friends, such as Kenyon and Mrs. Jameson, were, as ever, assiduous with attentions and hospitality. Mrs. Browning even liked that ambiguous figure, Geraldine Jewsbury, whose foolish devotion to Mrs. Carlyle so annoyed that spirited, irascible lady, and who, as one born out of due time, obstinately persisted in the writing of improper novels.

The meeting between Mrs. Browning and her relations-in-law proved eminently successful. They received her with every sign of affection, and she and Sarianna became the closest friends. " She is highly accomplished, with a heart to suit the head," was Elizabeth's verdict.

Wilson naturally wished for a holiday in order to visit her family after her long absence abroad, and the task of looking after Penini devolved upon Mrs. Browning. The child, aghast at the disappearance of his beloved " Lily," seemed to be stricken with fear lest his mother should vanish in like manner, so that she was seldom, if ever, able to leave him.

Arabel was, of course, eager to help her in the task, although even this did not give her much liberty. But, to her intense joy, all her brothers—Henry, Alfred, Sette and Octavius—went to see her. Stormie was still in Jamaica looking after the property. A letter to George went astray, but directly it reached him he, too, visited his sister. It made her happy to feel his arms about her again, and to feel, as she expressed it, that she was still something more to him than a stone thrown away. Moreover, he had always from the time of their first meeting liked and appreciated Robert Browning, which makes it still more difficult to understand his stubborn attitude of disapproval towards his sister after her marriage. But, given the circumstances, it was perhaps not easy for even a middle-aged, hard-headed barrister living under the paternal roof to adopt a policy at variance with that of Mr. Barrett.

The reconciliation with her brothers was thus effected without difficulty, but there the success of the visit ended. Instead of being permitted to see her father again, and put her little son into his arms to receive his kiss as she had always hoped to do, the profound estrangement between them was accentuated. She and Robert both wrote to Mr. Barrett entreating his forgiveness. Robert's letter was "manly, true, straightforward, everywhere generous and conciliating," but the answer he received was of a singularly violent and intemperate character. Moreover, Mr. Barrett placed within the packet all the letters he had received from his daughter since her marriage, intact, with their seals unbroken. Even those with black-edged envelopes had not been opened, thus she might have lost both husband and child, for all he knew. He would have returned them long ago, he wrote, had he known their address.

This untoward event cast a profound shadow upon Mrs. Browning's visit to England. From that moment all hope of an eventual reconciliation must have slowly perished in her heart. "I cannot of course write again" (she told Mrs. Martin in a letter). "God takes it all into his own hands, and I wait."

Mr. Barrett further gave evidence of his un-yielding temper by removing his family from London. This was an especial grief to Arabel, who, now that her two sisters were married, was the only daughter at home. Her intimacy with Elizabeth had always been of a singularly close character, and she delighted in the society of her adorable little nephew, an elf-like creature who lisped his baby sentences in Italian. Henrietta, however, came up from Taunton for a week to be near her sister, and thus Mrs. Browning had the joy of seeing all her family, with the exception of her father and the absent Stormie.

Mr. Bayard Taylor, an American who met the Brownings in London about this time, described Browning as almost more like an American than an Englishman, with his " lively, cheerful manner, quick voice, and perfect self-possession." Mrs. Browning, he said, had a pale face, bluish grey eyes, chestnut curls (she herself definitely described them as dark, as did most of her contemporaries), and a slight figure. He saw, too, the little Penini, with his flowing golden curls and blue eyes and rosy cheeks.

The Brownings left England at the end of September and for the next nine months remained in Paris.

" With such mixed feelings I went away ! Leaving love behind is always terrible, but it was not all love that I left, and there was relief in the state of mind with which I threw myself on the sofa at Dieppe. . . . Robert felt differently from me for once, as was natural, for it had been pure joy to him with his family and friends."

Carlyle accompanied them on their journey to Paris, although they had feared that little Penini with his ceaseless questions might annoy him. Luckily, he accepted the child quite good-naturedly, telling him, however, that he had as many aspirations as Napoleon.

" He left a deep impression with me " (Mrs. Browning wrote). " It is difficult to conceive of a more interesting human soul. . . . His bitterness is only melancholy, and his scorn sensibility."

From Carlyle's point of view the arrangement

must have been highly advantageous, inasmuch as Robert, with his knowledge of French, was able to deal with those minor disagreeables incidental to travelling, thus relieving Carlyle of all difficulty, and enabling him " to sit at ease with the women." Perhaps he envied Browning the serenity of his married life beside that equable and always adoring companion.

2

Paris suited Mrs. Browning's health far better than England had done. They found a charming sunny apartment in the Avenue des Champs Elysées, for which they paid two hundred francs a month.

After that first visit to England it must be observed that the Brownings were never again so retiring and unsociable. Robert, who had always enjoyed the society of his fellow-creatures, had probably eschewed it during those years in Italy out of consideration for his wife's health. But now she too appeared ready and even eager to go out more ; consequently they were to be seen at various houses in Paris that winter, at least as often as her always delicate health allowed. They attended Lady Elgin's receptions at the Embassy—functions which began at eight and lasted till midnight. There they met Madame Mohl, wife of the famous Oriental scholar, who, living on till the 'eighties, was still sought out by English pilgrims to France, and figures in the more recent memoirs of Mrs. Humphry Ward and Mr. Alfred Lyttelton. Her salon was then one of the most interesting in Paris. The Brownings' first attempt at seeing George Sand—to whom Mazzini had given them a letter of introduction— proved abortive, for on the occasion of her first visit to Paris after their arrival she was engrossed with the production and success of her new play, *Le Mariage de Victorine*. But their second venture was rewarded with a note written by the great lady herself, inviting them to visit her on the following Sunday, which, she said, was the only free day she had. Robert Browning was far less eager to make her acquaintance than was his wife, and on the previous occasion had firmly refused to pursue the lioness to her den at the theatre. " A strange, wild, wonderful woman," commented Mrs. Browning.

Browning was so little accustomed to knock at reluctant doors that, but for his wife's sake, he would have troubled no more about making the acquaintance of George Sand, who had returned to Paris to seek an interview with the President, in the hope of obtaining a reprieve for her friend Dufraisse, who had been sentenced to exile in Cayenne. I have often wondered if this incident suggested to Mrs. Browning the idea of sending a petition to Napoleon III on behalf of Victor Hugo. She wrote the letter, a rather touching and eloquent one, but for some reason or other it was never sent.

The February day was bitterly cold, and Mrs. Browning, with respirator complete and muffled in furs, drove in a closed carriage to George Sand's house in the Rue Racine at three o'clock. They found the sibyl surrounded by eight or nine young men. She received them graciously, and when Mrs. Browning would have kissed her hand said, "*Non, je ne veux pas!*" and stooping, kissed her mouth.

Stout for her height, and none too tall, she was dressed in grey serge with jacket buttoned to the throat and large linen collar and cuffs. She was not beautiful, though her large dark eyes were splendid ; her face—of a somewhat Jewish cast—lacked sweetness. Her manner was simple, with a touch of scorn ; her voice low and rapid. She adored her son, then a young man of twenty-three.

" I did not love her," wrote Mrs. Browning, " but I felt the burning soul through all that quietness."

At parting she kissed her again, and invited them for the following Sunday. Robert, who intensely disliked the crew of Bohemian young men who surrounded her, listening to her utterances as if to an oracle, only went there again to please his wife, although he resented the idea of her mingling with such persons. He had even declared that if another hostess had behaved as she did, warming her feet at the fire, he would have walked out of the room. Still, even to Mrs. Browning, determined to make every excuse, the society she encountered in the Rue Racine must have seemed a trifle queer. There was a Greek who "tutoyé'd" George Sand, and even—so Robert alleged—kissed her. There was " a vulgar man of the theatre " who fell on his knees before her, calling her sublime. *Caprice d'amitié*, she said disdainfully. She promised to go and see the Brownings, but left Paris without doing so.

Mrs. Browning, who had always had a tendency to hero-worship, was not altogether satisfied with the result of their intercourse. " We always felt that we couldn't penetrate—couldn't really *touch* her—it was all in vain."

George Sand's method of work seems to have been almost phenomenally rapid, for she had then just written a romance in fifty-two days, or rather nights, for she worked only at night.

The meetings between celebrities are rarely successful, much less fruitful, and it is certain that in this case George Sand with her promiscuous amours, her coterie of smoking and spitting Bohemians, was as the poles apart from a delicate, sheltered, refined woman like Elizabeth Browning. Even their great literary gifts were not of the kind that could draw them sympathetically together. They could have had as little in common as Goethe and Heine (who, in the presence of the master, could think of no more appropriate subject of discourse than the plums in the garden) ; or as Charlotte Brontë, tongue-tied in the presence of Thackeray, so long the hero of her dreams ; or even as Wordsworth, who, when he visited Sir Walter Scott, could find no more profitable employment of the time spent together than by reading his own poems aloud to him. Deep does not always call unto deep, and between men—and women—of genius, it would seem as if in some sort a veil often descends to obscure a clear vision.

Meeting George Sand later, when alone in the Tuileries Gardens, Robert offered her his arm and they walked together the whole length of the Gardens. She also sent them tickets for the first night of her play, *Les Vacances de Pandolphe*, which, however, proved a failure.

3

An appreciative article on Browning's poetry in the *Revue des Deux Mondes* led to a warm and lasting friendship with the author, Joseph Milsand, whose famous phrase concerning the English poet will perhaps never be forgotten : " *Quel homme extraordinaire, son centre n'est pas au milieu !* " But perhaps the remark would be applicable to many other poets, since there is always something a little abnormal about great genius.

Those were stirring days in Paris, for incipient revolutions seemed to dog the woman who had lain so long upon a secluded couch to which only faint rumours of the outside world had ever penetrated.

The President—afterwards Napoleon III—was not then so passionate an object of enthusiasm and admiration to Mrs. Browning as he afterwards became, but she was beginning to feel a deep interest in his ambiguous career.

Despite the fighting, Elizabeth showed no alarm either for herself, or—what is even more inexplicable —for her little son. (Penini, on his side, was only afraid that the soldiers might shoot Punch !) The Brownings seldom agreed on political matters, though both were Liberals. He had far less sympathy with revolutionary movements, and was wont to say, " in his self-willed, pettish way," that he hated all Buonapartes !

His father and sister spent some weeks in Paris to be near them. They had intended to leave for London in June, 1852, their apartment in Florence being still let, but Mrs. Browning had an attack of influenza, which rendered it necessary for them to postpone their journey. But at the end of June they were established in lodgings in Welbeck Street, in rather perilous proximity to Wimpole Street.

Elizabeth was changed in appearance and looked ill, proving the complete failure of her valiant attempt to winter in the north for Robert's sake. She had also overtaxed her strength, and realised that for herself a warm and dry hermitage was necessary in order to prolong life.

Mrs. Surtees Cook was also in London, and was only a few doors away from her sister, whom she saw constantly. Mr. Kenyon was among the first to be visited ; he had then as a guest the aged Walter Savage Landor. Mazzini, " with that pale spiritual face of his and those intense eyes full of melancholy illusions," came to see them. And Mrs. Carlyle, according to some recent Victorian memoirs, brought Mrs. Edward Twistleton to visit Elizabeth Browning.[1]

" She is very small," wrote that vivacious, astute, American lady, " shorter than I am, dressed in black and not with any particular care or nicety, but not at all sluttish either, only as if she did not spend money or thought upon the matter—she has very small hands and feet, beautiful thick brown hair but covered with a black cap behind, and worn in curls— soft grey eyes, a low gentle voice, and a quiet well-bred manner."

In London they once more found themselves surrounded by eager, welcoming friends. They went further afield this time, spending two days with Mr. and Mrs. Paine near Farnham, whence they went over to Eversley to see Charles Kingsley,

---

[1] *Letters of the Hon. Mrs. Edward Twistleton.* (Murray.)

accompanied by Penini and Flush. Wilson again
went home for her holiday, and Mrs. Browning was
left in sole charge of her little boy, who was unnerved
by the departure of his faithful " Lily." Even his
adoring aunts could not compensate for that untoward absence. " Will Mamma go away and leave
Penini all alone ? " was his troubled question.
Mrs. Browning could not but see that this child
of two poets was unusually sensitive and impressionable. But this year, having reached the mature
age of three and a few months, he indulged in no
outburst of screaming and crying, but struggled
to control himself when Wilson's departure was
accomplished.

While she was in charge of her boy Mrs. Browning
could, of course, pay no visits, and thus was unable
to fulfil her promise of spending a few days with
Miss Mitford. It was not very long since Miss
Mitford's *Recollections*, containing the unfortunate
allusion to Edward Barrett's death, had been published, and doubtless there must have been some
slight feeling of embarrassment which deterred Mrs.
Browning from any eagerness to effect the meeting.
Unfortunately, it was the last opportunity they had
of seeing each other, for Miss Mitford died before
Elizabeth's next visit to England.

Tennyson, whose little son had just arrived, sent
Mrs. Browning three such happy notes about the
event that she confessed she had never liked him
so well before. Monckton Milnes gave a large
luncheon on the occasion of his son's christening, to
which the little party were all bidden. Penini
behaved like an angel and looked very pretty, but
disgraced them by refusing to kiss the baby (who was
made to sweep in, in a mass of India muslin and
Brussels lace) on the ground that he was *troppo
grande.*

Ruskin was also among their visitors, and they
went to Denmark Hill to see his collection of Turners.
But they lingered on too long in England owing to
the inability of Wilson to return as soon as was

expected, and by October Mrs. Browning was so ill that a hasty departure for Paris was decided upon. Bad weather had revived the old lung trouble and she coughed ceaselessly.

After spending a few weeks in Paris they proceeded to Florence, where they arrived about the middle of November.

4

For the next three years the Brownings remained in Italy, spending part of the time in their apartment at Casa Guidi, with visits to Rome in the winter and to Siena or Bagni di Lucca in the summer.

It was ridiculous, their friends sometimes told them, for them to say they lived in Florence, since they left it in summer on account of the heat, and in winter on account of the cold.

Elizabeth Browning was engaged during those years in writing her longest and most ambitious work, *Aurora Leigh*, of which Swinburne said : " It is one of the longest poems in the world, and there is not a single dead line in it." Robert was then writing his *Men and Women*.

The return to Casa Guidi was pleasant.   They found the house actually improved after its long let, which is the happy experience of few landlords. The warm welcome from their Italian servants cheered them.   " *Dio mio, com' è bellino!* " Penini's nurse exclaimed on seeing him, the tears pouring down her cheeks.

Compared with Paris, Florence was dead.   But it was a beautiful death that contented her, Mrs. Browning said, although Robert was obviously pining for the gay boulevards, the contact with the fresh, energetic, intellectual life he had known in France.   He found Florence abnormally dull, and certainly it was no longer to him what it had been in the early days of their marriage.   Sometimes she confessed to feeling " like a weight round his neck," for the experiment of spending another winter in the north was out of the question for her.

Florence was at that time a hotbed of spiritualism, which indeed was prevalent in many countries, and was, moreover, practised by those in high places. Louis Napoleon, the Czar of Russia, and the King of Holland were all supposed to consult mediums. Mrs. Browning, with her love for the supernatural, her eager enthusiastic nature, embraced the new craze with a strange, uncontrolled fervour.

Browning disliked the whole thing intensely. It is related of him that once when his wife was discussing spiritualistic *séances* he burst out with an almost violent vehemence : " And what does it all end in ? In your finding yourself in a locked room with the keeper putting in his head and asking what you will be pleased to have for dinner ! " Mrs. Browning only protested with a half humorous, half deprecatory, " Oh, *Robert* ! "

With a less devoted couple their divergence on this point might have led to a serious schism, which was probably indeed only averted by Browning's good-temper and patience. But his sane, vigorous mind rejected the revelations of so-called mediums, and he ultimately took his revenge upon the whole unsavoury tribe by writing *Mr. Sludge the Medium*. He hated to see his wife so absorbed in this new enthusiasm, always so detrimental to character and judgment. Few people can seriously embrace spiritualism without a deplorable diminution of poise, both mental and moral. Once, indeed, a *séance* was actually held at Casa Guidi, when Mr. Lytton, who was then an attaché at the British Embassy at Florence, was present ; and among other guests were Frederick Tennyson (now settled in Florence with an Italian wife) and Villari. The experiment proved a complete failure, owing, Mr. Lytton said, to Browning's antagonistic, sceptical attitude.

Mr. Lytton, who subsequently had a most distinguished career in the Diplomatic Service and was afterwards Viceroy of India, met the Brownings after their return to Florence in 1852. He was a delicate, intellectual young man who made a name for himself as a poet under the *nom de plume* of Owen Meredith. He had a villa on Bellosguardo and was thus a neighbour of Isa Blagden. When summer came he gave evening receptions on his terrace overlooking Florence, when the guests were regaled with tea and strawberries and cream.

He encouraged Elizabeth in her growing interest in spiritualism, assuring her that the " rapping spirits " had been heard at Knebworth.

The winter passed quietly enough at Casa Guidi, although the trend of political events in Tuscany evoked from Mrs. Browning a fresh outburst against the " old serpent the Pope." Both she and her husband were busy with their books, and in addition she made some frocks for Penini, although he was now nearly four years old. She was well, quiet and occupied, reading, writing, working, playing with her child. The " rapping spirits " still intrigued her. " Fifteen thousand persons in all ranks of society and all degrees of education are said to be mediums, that is *seers*, or rather hearers and recipients, perhaps."

Mr. Lytton had been warned by several mediums that his father would meet with an accident, not fatal, but serious. Three months passed and he began to think they had made a mistake, " only it is curious that they should *all* make a mistake of the same kind precisely," when the news reached him that Sir Edward Bulwer Lytton had met with an accident to his arm which kept him away from the House of Commons.

Despite her interest in the subject, Mrs. Browning kept a level head about it, and she would never permit anyone to ask questions of the mediums on her own behalf. " As to the spirits, I care less about what they are capable of communicating than of the fact of there being communications. I certainly wouldn't set about building a system of theology out of their oracles. God forbid! They seem abundantly foolish one must admit. . . . "

Perhaps it was her fundamental scepticism on the point that kept her from any extravagant adherence to spiritualism.

They took on their apartment for another year. It was evident that Mrs. Browning was better in Florence than elsewhere, though probably a warmer, drier climate, such as that of Egypt, would have permanently improved her health. As it was, by March her cough had almost gone, and she was only taking cod-liver oil to please Robert. She was less thin, and he was triumphant.

They saw a great deal of Mr. Tennyson (the Laureate's elder brother), as well as of Mr. Lytton, and thus were gathering about them a literary coterie. Both the Brownings admired Frederic Tennyson's verses.

" They are full of *atmospherical* poetry and very melodious," Mrs. Browning wrote. " The poet is still better than the poems—so truthful, so direct, such a reliable Christian man."

She expected, too, great things of Mr. Lytton as a poet when he ripened into life and experience.

5

In the summer of 1853 the Brownings went again to Bagni di Lucca, taking the Casa Tolomei, which was sheltered by a group of splendid plane trees in which the *cicale* played their harsh, interminable, monotonous summer-music.

" Now it is cool by day and night. You know these beautiful hills, the green rushing river, which keeps them apart, the chestnut woods, the sheep-walks and goat-walks, the villages on the peaks of the mountains like wild eagles, the fresh

CASA TOLOMEI

(Bagni di Lucca)

Where the Brownings spent the summers of 1853 and 1857

p. 212

unworn, uncivilised world-before-the-flood look of everything."

William Wetmore Story,[1] the American sculptor, was living on the top of the hill with his wife and children, and a friendship was thus established which proved of permanent happiness to both families, lasting into the second generation, since Edith Story (afterwards Marchesa Peruzzi) was with Penini when he died in 1912 at Asolo. Mrs. Browning and Mrs. Story rode on donkeys to call upon each other, and sometimes they joined forces and explored in each other's company the mountain villages that crowned the hills like the eyries of wild eagles. For the rest they led a simple life in that beautiful solitude, devouring quantities of strawberries and milk. Both were busily at work. The cool mountain air of Bagni always suited Mrs. Browning; she was imbued with a new energy. Penini was excessively happy. Once when Browning pretended to keep a letter from Miss Mitford from his wife, the child flung his arms round his mother's neck, crying: " Never mind, mine darling Ba. You'll have it ! " And one night he was heard to pray that God " would make him good and take him on a donkey."

Mrs. Browning watched her child's development with delight, and was never tired of repeating his quaint sayings. He had a singularly happy, unrepressed childhood, and worshipped his mother, always calling her Ba at " coaxing times."

She had plenty of time for reading, but in regard to novels all was grist that came to her mill, for she bestowed almost equal praise upon *Villette* and the intolerable *Queechy*. Mrs. Gaskell's *Ruth* also charmed her, and of Dumas she never wearied.

She had a momentary irritation with Mrs. Martin for writing to say that George looked less young than formerly, adding that " we should

---

[1] See Appendix.

all learn to hear and make such remarks with
equanimity." Elizabeth showed little sympathy
with this opinion, protesting indeed indignantly
against its implications. " Be sure," she wrote
in reply, " that it is highly moral to be young as
long as possible. Women who throw up the game
early (or even late) and wear dresses ' suitable to
their years '—that is, as hideous as possible—are
a disgrace to their sex, aren't they now ? " She
also considered that people who asked : " Do you
remember in '20 ? " (as if anyone could !) were
the pests of society. Despite this, on looking
at her photographs one must acknowledge that
there is little evidence of any effort on Mrs. Browning's part to dress in a youthful manner. But
clothes of that day were voluminous according to
our modern notions, the bonnet that indicated
married rank was scarcely what modistes now call
" helpful " to the face, and the inevitable cap worn
indoors after a certain age had been attained, must
have removed all trace of girlishness from the
wearer.

In August they entertained a visitor in the person
of Mr. Lytton from Florence. He lost nothing
from the test of house-intimacy, Mrs. Browning
averred. But her prophecies concerning his future
were singularly at fault, inasmuch as she said she
did not think he would ever become a successful
diplomatist. This of the man who was afterwards,
as Lord Lytton, to be Ambassador to France and
Viceroy of India ! Still, his was a many-sided
and extraordinarily gifted personality, for he
achieved fame also as the poet, Owen Meredith,
and some of his lyrics will not easily be forgotten.
Probably in that quiet, literary household and in
such company his poetic complex was in the ascen-
dant. He was then only twenty-one and had
already published some poems. He struck his
hostess as dreamy, excitable and delicate. Once
after a fatiguing excursion to Prato Fiorito, six
miles there and six miles back, with steep hills the

whole way, she turned to him as they neared home and said : " I am dying. How are you ? " He answered, " I thought a quarter of an hour ago I could not keep up to the end, but now I feel better." But if the story indicates a lack of physical endurance on the part of the young man it throws an extraordinarily vivid light upon the increased vigour of Mrs. Browning. Robert pretended not to be tired, but no one believed him.

By October they were all back in Florence, when Reade persuaded Robert to sit to him, and then they both insisted upon Mrs. Browning's having her portrait painted. She wished that Penini had been chosen instead ; for herself she disliked the process. " When gone from hence may nobody think of me again, except when one or two may think perhaps how I loved them ! "

She was delighted, however, to find herself back at Casa Guidi. She was better in health, and was able to attend a performance of Verdi's new opera " Trovatore " at the Pergola. But they did not remain long in Florence. Their new intimacy with the Storys encouraged them to go to Rome, which she had never as yet seen. She hoped to obtain a little rest there from the constant flow of visitors to which they were exposed in Florence. They had lived a disturbed life at Casa Guidi since their return, and were eager to get back to work. Robert's book was, however, more advanced than hers. *Aurora Leigh* was still very far from completion. Her outdoor life amid the beautiful scenery and in the delightful summer climate of Bagni di Lucca had proved little conducive to sustained literary effort. With her new interests, the love of husband and child, the literary and artistic friends that surrounded her, poetry had ceased to be the first impulse of her life.

CHAPTER XV

I

THEY went to Rome in November, and stayed at No. 43 Via Bocca di Leone, in the big yellow palace that stands at the corner of the Vicolo del Lupo. An old faded fresco of Our Lady of Seven Dolours is painted on a shield upheld by *putti* upon the angle of the house, illuminated by a great iron lantern. A memorial tablet was placed on the walls by the Roman Municipality in 1912 to commemorate the Brownings' residence there, on the first centenary of Robert Browning's birth. The inscription runs as follows :—

> Questa Casa Ospitò
> Roberto e Elisabetta Browning
> Che l'Italia ebbero Patria ideale
> E in Carmi imperituri
> Ne profetarono i nuovi destini
>
> Compiendosi il primo Centenario
> dalla Nascità del Poeta
> Il Municipio di Roma
> Pose
> VII Maggio MCMXII

Le Sue Memorie Eterne	Aprendo il mio Cuore
Attestano che l'Italia è immortale	Vi trovereste inciso ITALIA
E. Barrett Browning	R. Browning

At the unveiling of this tablet the British Ambassador, Sir Rennell Rodd, assisted, and there was also present Miss Alice Moulton Barrett, the daughter of Mr. Alfred Moulton Barrett and niece of the famous poetess.

The Brownings travelled to Rome by way of Perugia.[1] They visited Assisi, where they stopped to see the famous triple church. Their route lay through Terni with its wonderful waterfall—" that passion of the waters which makes the human heart seem so still." They entered Rome in the highest spirits, Robert and his boy actually singing. They found the apartment made ready by the Storys —who had taken it for them—with wood fires blazing and lamps lit. The rooms, which were sunny and well carpeted, were on the third floor, and were approached—and indeed still are for that matter—by a cold and cheerless steep stone staircase. But their six south windows caught every gleam of sunshine. Indeed, Mrs. Browning used to say that the only disadvantages of the apartment were its height and the smallness of the rooms. Still, as they were able to entertain twenty people at a time, they were perhaps only small in comparison with the more palatial ones of Casa Guidi.

It was unfortunate that tragedy should have darkened their first days in Rome. On the 23rd of November, the very day after their arrival, little Joseph Story, who was then only six years old, was taken suddenly ill with convulsions ; he never rallied, and died that same night. Little Edith Story had been sent round to the Brownings to be looked after during her brother's illness, but to Mrs. Browning's indescribable terror she too was taken ill with precisely the same form of gastric malady that had killed her brother. Her life was despaired of, and it was impossible to take her back to her home. As there was no room in the Brownings' flat for her she was carried down to a lower floor to that of Mr. Page, the artist, who lived in the same house. Almost immediately his youngest child, Emma Page, sickened of the same complaint, which was described as gastric fever affecting the brain.

---

[1] See Appendix:

Mrs. Browning was not only deeply grieved for her friends' loss but she was terrified and panic-stricken. To see child after child stricken by this fatal and mysterious malady made her tremble for little Penini's safety. He was naturally her first thought, and had she been able to do so she would have carried him off to the ends of the earth, undeterred, as she said, by the hooting after her of all Rome.

Little Pen, on hearing of Joe's death, gravely asked if " Papa had seen the angels when they came to fetch Joe ? " On being told " no," he burst into tears, sobbing : " Then did Joe *go up* by himself ? "

The doctor reassured Mrs. Browning, telling her that the disease was not infectious. Rather reluctantly she consented some days later to accompany Mrs. Story to visit the child's grave, close to the burial-place of Shelley's heart amid the blossoming violets and late roses of the beautiful Protestant cemetery near the Gate of St. Paul. But the expedition was not to her taste. She was horribly weak about such things, she declared, disliking to contemplate the " earth-side " of death, preferring to look *over* death and upwards. . . . " All this has blackened Rome for me."

Despite these calamities, Rome suited them all admirably during the winter months. Penini's cheeks were red as apples ; Robert was well ; she herself walked out daily. They met various celebrities—Thackeray, who was there with his two daughters ; Lockhart, travelling with the aged Duke of Wellington ; Adelaide and Fanny Kemble, the former better known as Mrs. Sartoris ; the artists, Gibson and Page ; Hatty Hosmer, the young American sculptress; and Mrs. Archer Clive, who subsequently achieved considerable fame with her novels *Paul Ferroll* and *Why Paul Ferroll Killed his Wife*. Mrs. Browning, in describing her, said that she was very peculiar indeed to look at—a peculiarity that extended to her voice and bearing and of which she seemed entirely unconscious. Miss Hosmer's memoirs afford us a last glimpse of " Flush—My Dog." Sadly changed, in extreme old age, he would still wag the remains of his tail to greet the Brownings' visitors as they entered the rooms at No. 43 Bocca di Leone.

They saw much of Thackeray and of Lockhart, who approved of Browning, saying that he wasn't at all like a " damned literary man." They heard excellent music once or twice a week at Mrs. Sartoris's, where all that was best of English and American society in Rome gathered regularly. They admired Page's work, and were, very properly, a little dubious about Gibson's *Tinted Venus*.

About this time George Barrett sent her a " stupid, blind, cur-dog, backbiting " notice of her from an American paper. So indignant was he at its content that he advised her to write and contradict it. But Elizabeth, in her safe sheltered position, refused to do any such thing. She treated the matter lightly, and urged George, if he should ever marry, not to choose a woman who had published books.

Spiritualism still engrossed her, to what an extent, alas ! we can gather from her amazing statement that when present at a *séance* the " shivering of the dead dumb wood, the human emotion conveyed through it—by what ? " had a greater significance for her than St. Peter's. Fortunately she herself had no power as a medium, although sometimes when she tried to practise automatic writing the pencil stirred in her hand.

Both Robert Browning and his little son were painted by Fisher, the English artist. The portraits were eminently saleable, Mrs. Browning said, but she considered that the child's hardly did him justice, although it portrayed the beauty of his blue eyes and " innocent face emplumed in golden ringlets." People told her he was the most attractive child they had ever seen, and this can readily be believed when one looks at the pictured face, thoughtful, chubby, intelligent, and remembers the quaint sayings, the quick sensitive affection.

" He is so full of sweetness and vivacity together, of imagination and grace. A poetical child really, and in the best sense."

They must have wearied of having their portraits painted. Mrs. Browning sat to Miss Fox for a crayon-drawing, which was pronounced successful— at any rate as regards the hair.   It was during that winter, too, that Hatty Hosmer—a pioneer of modern women students, since she lived in Rome exactly as a young man might have done, having her own studio and working assiduously as a sculptor —executed the beautiful and now famous model of the *Clasped Hands* of Mr. and Mrs. Browning. Mrs. Browning only consented to have them done if Miss Hosmer herself would cast them—she refused to sit for the *formatore*. In the *Marble Faun* Hawthorne alludes to it, saying : " Harriet Hosmer's *Clasped Hands* of Browning and his wife symbolises the individuality and heroic union of two high poetic lives."

But Rome, with its superior social attractions, its gay coterie of artists and writers, proved even less conducive to regular work than Florence. Neither Mrs. Browning nor her husband could have made any substantial progress with their books, although Robert Browning was learning the city by heart and storing up intimate impressions of it to bear fruit later in *The Ring and the Book*. Via Vittoria, where Pompilia lived with her adopted parents, was but a stone's throw from the Brownings' abode, and the Church of S. Lorenzo in Lucina, where the unfortunate girl was married and where as a child she had always feared the lion emerging from the wall with a man in its paws, on the right side of the entrance, was not far away across the Corso.

As spring advanced there were excursions into the Campagna, where they spent long hours with their friends, on morns of " Rome and May," to which that marvellous poem, *Two in the Campagna*, must have owed its inception.

> The champaign with its endless fleece
>   Of feathery grasses everywhere !
> Silence and passion, joy and peace,
>   An everlasting wash of air,—
> Rome's ghost since her decease !
>
> Such life here, through such length of hours,
>   Such miracles performed in play,
> Such primal naked forms of flowers,
>   Such letting Nature have her way
> While heaven looks from its towers.

These expeditions were usually organised by Mrs. Sartoris and Fanny Kemble, their fellow guests being Ampère, Mr. Lyons, and the Austrian Minister, M. Gorze. The talk was " almost too brilliant for the sentiment of the scenery," Elizabeth told Miss Mitford in a letter, " but it harmonised entirely with the mayonnaise and champagne." The Kembles, as she called them, " were their great gain in Rome." She described them as noble and upright women, preferring, however, Mrs. Sartoris to her sister, because she was the more tender and tolerant, the more lovable and sympathetic of the two.

Mrs. Page, the artist's wife, gave a sumptuous birthday party for Penini in March. He was then five years old, and sat at the top of the table doing the honours with a perfect freedom from shyness or self-consciousness. There was an immense cake with *Penini* inscribed upon it in sugar. The child was overwhelmed with gifts and attentions and was regarded as the king of the children there. He was fearless and independent, generally telling Wilson to come to fetch him " velly late." He would talk to Fanny Kemble, who inspired most people with awe. " I not aflaid of nossing," he used to boast.

But the little circle broke up as spring advanced. Thackeray took his two daughters to Naples, where

they had scarlatina.   Lockhart went away with the
Duke of Wellington—then eighty-four years of
age—who was troubled as to what he should do if
his companion, who looked appallingly ill, should
die on the road.   Should he send the body to
England for burial ?   Would it be delicate to ask
Lockhart what he would like done about it ?   However, the critic survived, and recovered on his return
to England, revived, so it was said, by his native
beef and beer.

2

They stayed on in Rome until the 22nd of May.
The weather was cold, which Mrs. Browning described
as " abnormal," but which shows that the climate of
Rome has changed less than many persons suppose.
Cold spells often occur astonishingly up till the end of
April, and there is an Italian proverb akin to the
Scottish one which warns the unwary not to be too
ready to doff their warmer clothing during May.

Towards the latter part of their stay Penini's
health flagged, and a physician was called in three
times to attend him.   He was pale and looked delicate, there were blue marks under his eyes, but he
recovered quickly when he returned to his native
Florence.

Robert had begun to go grey, a fact which Mrs.
Browning could hardly have regretted, for she was
six years his senior and her own dark clustering curls
were still untouched with silver.   But Robert, it
seemed, had shaved off his beard in a fit of momentary irritation, and the sight of him without it filled
his wife with horror.   He grew it again, but as a
retribution for the hasty act it came white.

They were delighted to be back among their old
friends.   They spent an evening with Lytton, and
walked home to the song of nightingales by " star-
light and firefly light."   Elizabeth confessed that
Florence looked more beautiful to her than ever after

Rome, for never did English exile care in the same
way for both cities.

The Brownings had planned to go to England
that summer, but the journey had to be abandoned
on account of financial difficulties. " A ship was to
have brought us in something and brought us in
nothing instead, with a discount." There was
nothing to be done but to remain quietly in Florence,
living on bread and macaroni and fruit. Probably
they had spent too much in Rome, where, then as
now, living was more expensive than in Florence.
Still, they passed the summer pleasantly enough
" among their own nightingales and fireflies."

" Both light and love," Mrs. Browning wrote,
" seemed stronger with her at Florence than elsewhere."

Penini flourished despite the hot weather. " I
wish I could show you my Penini," she wrote to Miss
Mitford later in the year, " with his drooping golden
ringlets and seraphic smile and his talk about angels."
The child adored his mother, calling her " my sweetest little mamma, my darling *dearlest* little Ba."
Indeed, there was more than common sympathy
between them, and she made his childhood as unlike
her own as possible, absolutely free from coercion
and with as little repression and restraint as was
necessary for his own security and well-being.

But bad news reached her from Wimpole Street.
Mr. Barrett had met with an accident and injured
his leg, and it was believed that this would result in
permanent lameness. To a person of active habits
and tireless energy the prospect was appalling,
especially as he firmly refused to go out for a drive,
saying that never in his life had he driven out for
mere amusement. Arabel found life inexplicably
dreary in Wimpole Street with her morose and bilious
father on her hands. It was the winter of the
Crimean War, and that dreadful, tragic calamity
was pursuing its tedious, dismal course. The bitterly
cold winter enhanced the sufferings of the troops and
added to the anxious misery of those at home.

No one cared for literature in those days ; people only read the newspapers. Poets and authors must have felt the pinch as later they were destined to do when the Great War devastated the fair countries of Europe.

Cold weather with frost and snow prevailed in Florence. The first tramontana of November brought back Mrs. Browning's cough. Her own health occupied her attention more than usual that winter, and she suffered from the worst bronchial attack she had had since her marriage. In the backwater of Florence the war—apart from its political significance—seemed scarcely to touch her. She was never one to dwell upon unpleasant subjects such as old age, disease, death ; the proximity of such things flung her into a state of nervous panic. Nor were her sympathies always with England in those dark and anxious hours. "England deserved her humiliation——" but perhaps the faint acidity that characterised her letters at this period was due to her own indifferent health. Her remarks about Florence Nightingale, whom she had met in London, showed a certain acerbity. "Every man is on his knees before ladies carrying lint, calling them 'angelic she's,' whereas if they stir an inch, as thinkers or artists, from the beaten line (involving more good to general humanity than is involved in lint), the very same men would curse the very same women. . . . I acknowledge . . . that I do not consider the best use to which we can put a gifted and accomplished woman is to make her *a hospital nurse.*" Still, as in the late War, the palm went—and very properly—to the active woman who could help, whether by nursing or otherwise, rather than to the poet and thinker whose wares for the moment were at a discount.

Robert Browning, who, unlike his wife, was vigorously and robustly English in his sympathies, lamented the mistakes and disasters that attended the Crimean War. He was deeply affected by the course of events, and I imagine there must have come to him, as to all strong, energetic men, a desire for a more active participation in the war that was bringing calamity upon Europe.

In any case, however, it would have been quite impossible for him to leave his wife, who was ailing throughout the winter and unusually depressed. " Except for love's sake it wouldn't be worth while to live on at the expense of so much harm," she wrote. " Not only do I die hard, but I hardly die."

Spring came and with it renewed health. The weather was beautiful, and Mrs. Browning was able to walk out again and to discard the nauseous cod-liver oil. She was fatter, and even her hair curled differently. Robert was very busy, dictating four hours a day to a friend who transcribed his poems for him. He had completed eight thousand lines. Penini was radiant. Spiritualism still intrigued the English colony in Florence, and messages from Dante and Savonarola had come through to these credulous devotees. Mrs. Browning had been out shopping for her " two treasures," and had helped to frill and tuck some little trousers for her boy. She also gave him his lessons, so that it was highly creditable of her to have finished seven thousand lines of *Aurora Leigh* in addition to these purely domestic activities.

Penini made excellent progress. At six years old he could read both English and Italian, and was able to write without lines. He had even written some little poems—" the very prattle of the angels," his mother said. He was proud of having been born in Florence. " *Sono italiano, voglio essere italiano !* " was his cry. And, indeed, his love for Italy remained one of his chief characteristics until his death at Asolo in 1912.

For the rest he was " very well, imaginative and noisy," as Robert Browning told Miss Hosmer in one of his letters, adding that he had just gone up to see Miss Blagden—who had been very ill—to give her the benefit of those qualities.

Among the illustrations of a recently-published book, *The Story Without an End*, there was the

P

picture of a child who exactly resembled Penini.
Others besides his mother noticed the striking likeness. The little boy was still excessively sensitive,
and burst into tears when he first heard the history
of St. John's exile on Patmos. " Just like poor
Robinson Crusoe ! " he sobbed, and his mother did
not know whether to laugh or to cry.

Penini possessed so many of her characteristics
of imagination, sympathy and acute sensibility, that
she was able to enter into the workings of that
childish mind with an ease not always given to
mothers. In her dealings with both her " treasures,"
as she called them, she showed a rare quality of
imaginative insight that has seldom been surpassed

3

Robert Browning's book, *Men and Women*, with
its beautiful and touching dedication to his wife,
intended perhaps as an answer to her *Sonnets from
the Portuguese*, was now finished. Elizabeth had been
prevented by her long illness that winter from
finishing *Aurora Leigh*, and it was not published until
the following year, 1856. But her husband's work
was ready, and it was of a finer quality than anything he had yet achieved. *Evelyn Hope, By the
Fireside, A Toccata at Galuppi's, Any Wife to Any
Husband, A Serenade at the Villa, Too Late, The
Statue and the Bust, An Epistle, The Last Ride
Together, The Patriot, Old Pictures in Florence, Two
in the Campagna*, and *One Word More*, comprise
perhaps all that is best known and most enduring
of his shorter poems. In their human content they
are for all time, while in their subtle psychology
they have made perhaps a deeper appeal to recent
generations than they ever did to his own contemporaries. The tender glimpse he allowed the world
to see of their beautiful married life could not
have found more perfect expression than in the
penultimate stanza of *One Word More*.

This I say of me, but think of you, Love !
This to you—yourself, my moon of poets !
Ah, but that's the world's side—there's the wonder—
Thus they see you, praise you, think they know you.
There in turn I stand with them and praise you,
Out of my own self, I dare to phrase it.
But the best is when I glide from out them,
Cross a step or two of dubious twilight,
Come out on the other side, the novel
Silent silver lights and darks undreamed of,
Where I hush and bless myself with silence.

For this once, he said, he would speak in his own
person.

Take these lines, look lovingly and nearly,
Lines I write the first time and the last time.

And never again did he in any of his poems use
that precise rhythm and metre.   He had only verse
to give her, he told her in words of delicate music,
but they should be of a quality that he would never
again write.
There is internal evidence in the poem that it
was written in London after their return there in
1855. But when he wrote it he seemed to be
watching the moon hanging above San Miniato
while the nightingales were singing and the fireflies
illuminating the corn, as on summer nights among
the olive groves that girdle Florence.

4

The Brownings arrived in London in July and
were soon settled in rooms in Dorset Street. They
saw during their stay a number of celebrities, including Tennyson, Carlyle, Ruskin, Leighton, King-
lake, the Procters, and of course their friend and
benefactor, Mr. Kenyon. But of her own family
Elizabeth saw very little indeed. Henrietta could
not afford to make the journey to London, and Arabel

was promptly whisked out of sight by her father. One of the younger sons, Alfred, had just committed the dire offence of marrying, his bride being his cousin, Lizzie Barrett. He was the first of Mr. Barrett's sons to defy him in this respect, incurring thereby his unforgiving anger. Like his two sisters he was thenceforward banished from the paternal home in Wimpole Street.

Fortunately for Arabel no scenes had attended this act of insubordination. Alfred wrote to his father a few days before the wedding to announce his intention of getting married ; he received no answer, and followed it by a second letter to say that the ceremony had taken place in Paris.

Mrs. Martin again urged Elizabeth to come and stay with them at Malvern, but she refused as firmly as ever. She could not go to Herefordshire, she said, even if she were rational, which she was not. And then for the first time she revealed what must have tortured her through all the long years that had elapsed since the death of her beloved Bro. She said she could as soon open a coffin as return to Malvern, because the thought of that face which never ceased to be present with her, and *from which she had parted for ever in her poor blind unconsciousness with a pettish word,* would rise up and prevent her from having a single moment of ordinary calm intercourse with Mrs. Martin or anyone else. Of course she was morbid, she said so herself, but she realised her own limitations and knew exactly what must prove unbearable. The remembrance of that " pettish " word must have haunted all her thoughts of Edward, filling them with bitter self-reproach, but she should have remembered, too, that he would have been the last to blame her for any temporary exhibition of irritation.

To go back to scenes where one has been very happy requires always a certain degree of courage ; it must be done, too, at once or not at all. Even so, it holds another danger of inciting the mind to dwell too profoundly upon that irretrievably lost happiness, with something of Ben Jonson's piteous anguish voiced in his *Sad Shepherd* :

Here she was used to go, and here, and here. . . .

In the end the Brownings remained in London during the whole of their visit, partly for economy's sake, since their finances were not very brilliant, and partly because Robert was immersed in the correction of proofs.   They refused attractive invitations to Knebworth and elsewhere, and stayed in London till October.

Wilson had married a Florentine, Ferdinando Romagnoli, who on this occasion accompanied them to London.   *Povera gente, che deve vivere in questo posto !* was his first exclamation, echoed, I fear, by thousands of Italian immigrants who have left their own blue skies and sunshine for the first time to sojourn in the grey, stern north.   He and Wilson served the Brownings and their son faithfully to the end, dying many years later in the Palazzo Rezzonico at Venice, where Robert Browning also breathed his last in 1889.   Ferdinando survived his old master about four years and was himself survived by " Wilson."

Mrs. Browning was ill and melancholy and inclined to dislike England.   She was a little overdone with people and longed for the quiet of Florence. Still, there were compensations.   Tennyson came to dine with them, and ended by reading *Maud* aloud to them from beginning to end, only leaving at half-past two in the morning.   Every now and then he would stop to ejaculate a characteristic comment. " There's a wonderful touch !   That's very tender ! How beautiful that is ! " and it certainly was tender, wonderful and beautiful, Mrs. Browning said, and he read it exquisitely in organ-like tones that resembled music rather than speech.   Dante Gabriel Rossetti, who was present, and who had an almost reverent admiration for Mrs. Browning, amused himself by sketching the Laureate as he read. *Maud* was having a great success, and five thousand copies had already been sold.

Meanwhile, the first half-volume of Robert's poems was in proof and looked all the better in print, as " all true work does brought into the light." He had read the proofs to Mr. Fox (of Oldham), who considered the poems were " at the top of art in their kind," a criticism with which few would now be disposed to disagree.

But, despite these amenities, the fact remains that this visit to England was not a success. Mrs. Browning had hoped to join Arabel at Eastbourne, but this proved to be impossible. Work and the lack of means compelled her to remain in London, where Penini gave himself airs about the superiority of Florence and discoursed on the glories of the Cascine to anyone who would listen to him. It was with something of relief that Mrs. Browning left London in October for Paris.

The first days of their stay in Paris were disastrous. A friend had taken rooms for them in the Rue de Grenelle, which, with their sharp easterly aspect, soon took toll of Mrs. Browning. By December they were settled in another apartment in the Rue du Colisée, where she recovered and was able to resume her long, patient work on *Aurora Leigh*. " I hop about from one side to the other like a bird in a new cage. The feathers are draggled and rough, though. . . . And this time I shall not die, perhaps, indeed I think not. . . ."

The new rooms suited them exactly, being warm and sunny, with plenty of sofas and comfortable chairs. They saw, among other friends, Lady Elgin, Hamilton Aidë and Madame Mohl.

I cannot help sympathising deeply with Elizabeth in the matter of the clock which her friend Miss Haworth had asked that Robert might choose for her in Paris about this time. Persons who habitually live abroad must present a firm front against the execution of such commissions, or they would find the encroachment upon their leisure incredibly formidable.

" If you knew Robert " (wrote Mrs. Browning),
" you never would have asked him.   He has a sort of
mania about shops and won't buy his own gloves."

She herself was shut up in her winter prison,
and her sister-in-law, Sarianna Browning, who
was with them in Paris, very properly declined the
responsibility.

News reached them from Florence that Mrs.
Trollope—hitherto an ardent devotee of that sinister and ambiguous figure—had thrown over Daniel
Home (or Hume), the medium, on account of his
moral character.   Mrs. Browning admitted that the
young man, who was weak and vain, deserved his
fate.   But she still clung to the authenticity and
genuineness of his mediumistic powers.   It was
a physical faculty, she alleged, like an electric wire.
At Florence, however, the camps were divided, and
" everybody was quarrelling with everybody on the
subject."

Mrs. Browning was exceptionally busy that winter,
for besides her long poem, at which she worked when-
ever her health permitted, she still continued to
teach Penini.   It was difficult to keep his attention
for more than a few minutes at a time, but, when
rebuked, he would only fling his arms about his
mother and cry : " Oh, you little pet ! *Dive* me
one chance more.   I really will be *dood* ! "   And
despite the lack of concentration, he was extraordinarily quick, and in less than two months had learned
to read French, although he was little more than
seven years old at the time.   He wrote, too, a little
poem on the war and the peace, entitled *Soldiers
Going and Coming*, which elicited the proud admiration of both his poet-parents.

Robert Browning tried to revise *Sordello*, an
attempt which he finally abandoned in 1864.   In
Paris he passed through one of his periodical fits
of complete idleness, when it seems to have been
peculiarly difficult to amuse him.   Strange to say, he
was no reader, unlike his wife, who was always able

to occupy her leisure with novels, English, French and Italian. She was an omnivorous reader, but Robert, when not writing poetry, was prone to seek other forms of self-expression. Thus, in Paris he studied drawing, as later on in Rome he took up modelling. In less than a fortnight he had produced " some quite startling copies of heads," which was scarcely astonishing considering that drawing with him had been a passion in childhood. His family and friends were inclined to disapprove of these excursions into other arts, but Mrs. Browning very wisely encouraged him. She was aware that he was miserable when idle, and really required some interesting occupation apart from his poetry. He was apt to get depressed when he had nothing to do, and it was often difficult to induce him to take sufficient exercise.

He went out a good deal in Paris, dining on one occasion with his old friend, Monckton Milnes, in company with Cavour, Miguet and George Sand, who wore a wreath of ivy in her black hair. An empty chair had been placed at the table for Lamartine.

By this time Mrs. Browning had arranged and transcribed five books of *Aurora Leigh*, six thousand lines of which were now ready for the press. She wished to finish it before their return to England in June. She told Mrs. Jameson that when she had read this book she intended her to put away all her other poems and know her only by the new one. But authors, as is well known, always prefer the latest fruits of their genius, and are inclined to compare all former work unfavourably with the new-born.

" Oh, I am so anxious to make it good," she wrote. " I have put much of myself in it—I mean to say of my soul, my thoughts, emotions, opinions. . . ."

By May she was hard at work on the last book, practically all the others having been transcribed. Robert spoke well of it and encouraged her greatly.

Towards the end of their stay in Paris, disquieting news reached them of their old friend, Mr. Kenyon.
Robert was anxious to start off at once to be with
him, but feared to intrude.   He longed to sit up with
him, hold his hand, speak " a good loving word "
to this man who had shown him such practical
sympathy, but the suggestion was negatived by
Kenyon himself.

5

The Brownings arrived in London at the end of
June.   Mr. Kenyon had by then been moved to the
Isle of Wight, but he generously placed his house in
Devonshire Place at their disposal.

Mr. Barrett, still unrelenting, banished Arabel
when he heard of his eldest daughter's arrival.
Arabel, however, " brought her praying eyes to bear
on Robert," and he promised to spend a fortnight in
the Isle of Wight, the place of her banishment.
Arabel was aggrieved at being sent away in this
manner, but apparently there was no appeal from
any of Mr. Barrett's acts of tyranny.   Elizabeth, however, considered that her sister required change of
air and rest, for she had been overworking herself
in London with schools and refuges and societies.
She had been very unwell during the previous
winter and was at all times thrown too much on her
own resources, which were invariably of a somewhat
depressing nature.   Mrs. Browning declared she
would have given her right hand to take her back to
Italy with them, but such a step would, of course,
be out of the question.   Fortunately, Mr. Barrett
elected to remain in London himself, and told his
daughter that probably he should not join her at
Ventnor for a week or two, thus unconsciously leaving
the path clear for the Brownings.   The sons were
also exiled with Arabel.

Penini, who was now in his eighth year, realised
with a child's quick intuition that something was
wrong, really radically wrong, between his mother

and her own father.   She never saw him, and clearly she must have committed some dreadful crime to merit such punishment as that, for he himself was never parted from his parents for a single day or night.   One day he said to her coaxingly : " Mamma, if you've been very naughty, if you've *broken china,* I advise you to go into the room and say, *Papa, I will be dood!* "   That simple expression of contrition had always served for his own nursery sins, and he could not believe that anyone could listen to it without instantly relenting.   And for one moment she did seriously contemplate adopting little Pen's advice. But she had written, and no notice had been taken of the letter.   There was the remembrance, too, of that packet of letters returned with all their seals unbroken. The position was then, as always, hopeless.

But although she did not dare to go herself she made a last and most pathetic attempt at reconciliation, which she confided later to her intimate friend, Mrs. Story.   She dressed Penini in his little velvet suit with the lace collar, in which he always looked so adorable, and sent him round to Wimpole Street, begging that her father would receive him.   As a mother she felt that no one could resist the beauty and charm and quick keen intelligence of her boy. But the little messenger of love was turned back from the door without a word.   After that rebuff she knew that there was no hope. . . .

The weeks at Ventnor were very peaceful ones, and they were the last Elizabeth Browning was ever destined to spend with her own family.   She never afterwards returned to England, and it is doubtful if she saw any of her brothers and sisters again except George and Arabel.   Her brothers were delighted with Penini, despite " his being an Italian and wearing curls," appreciating his fearlessness and pluck.   They played with the child and carried him on their backs, and he on his side thoroughly approved of " mine uncles."

Although it was only September, Mrs. Browning's cough returned, and it was impossible to suppose that she would be able to stay much longer in England.   From Ventnor they proceeded to Cowes to see Mr. Kenyon, who then had little more than two months to live.   He was even then a dying man. Sometimes they would find him leaning on the table ejaculating :   " My God, my God ! "   At others he would pray audibly to die.

From Cowes they went to Taunton to see Henrietta, little dreaming that this too was a farewell visit.

Kenyon died in December, and in his will he left the Brownings eleven thousand pounds—the largest of any of his bequests—thus placing them beyond all fear of financial stress.   Apart from their earnings, they must now have had between nine hundred and one thousand pounds a year, a sum upon which, in Florence, at any rate, they could at that time live almost like princes.   They were thus relieved, too, of any anxiety regarding the future of their son.   Mr. Kenyon also left a small legacy to Mrs. Surtees Cook, but when the executors applied to Mr. Barrett for her address he refused to give it.

CHAPTER XVI

I

DURING her stay at Ventnor, Mrs. Browning had received and corrected the final proofs of *Aurora Leigh,* and the book was published that autumn. Its success was immediate and three editions were called for within a few months. It was dedicated to Kenyon, in whose London house the last pages had been written.

" Ending, therefore, and preparing once more to quit England, I venture to leave in your hands this book, the most mature of my works, and the one into which my highest convictions upon Life and Art have entered ; that as, through my various efforts in literature and steps in life, you have believed in me, borne with me, and been generous to me, far beyond the common uses of mere relationship or sympathy of mind, so you may kindly accept, in sight of the public, this poor sign of esteem, gratitude and affection, from
Your unforgetting
E. B. B."

It was dated from Kenyon's house, 39 Devonshire Place, the 17th October, 1856.

Aurora Leigh very naturally came in for a great deal of adverse criticism, published as it was at a time when equivocal subjects were avoided and even the mention of them tabooed. It was hardly surprising that, like her famous contemporary, Charlotte Brontë, Mrs. Browning should be accused of coarseness and even of indecency. Elderly ladies of sixty declared they had never felt pure since reading the book—an affirmation which cannot fail to astonish a less sensitive generation. Anxious mothers kept it sedulously from their daughters, but the daughters got hold of it and approved.   It is noteworthy that it challenged comparison with *Jane Eyre*, because it, too, possessed a blinded hero whose house had been burnt down.   It was a comfort to poor Mrs. Browning when Robert assured her " she couldn't be coarse if she tried."

She had written the book of deliberate purpose to call attention to the state of unfortunate women in great cities.   She would not have altered a single line that referred to them, so deeply and strongly did she feel on this subject.   Nor would she soften her words to make them more palatable.   She intended to say exactly what she had said.   And she was gratified when Ruskin acclaimed it as " the finest poem written in any language this century."

It is possible that the poem is no longer greatly read except by students of English literature.   It is very long, and the interest is never very enthralling.   But it is well worth the effort, for it contains some of the most exquisite and accurate descriptions of Italian scenery that have perhaps ever been written by any poet.

> The old miraculous mountains heaved in sight,
> One straining past another along the shore,
> The way of grand dull Odyssean ghosts,
> Athirst to drink the cool blue wine of seas
> And stare on voyagers.   Peak pushing peak
> They stood ;   I watched beyond that Tyrian belt
> Of intense sea betwixt them and the ship,
> Down all their sides the misty olive-woods
> Dissolving in the weak congenial moon,
> And still disclosing some brown convent-tower
> That seems as if it grew from some brown rock,
> Or many a little lighted village, dropt
> Like a fallen star upon so high a point
> You wonder what can keep it in its place
> From sliding headlong with the waterfalls
> Which powder all the myrtle and orange groves

With spray of silver.   Thus my Italy
Was stealing on us.   Genoa broke with day,
The Doria's.long pale palace striking out
From green hills in advance of the white town,
A marble finger dominant to ships,
Seen glimmering through the uncertain grey of dawn.

This very perfect passage exhibits the enormous strides she had made in her art.   Its fluency was controlled, its form disciplined ; her wider vision, released from its old trammels, imbued her poetry with a strange, new, wonderful quality.   She, the London prisoner, with so little hope of escape, had gone out into the beautiful radiant world that is Italy, ever the land and home of poets, and had received those new impressions, embracing them with a kind of passionate ardour, and weaving them into the very texture of her verse.   *Casa Guidi*, with its many beautiful and suggestive lines, failed as a poem because of the limited appeal of its political content.   But in *Aurora Leigh*, Elizabeth Browning did in many respects excel all that Elizabeth Barrett had ever accomplished, with the single exception of the *Sonnets from the Portuguese*, which must always remain the apex of her art, challenging, as they undoubtedly do, comparison with all the great sonnet-sequences the world has ever seen.

Much of the first book is autobiographical, and we have an intimate description of the little room of her girlhood at Hope End.

I had a little chamber in the house,
As green as any privet hedge a bird
Might choose to build in, though the nest itself
Could show but dead brown sticks and straws ; the walls
Were green, the carpet was pure green, the straight
Small bed was curtained greenly, and the folds
Hung green about the window which let in
The outdoor world with all its greenery.
You could not push your head out and escape
A dash of dawn-dew from the honeysuckle. . . .

Tender and beautiful, too, are her descriptions

of the Herefordshire scenery where all her childhood and girlhood were spent.   She went back to those early days with their thoughts and dreams, so that we are made to realise as never before the little poet-child.

> I used to get up early, just to sit
> And watch the morning quicken in the grey,
> And hear the silence open like a flower
> Leaf after leaf—and stroke with listless hand
> The woodbine through the window, till at last
> I came to do it with a sort of love. . . .

But her memories of England were sad ones, too poignant almost to be touched upon, and the little *Aurora* was always a sad and dreamy child.   When she wrote of Florence, however, something of the great happiness she had known there touched her verse to a greater warmth, even to something of passion for its ever-arresting loveliness.

> I found a house at Florence on the hill
> Of Bellosguardo.   'Tis a tower which keeps
> A post of double-observation o'er
> That valley of Arno (holding as a hand
> The outspread city) straight toward Fiesole
> And Mount Morello and the setting sun,
> The Vallombrosan mountains opposite,
> Which sunrise fills as full as crystal cups
> Turned red to the brim because their wine is red.
> No sun could die nor yet be born unseen
> By dwellers at my villa ; morn and eve
> Were magnified before us in the pure
> Illimitable space and pause of sky,
> Intense as angels' garments blanched with God,
> Less blue than radiant.   From the outer wall
> Of the garden drops the mystic floating grey
> Of olive trees (with interruptions green
> From maize and vine) until 'tis caught and torn
> Upon the abrupt black line of cypresses
> Which signs the way to Florence.   Beautiful
> The city lies along the ample vale,
> Cathedral, tower and palace, piazza and street,
> The river trailing like a silver cord
> Through all, and curling loosely, both before
> And after, over the whole stretch of land
> Sown whitely up and down its opposite slopes
> With farms and villas.

It is a faithful picture, as all visitors to Florence who have stood upon those heights must know.

And surely it was of little Penini of whom she was thinking when she wrote that, before she was awake, Marian's child would bring Aurora flowers to fill her vases, the gorgeous wild flowers of a Tuscan spring.

> My grandiose red tulips which grow wild,
> Or Dante's purple lilies, which he blew
> To a larger bubble with his prophet breath,
> Or one of those tall flowering reeds that stand
> In Arno, like a sheaf of sceptres left
> By some remote dynasty of dead gods. . . .

Nature always meant more to her than art ; she was never much of a judge of pictures or sculpture, but in her close scrutiny of nature she never sounded a wrong note.

> I knew the birds
> And insects—which looked fathered by the flowers
> And emulous of their hues ; I recognised
> The moths, with that great overpoise of wings
> Which make a mystery of them how at all
> They can stop flying ; butterflies that bear
> Upon their blue wings such red embers round,
> They seem to scorch the blue air into holes
> Each flight they take ; and fireflies, that suspire
> In short soft lapses of transported flame
> Across the tingling Dark, while overhead
> The constant and inviolable stars
> Outburn those light-of-love : melodious owls
> (If music had but one note and was sad
> 'Twould sound just so) ; and all the silent swirl
> Of bats that seem to follow in the air
> Some grand circumference of a shadowy dome
> To which we are blind : and then the nightingales
> Which pluck our heart across a garden wall . . .
>
> And I knew
> The harmless opal snakes, the large-mouthed frogs
> (Those noisy vaunters of their shallow streams) ;
> And lizards, the green lightnings of the wall. . . .

In her backwater at Florence it is possible that she paid less heed to adverse criticism than she could have done in London. Surrounded by admiring, approving friends, she was less sensitive to the outcries of the Press at home. The book was safely launched on its somewhat stormy voyage, and she could resume those domestic activities of looking after her husband and child, which, after all, were dearest to her heart.

At Christmas the little boy was overwhelmed with presents. From his mother he received a sword with a bright blade, and from his father a box of tools, a carpenter's bench, and a copy of Robinson Crusoe, in addition to sleeve-links and a silver pencil. He described himself as exceptionally happy—this child whose boyhood must have been as nearly cloudless as it is possible to be. But then, neither Robert nor Elizabeth Browning were in any way typical Victorian parents.

Penini was deeply attached to Wilson's husband, Ferdinando. On one occasion he accused his mother of preferring himself to Ferdinando, adding that the latter had too much work to do. When she could not deny that she preferred her own little boy to the faithful Italian manservant, he burst into tears. " Indeed, indeed, Mamma, you are unjust ! Ferdinando does everything for you, and I do nothing except tease, and then sometimes I am a very naughty boy ! "

I think she must often have felt anxious about her child, with his over-developed sensibility, his precocious intellect, his nervous excitability and excessive devotion to herself and those about him.

During the Carnival that year Penini pleaded for a domino—a blue one trimmed with pink. " Almost never in all my life have I had a domino," he said. Of course she let him have his way, and he was enraptured, running about the streets with Wilson and crying : " Now, Lily, I do pray you not to call out Penini ! " But the English child with his flowing golden curls was too well known in Florence, and his desire to pass unrecognised even when masked amid the throng of merrymakers was unlikely to be fulfilled however much Wilson might refrain from calling to him.   Lessons were impossible just then.   Florence was a gigantic pantomime, and even Mrs. Browning was infected by the universal madness, as she called it, and although she had not left the house for three months, she persuaded Robert to take her to the grand ball at the Opera in domino and mask.   He had already secured a box intending to invite some of their friends and thus make some return for the hospitality they had both received, but there had been no question of her accompanying him.   A favourable change in the weather induced him to allow her to go, and she appeared in a hired domino and mask because there was no time then to buy such things.   Nor was she content with watching the brilliant scene from the box ; she must needs descend and mingle with the gay, masked throng below.   Someone struck her on the shoulder crying *Bella mascherina!*   She stayed till two o'clock in the morning—I am sure she had never done such a thing in her life before—while Robert and his friends remained until four.

In April there was a sudden burst of summer, not an unusual thing in Tuscany at that season, and she was able to drive in the Cascine and drink tea on the terrace of Miss Blagden's villa at Bellosguardo.   They met and liked Mrs. Beecher-Stowe then at the height of her fame.

Mrs. Browning had revived a little and was able to enjoy life once more after her winter hibernation, when a sudden blow struck her.   George Barrett wrote communicating the news of his father's death at the age of seventy.   He had passed away after a short illness of which they had already heard from Arabel, not suspecting, however, any danger.   Unforgiving and unrelenting to the last, he left no farewell messages either to Elizabeth Browning or to

his other married children.   Many people, including
Mrs. Martin, had tried to effect a reconciliation.
But this end, so eagerly desired on the one hand,
so sternly refused on the other, was never attained.
Nor had there been any kind answer, or indeed any
answer at all, to those piteous entreaties which
Robert had seen his wife write over and over again
to her obdurate father.

Mr. Barrett was buried with his wife at Ledbury.

"I believe hope died in me long ago, of reconciliation in this world" (Elizabeth wrote to Mrs.
Martin).   Indeed, there had been nothing upon
which the most sanguine person could have based
any substantial hope.   Nearly ten years had passed
since the eventful day when she had slipped secretly
out of her father's house in Wimpole Street, accompanied by Wilson and Flush, and since then there had
been an absolute and relentless and obstinate
silence on Mr. Barrett's part, except for the one
cruel little note to Robert when he had returned
all her letters with their seals unbroken.   It was a
strange complex, this of Mr. Barrett's, to cherish
an enduring anger against those of his children who
dared to marry, but although it seems inexplicable
to us now, it was no uncommon trait in fathers of
that date.   Mr. Brontë, as we know, stood in the
way of Charlotte's marriage to Mr. Nicholls for some
years, and only gave way at last because he needed
a reliable curate to do the work of his parish.

3

Mrs. Browning was deeply distressed about this
time because Miss Haworth, whom she had encouraged
to become an ardent devotee of spiritualism, sent
her some *soi-disant* messages from the "rapping
spirits."   Whether they purported to come from Mr.
Barrett was not disclosed in the correspondence, but
Elizabeth wrote entreating her never to tell her
anything of the sort again.   "The truth is I am made

of paper and it tears me." Quite possibly the messages may have been believed to emanate from Edward, but it is much more likely they were expressions of forgiveness and sorrow from her father. She begged, too, that Miss Blagden might not be told, and that the subject should never again be mentioned to her. Miss Haworth was not even to express regret, the matter must be completely dropped.

"Tell me all about the spirits, only not what they say of *me*," she wrote. "The drawback is that without any sort of doubt they personate falsely. Forgive my poor little body, which shakes and breaks."

She did not quickly recover from the undoubted shock the news of her father's death had had upon her frail physique. For a whole month she did not leave the house, and she saw no one save Isa Blagden. The summer proved unusually hot, which still further sapped her strength, and in July the whole family migrated to Bagni di Lucca, where they again stayed at Casa Tolomei. Mr. Robert Lytton and Miss Isa Blagden followed them thither for the sake of their company. Disaster seemed at that time to dog their footsteps, for almost immediately after his arrival, Lytton, who had been feeling unwell in Florence, was laid up with a very serious illness, probably of a typhoidal character. Miss Blagden refused to have a nurse for him, " through sentimentality and economy combined," which annoyed Mrs. Browning very much, especially as it entailed her Robert sitting up four out of five nights with him, in addition to spending the greater part of the day beside his bed.

For many days they were consumed with anxiety as to the outcome of the illness, Lytton being at the best of times a delicate, highly-strung man. When he had been ill for sixteen days the doctors were able to pronounce that there had been some progress, but during that time Browning had remained with him for eight nights and Miss Blagden for a similar number. Her devotion to him was complete, but she, too, was becoming worn out with these protracted vigils, and finally they persuaded her to call in a nurse for the night duty. Lytton was terribly weak and apprehensive about himself ; he was prone, too, to discuss divine things and the state of his soul, and to dwell upon the Love of God, which Mrs. Browning evidently regarded as ominous symptoms.

He, however, rallied, and by the end of August was able to drive daily with Robert Browning and the nurse. But he was still very weak and exhausted and emaciated, with hollows in his temples, although he was now able to think of such things " as poems and apple-puddings in a manner other than celestial."

Browning and his son thoroughly enjoyed the fine mountain climate of Bagni di Lucca. The poet bathed daily in the river at half-past six in the morning, an hour at which the water must have been icy-cold. Still, he declared that he derived great benefit from the practice. Penini was " like a rose possessed by a fairy." He, too, bathed in the river— the Lima, a rushing mountain stream forming here and there deep pools well adapted for swimming. The father and son went for excursions, riding on donkeys or mountain ponies. Penini, despite his sheltered, somewhat coddling upbringing, was as bold as a lion on horseback. They were often accompanied on their expeditions by Miss Annette Bracken and a wounded Crimean officer.

Mrs. Browning confessed to Mrs. Jameson that her sisters' letters at that time made her feel *froissée* all over. But she had had some tender words from Stormie, who had now at his father's death inherited the West Indian estates. He had returned from Jamaica and had taken a place on the Welsh borders for three years.

In September. Lytton returned to Florence accompanied by Miss Blagden. He was to stay with her at the Villa Bricchieri on the heights of Bellosguardo to be nursed back to health and strength.

One imagines that the vivacious little elderly lady must have cherished a certain *tendresse* for him, such as women of her age are prone to feel for a young, gifted and delicate man.

The Brownings remained on at Bagni di Lucca ; it was really still too early to return to Florence. They were already beginning to weave plans for future journeys, intending to go to Rome and Naples, and perhaps even to Egypt and the Holy Land. Mr. Kenyon's legacy had placed it within their power to realise these dreams, although they never in fact went further afield than Rome.

There had come a slight change in Mrs. Browning's attitude towards spiritualism, as if she were beginning to realise its dangers. In particular she was anxious about its permanent effect upon her friend, Fanny Haworth.

" Don't let them bind you hand and foot. Resist. Be yourself," she wrote. " Also where (as in the medium-writing) you have the human mixture to evolve the spiritual sentiment from, the insecurity becomes doubly insecure."

For herself, she added, she could never consent to receive her theology or any kind of guidance from the spirits—the submission of the whole mind and spirit was to be avoided at all costs, since it carried the devotee either " to the pope or the devil ! " She seems to have been wholly unaware that spiritualistic practices have always been strictly prohibited by the Catholic Church. But this warning to her friend shows that her interest in the matter was purely objective and her own attitude one of enquiry. Her mind was fundamentally too sane and well-balanced to suffer permanent injury from her rather ineffective dabbling in occult science.

4

Before they left Bagni, however, another calamity
befell them in the illness of little Penini.   One day
he walked too far and too fast in the sun, and returned
heated and chilled, a condition towards which the
early morning bathe may well have contributed.
He had a slight attack of fever, but in the morning
seemed better and accompanied his parents to dine
with some friends in the mountains, a distance of
thirty miles, twenty of which were accomplished
in a carriage and the remaining ten on donkeys.   It
is not surprising that the fatigue combined with the
burning September sun should have adversely affected
an already ailing child, and it speaks well for the
improvement in Mrs. Browning's health that she
was able to endure it with impunity.   Penini arrived
back in high spirits, singing at the top of his voice ;
he was probably even then " running a temperature."
On the following day he was seriously ill, and was
supposed at first to be sickening for scarlatina or
measles.   But very soon the doctor pronounced the
malady to be the same form of gastric fever from
which Mr. Lytton had suffered, and which had indeed
almost ended prematurely his brilliant career.

Penini's sweetness and patience tore his mother's
heart.   " You pet !   Don't be unhappy for me.
Think it's a poor little boy in the street and be just
only a little sorry and not unhappy at all ! "

As in all typhoidal attacks he was only allowed a
few spoonfuls of thin broth during the day, although
he was savagely hungry and his imagination was
conjuring up visions of beefsteak-pies and buttered
toast.   " Per Bacco, ho una fame terribile, e non voglio
avere più pazienza con questo dottore ! " he told the
flower-girl who was allowed to come in and see
him when he was better.

All plans for extensive journeying were naturally
in abeyance, nor was Mrs. Browning attempting to
do any work.   " We think little of Jerusalem or any
other place except our home in Florence," she wrote.

Still, by the end of September Penini was con-
valescent, although the rosy cheeks, the round fat
little shoulders, the strength and spring he had shown
a month before, were now so sadly changed.

They returned to Casa Guidi and the winter
passed quietly enough. After an unusually hot
summer the winter months proved, as is often the
case, exceptionally cold, and for the first time for
ten years there was ice on the Arno. Influenza
swept remorselessly over Italy, and both Robert and
Penini were laid low with it. Mrs. Browning
escaped with only her usual cough. But with so much
illness prevalent everywhere, it is scarcely astonishing
to find that they preferred to spend the winter within
their own four comfortable walls at Casa Guidi.

The situation in Italy had already begun to give
rise to anxiety, and Sarianna Browning displayed
some little fear for their safety. " I should never
think of running away, let what might happen,"
was Mrs. Browning's answer, for had she not been
in a far more dangerous situation in Paris in 1852
and 1853 ? Also Mazzini had voiced his opinion
that people stood on ruins in England where at any
moment there might be a crash ! She did not in the
least share Mrs. Carlyle's passionate admiration for
Mazzini, declaring that she felt indignant with him
and " all who name his name and walk in his
steps," and stigmatising him too as " that man of
unscrupulous theory."

Meantime she quietly continued Pen's education.
He was now nine years old and showed a remarkable
facility for languages, to which his Continental upbringing had no doubt largely contributed. Already
he was able to read Italian, French and German as
well as English. He played remarkably well on
the piano, and wisely they allowed him to give the
greater part of the time allotted to his studies to
music. Elizabeth described him as a very sweet,
gentle child, sweet to look at and to listen to,
affectionate, and good to live with. While girlish
in aspect by reason of the long curls which she still

permitted him to wear, he was active, fond of riding, and quite fearless.

She employed her leisure, as was usual with her during times of literary idleness, in reading innumerable novels. " For months I have done nothing but dream and read French and German romances ; and the result of learning a good deal of German isn't the most useful thing in the world one can attain to."

She rather shrank from going to England that summer, although one would have thought that after her father's death she would have enjoyed the prospect of seeing as much of her sisters as she chose. A little cloud, however, seemed to have arisen between them, though of its nature we are permitted no exact knowledge. And after all they were perfectly free—as free as she was—and could seek her out in Florence if they wished to do so. Perhaps they, too, had taken fright at the trend of affairs in Italy, and were urging her to return home. But why they none of them ever attempted to visit her at Casa Guidi after their father's death, when all obstacles to such a course were automatically removed, remains an inscrutable mystery.

The medium, Hume, was still in Italy. He had been left an annuity of £240 by an Englishwoman, and on his return to Florence discharged all his debts, even returning their valuable gifts to such donors who had subsequently discovered his fraudulency. His manners as well as his morals were much improved. Meantime it was said that the Empress Eugénie was paying for the education of his little sister in Paris. . . . While he was in Tuscany his power seemed to be leaving him, but he had now recovered it tenfold, and his foolish dupes no doubt multiplied in like proportion. Robert Browning's hatred of the whole thing was no less violent than it had ever been, but he refrained from giving public expression to it during his wife's lifetime. It was only after her death that he dipped his pen in gall and wrote *Mr. Sludge, The Medium.*

5

The Brownings went to France that summer with the principal object of being near the poet's father and sister who were then settled in Paris. For the sake of economy, they travelled by sea to Marseilles and had a very stormy voyage. From thence they went by easy stages to Paris, halting at Lyons and Dijon.

Mrs. Browning was an excellent traveller, being one of those fortunate persons to whom a journey provides a real rest. She rejoiced in the complete immunity from visitors, unpleasant letters, and the expectation of bad news. Still, it was cold in Paris, although it was the month of July. " No more cypresses, no more fireflies, no more dreaming repose on burning hot evenings." She was the child of generations of people who had lived and basked in the tropical climate of the West Indies ; the love of the hot sunshine was in her blood. But she was never again after that year—1858—to leave Italy for the grey north. She confessed that she had a weakness for Paris and a passion for Italy, and she could quite easily have gone on living in Paris if there had only been sufficient sunshine. " If you knew how happy I think you for being in Italy," she wrote with something of nostalgia to Miss Haworth, who was then settled in Florence.

The new Paris fashions intrigued her, and she warned Miss Haworth to draw her bonnet down more over her face ! The mention of this change in the fashion of bonnets, and the novel manner of wearing them approved by Paris, inspired Miss Haworth to invite Mrs. Browning to bring her back one of these delectable models. This Elizabeth very wisely refused to do.

" Now, dearest Fanny, let me confess to you. I have not brought the bonnet. A bonnet is a personal matter, and I would not let anyone choose one for me. Still, as you had more faith in man (or woman) I should have risked displeasing you, only Robert would not let me.   He said it was absurd —I did not know your size—I could not know your taste—in fact he would not let me."

To console her she should, however, be permitted a glimpse of Mrs. Browning's new one, which was the " last novelty."   Hats were at that time not worn at all in Paris except on the heads of young girls, although they appeared at the sea-side.   Bonnets were larger. . . . It will be seen that Mrs. Browning had lost nothing of her passionate interest in dress.

While they were in Paris they saw Lady Elgin, who had just had another stroke from which, however, she rallied.   Robert and Elizabeth sat with her and talked, but she was unable to utter a word, only looking at them with her bright eyes and smiling. Robert fed her with a spoon from her soup-plate, and she made a sign before he left that he should kiss her forehead.   " She was always so fond of Robert, as women are apt to be, you know—even *I* a little," wrote Elizabeth.

After a fortnight in Paris they went to Havre, Etretat having proved too expensive.   They were all housed in the Rue de Perry, old Mr. Browning and Sarianna occupying another apartment, although the whole party met in the dining-room for meals. Warm sea-baths had been recommended for Mrs. Browning, and here she was close to the sea and could creep down to the shore in a few minutes.   Of late she confessed to having felt very weak and unwell, but the sea air and baths proved beneficial.

They returned to Paris in September and were joined there by George and Arabel.   They took an apartment in the Rue de Castiglione, and Arabel remained with them until they left for Italy.

In October they were back in Florence, having taken nine days to complete their journey, which plainly showed Mrs. Browning's failing health.   A lady had requested to be allowed to accompany them, but Robert altogether declined to allow such a thing. Probably he thought his hands were already too full, what with a delicate wife and a young child, for him to undertake further responsibilities. On their way they spent the day at Chambéry—that favourite halt of literary travellers—in order to visit Les Charmettes, where Robert played the " Dream " on the old harpsichord.

They went from Genoa to Leghorn by sea, and their voyage was such a stormy one and their boat so delayed—taking, indeed, eighteen hours to accomplish the short journey—that their friends in Florence gave them up for lost. They were so exhausted by their experience that they stayed at Leghorn instead of proceeding immediately to Florence.

Mrs. Browning wrote that she was so glad to be back—so glad—so glad. . . .

It was still summer in Florence when they arrived in November, but the warm weather was of brief duration and was followed by snow and piercing cold. They all felt, she confessed, a little languid about further travelling, but the early onslaught of winter constrained Robert to carry out their original intention of going to Rome. In the meantime he had bought a bust of Penini, the work of one Monroe, which was to be exhibited in London the following May. " The likeness, the poetry, the ideal grace and infantile reality, are all there," Elizabeth wrote to Miss Browning. The artist was generous, only charging them his out-of-pocket expenses amounting to twenty-five guineas. She would have given up Rome to possess it, she said.

Indeed, despite the legacy, they were none too well off just then, and but for the fact that their American friend, Mr. Eckley, had placed his empty carriage at their disposal for the journey, they might even have been forced to abandon the thought of going to Rome at all. These friends were extraordinarily kind and generous to the Brownings. " They humiliate me by their devotion," she wrote. " Such generosity and delicacy combined with so much passionate sentiment (there is no other word) are difficult to represent."

So perhaps it was not altogether by some fortunate accident that the Eckleys' carriage happened to be proceeding empty to Rome just then, enabling them to accomplish the journey without any more expense than was entailed by their various stoppages on the road.

CHAPTER XVII

I

THE Brownings left Florence for Rome in November, taking seven days to accomplish the journey. They slept at Poggio Bagnoli, Camuscia, Perugia, Spoleto, Terni, and Città Castellana. At Terni Robert visited the famous falls with Mr. Eckley, and found them swollen by rain and melted snow. His wife was too tired to accompany him. As usual, however, she bore the journey extremely well, for she was out of doors practically the whole of each day, travelling with the windows of the carriage wide open.

In Rome they found themselves in their old quarters in Via Bocca di Leone, for which they had to pay two pounds a month more than they had done on their previous visit. Still, the house had been thoroughly renovated and the monthly rent of £11 which they now paid for it does not sound extravagant to our modern ears.

They were soon surrounded by friends. Besides the Eckleys, who continued to show them the most generous kindness, they saw Hatty Hosmer, Leighton, Miss Cushman, the Storys, Mr. Page with his third wife, and Gibson of *Tinted Venus* fame. Ferdinando, who had gone by sea with the luggage, was waiting in Rome to receive them.

On Christmas Day Mrs. Browning attended the Pope's Mass in St. Peter's. She heard the famous silver trumpets, and admitted that she never once thought of the Scarlet Woman!

The winter proved a very severe one. The famous fountains were frozen. Robert caught cold,

but still insisted upon going for a walk every morning
at six o'clock with Mr. Eckley, and this in the early
days of a bitterly cold January when Rome must
have been plunged in darkness, the flickering lamps
scarcely illuminating the narrow streets.   The regular
exercise, however, proved on the whole beneficial,
and his enormous appetite at breakfast delighted
his wife, who said that the " loaf perished by Gargan-
tuan slices."   Moreover, he was full of engagements,
had been out every night for a fortnight, with sometimes two or three parties on the same night.   Mrs.
Browning did not accompany him; such dissipation
would at any time have been too much for her, and
she took the opportunity of going to bed early.

Penini, who had inherited her passion for reading,
was now deep in Dumas' *Monte Cristo*, which he
was reading in an Italian translation.   " Magnificent,
magnificent ! " she could hear him murmur.   One
day at breakfast he astonished her by saying :
" Dear Mamma, for the future I mean to read *novels*.
I shall read all Dumas' to begin with.   And then I
shall read Papa's favourite novel, *Madame Bovary*."

They were both convulsed with laughter at his
infant precocity.

In February 1859 the Prince of Wales, afterwards
King Edward VII, paid his first visit to Rome,
staying with his suite at the Hôtel d'Angleterre,
which is also situated in the Via Bocca di Leone, a
few paces from the Brownings' abode.   The chief
purport of the royal visit was educational, the Prince
being then only in his eighteenth year.   Through
Gibson, the veteran English sculptor, he saw something of the literary and artistic life of Rome.   It
is said that he was especially attracted by the work
of the two famous American sculptors—Story and
Hatty Hosmer.   He visited Leighton's studio, and
was at once captivated by his charm, describing him
as a " young painter of great merit, under thirty."
He purchased from him a picture called *Nanna*.   Of
literary men the Prince—who won all hearts by his
good looks and charming simplicity—met the French

archæologist and historian, Ampère ; Motley, the American writer, then at work on his *History of the Netherlands*, and aggrieved because he was refused access to the Vatican archives, which is perfectly comprehensible in view of his savage attacks on the Papacy in his famous *Dutch Republic* ; and Robert Browning, who had been warned by his wife " to eschew compliments and keep to Italian politics." Sir Sidney Lee [1] amazingly attributed this injunction to the Prince's equerry, Colonel Bruce, whereas Mrs. Browning wrote at the time and told Miss Blagden she had thus warned her husband, having recently had a somewhat bitter experience of his well-intentioned but equivocal flatteries.

Colonel Bruce called upon Mrs. Browning, and told her that, although the Prince was not to be exposed to the influence of mixed society (for which purpose the assistance of Mr. Odo Russell, afterwards Lord Ampthill, was enlisted), the Queen was desirous that he should meet some of the most eminent men in Rome, and that it would undoubtedly gratify Her Majesty if her son were to make the acquaintance of Mr. Browning. Elizabeth felt—as indeed any wife would have done—immensely flattered by the royal recognition.

The young Prince, however, did not speak of politics. He sat almost silent, listening while the burning topics of the day were discussed by his suite and guests. Robert described him as a gentle, refined boy.

There is no doubt that Browning enjoyed the gaiety and numerous parties to which he was invited. " Plenty of distraction and no Men and Women," was her epitome of the situation. But she was perfectly satisfied, having the sense to see that this man, six years her junior and in the prime of life, required amusements of a kind in which she could not possibly participate. Even an evening spent at home with her was in a sense a dissipation, so rare had it become.

---

[1] *King Edward VII : A Biography*, by Sir Sidney Lee, p. 63. (Macmillan.)

2

The political crisis became acute in Italy that year, and accelerated the departure of the Prince of Wales from Rome. England wished to convene a European Congress to arrange a general disarmament in the face of these rumours of wars. In 1859, as seventy years later, the burning question of disarmament as a precursor to universal peace was uppermost in men's minds. The long tragedy of the Crimean War had left its wounds upon Europe, and England had suffered further bitter loss and bereavement in the Indian Mutiny that so swiftly followed it.

During those troublous years Elizabeth Browning had lived for the most part in her backwater at Casa Guidi, with but few contacts to bring the war personally home to her. It aroused within her more vehement annoyance than sorrow. But her keen enthusiasm for Louis Napoleon, coupled with her passionate desire for Italian unity, and emphasised by her intense dislike of the Papacy and her complete ignorance of its significance, made her desire war to achieve that unity even if it were to be fought at her very doors.

England still distrusted Louis Napoleon, but even the peace of Villafranca, and the French demand for Nice and Savoy as the price of their assistance in expelling the Austrians from Italy, could not diminish Mrs. Browning's enthusiastic and even exaggerated admiration for the Emperor of the French. Her husband did not see eye to eye with her politically, any more than he did in the matter of the "rapping spirits." These ill-proportioned enthusiasms of hers left him cold. In regard to the Emperor's intervention he merely remarked : " It was a great action, but he has taken eighteenpence for it ! "

This intense preoccupation with Italian affairs led Mrs. Browning into a regrettable antagonism for her own country. She must be forgiven for this

R

(though many people have found it hard to forgive her), because when her vivid imagination had grasped a particular point of view her mind was no longer sufficiently well-balanced or poised for her to be able to envisage the other side. Her estimate of the characters of Victor Emanuel and of Louis Napoleon has not indeed been endorsed by history, but because their policy was hers she exalted them both to the skies.

On one occasion she received a visit from Massimo d'Azeglio, who some years previously had been Prime Minister of Piedmont. He spoke with bitterness to her of English policy, and I am sorry to say that she agreed with him, although she found herself less in accord with him when he averred that Louis Napoleon had made himself great simply by comprehending the march of civilisation and leading it. Nevertheless, she felt an intense sympathy for Azeglio, and in Swedenborgian language attributed to him, " a large, clear, attractive sphere."

Robert Browning had a far deeper love for his own country than had his wife. Never did he display an unpatriotic spirit, and it was solely due to his tactful handling of the situation that their mutual love was unimpaired by such drastic divergence of opinion on this as on other subjects.

War broke out in May—always a popular month in Italy for military adventure—and the Brownings returned to Florence, from which the Grand Duke had now departed. Magenta and Solferino were fought in June, and then came the sudden—and to Mrs. Browning disastrous—armistice, the encounter of the two emperors at Villafranca, and the subsequent peace. She suffered both in health and spirits from this blow to her hopes, although even then her blind faith in Napoleon III's disinterestedness was undiminished.

Penini was charmed with the French soldiers in Florence and loved to watch them playing Blind Man's Buff. Imbued with something of his mother's

enthusiasm, he declared that he wished he were
" great boy enough to fight."

It is a little trying, even after all these years,
for an English student to see how completely and
unjustifiably Mrs. Browning blamed her own country
for the peace. " Not only the prestige but the
very respectability of England is utterly lost here,"
she wrote. And to Ruskin : " England has done
terribly ill, ignobly ill, which is worse." But the
Emperor was still " sublime."

She was definitely ill when the news of the
peace reached her, and declared that many young
Italians in Florence were ill in bed and from the
same cause. Every picture and bust of the French
Emperor vanished as if by magic from the city,
as at a more recent date all traces of President
Wilson were obliterated from the streets and squares
that had been named after him in Italian towns !

Mrs. Browning suffered from significant dreams
coupled with insomnia. Once she followed a mystic,
masked, white-clad woman down a long suite of
palatial rooms, and although she could not see her
face she felt assured she was Italy. She had
political dreams, too, in which she saw " inscrutable
articles of peace and eternal provisional govern-
ments "—always the dismal aftermath of war.
Naturally her weak spot reacted to her overwrought
mental condition, and her lungs were affected.
A blister was applied to her side, while all the old
symptoms of debility and cough returned.

The heat in Florence was intense, and in July
it was deemed advisable to move her to Siena.
They were followed thither by a Prussian doctor,
Gresonowski, to whom she had roundly abused
Germany on Isa Blagden's terrace at Florence,
permitting him, alas! in return to say anything
he liked against England. But he evidently bore
her no ill-will for her vehement animadversions, since
he attended her without charge for several days after
her arrival in Siena.

She continued to blind herself to the real and

solid friendship that had for so long existed between England and Italy. " I can never forgive England for the damnable part she has taken in Italian affairs, never ! " she cried. But her case is not altogether singular, for despite the acute sense of race-consciousness, developed and emphasised by the Great War, it is still possible to meet Englishmen —and women—in Italy who are more Italian than the Italians, associating themselves passionately with its political movements—which are really not their concern at all—or violently opposing such measures which their own views stimulate them to dislike or disapprove of. This peculiar complexity of vision is almost always—as in Mrs. Browning's case—combined with an intense dissatisfaction for the policy of their own country when opposed to their personal views, which, pushed to its farthest limits, engenders a lack of patriotism altogether incomprehensible to the logical Latin mind. I suppose it is impossible to live for a long time in a foreign country without learning to sympathise with its anxieties and aspirations, but to participate actively in any foreign political movement is almost always disastrous to the Englishman.

Yet we who have witnessed other happenings in another century in Italy—that land so beloved of English poets and writers—can surely cry with her : " This country is worthy of becoming a great nation ! "

3

At Siena they were lodged in the Villa Alberti, from which their windows commanded " sunsets and night-winds." Mrs. Browning slowly revived in that fresher air ; her cough left her. She could hardly stand unsupported when she arrived there, but in a few weeks something of strength had returned to her.

Robert, who had nursed her faithfully night and day throughout her illness, had not slept for three weeks on account of her cough, and the alarming symptoms almost amounting to angina pectoris that accompanied it. He, too, must have been glad of the change.

Mr. and Mrs. Story were spending the summer on the opposite hill with their children, and in a smaller *villino* quite close to them was housed poor old Walter Savage Landor, who had taken refuge from the " buffetings of his family." Not long before he had appeared at the door of Casa Guidi vowing he would never return home. He was then scarcely able to walk a hundred yards, and looked as if he were dropping into the grave.

Mr. and Mrs. Thomas Crawford—the parents of the afterwards famous novelist Marion Crawford—were also spending that summer in Siena with their children. Like Story, Crawford was a sculptor of some repute. Their second little girl, Mary (afterwards Mrs. Hugh Fraser and the author of many delightful books), was at that time about nine years old, a thoughtful, observant child, two years younger than Penini. These children, with the Storys and Penini, played together, often in the Crawfords' garden, during the hot summer days of 1859. Mary Crawford described Penini as a " beautifully dressed child with long chestnut curls, and as spoilt as the only son of two such people was bound to be."

On one occasion her mother took her to see Mrs. Browning, which in later years she described as an awesome experience, and indeed hers is the one dissentient voice in the chorus of praise and admiration with which her contemporaries invariably alluded to Elizabeth. But the reactions of a child of nine, recounted long afterwards when a deeper knowledge had obviously coloured those impressions, must not be taken too seriously.

They went into a great dark room in which the little girl was only just able to discern a figure lying on the sofa and holding out a hand to her. The heat and airlessness of the shuttered room affected the child disagreeably, though it is a normal condition during Italian summers, when the sun's rays so often have to be rigorously excluded by closed windows and wooden shutters.

" The poetess was everything I did not like," wrote Mary Crawford years later, when she was Mrs. Hugh Fraser. " She had great cavernous eyes glowering out under two big bushes of black ringlets, a fashion I had not beheld before. She never laughed or even smiled once during the whole conversation, and through all the gloom of the shuttered room I could see that her face was hollow and ghastly pale. All that day and long afterwards I pondered in my own silent busy way over the strange problem—why should that nice happy Mr. Browning have such a dismally mournful lady for his wife ? " [1]

Penini was extraordinarily happy at Siena. He was a familiar sight galloping about the lanes on a Sardinian pony, " the colour of his own curls, like Puck on a dragon-fly's back." Robert gave him such lessons as he was capable of during the hot weather, since his mother was too weak now to teach him. For the rest he passed his time in exciting games with the Story and Crawford children, leading a healthy open-air life, making friends with the peasants, helping to guard the sheep, catch the stray cows, and drive the great white oxen in the grape-carts upon which he used to sit perched like some young Bacchus surrounded by heaped-up bunches of the purple fruit. And in the evening he would read and expound the revolutionary songs of the Venetian poet, Dall'Ongara, to the assembled *contadini*. But he ate so many grapes during the vintage that he lost appetite for anything else !

He continued to make rapid progress with his music, and was now able, at ten years old, to play Beethoven's *Sonata in E Flat* and the first four books of Heller.

---

[1] *A Diplomatist's Wife in Many Lands*, by Mrs. Hugh Fraser (Hutchinson):

While they were in Siena that summer Mr. Hamilton Wilde, an American artist who was staying with the Storys, painted the well-known picture of Penini riding about the lanes with his curls hanging down his neck from beneath a picturesque plumed hat. His somewhat girlish blouse and lace collar, white loose knickers and socks, seemed to form a costume that was hardly compatible with the resolute eager little face.

One day when Mrs. Browning was looking over his diary she came upon this significant entry : " This is the happiest day of my *hole* life, for now dearest Victor Emanuel is *nostro re.*" Thus early had he imbibed her political enthusiasms.

Landor, after those devastating domestic disputes which, as we have seen, had ended in his being practically ejected from the villa at Fiesole, was now living under the ægis of Wilson, who seems to have temporarily left the Brownings' service for this more exacting if more remunerative post. She received thirty pounds a year instead of sixteen, but the old gentleman was not an easy person to live with, and she must have felt that she earned the money. He employed his time sitting under the trees and writing Latin alcaics on Garibaldi and the wickedness of Louis Napoleon, and also upon that very fruitful subject, his own wife. When he disliked his food he would dash the plate with all its contents upon the ground, sometimes even flinging it, as Keats had done, out of the window.

Mr. Odo Russell spent a couple of days with the Brownings on his way back to Rome, where they had met him during the previous winter. It speaks well for his diplomatic reticence that he left Mrs. Browning with the impression that he " knew nothing," and understood the Italian situation less well than she did herself ! His sole admission seems to have been that Louis Napoleon had proved *trop fin* for the British Government. He himself at that time had been sent on a special Mission to the Vatican, which had not then any official representative from England. It is noteworthy that in quite recent years his son and namesake held the post of Minister to the Holy See during the Pontificate of Pius XI.[1]

During the latter part of her stay Mrs. Browning was able to enjoy some drives in the lovely country around Siena in the company of her husband, while Pen galloped alongside on his pony. She visited Siena and even ventured into the Gallery to see Sodoma's " divine Eve " again, but the Cathedral was impossible for her on account of the steps. They thus had a peaceful *villeggiatura*, and even from her ears the sounds of war, the even more baleful echoes of peace, gradually died away.

4

She was much better by the time they returned to Florence in October, although the doctor would not hear of her wintering there. The condition of the lungs, coupled with the persistent cough, had weakened her heart. She was aware how hardly a renewal of her last illness would go with her, otherwise she would have been thankful to remain within her own four walls at Casa Guidi for the winter. Both she and Robert were a little tired of wandering, nor did they work so well amid the manifold distractions of Rome.

Penini induced his parents to buy the pony for him. " If Papa speaks to you about the pony please don't discourage him," he entreated his mother. The pony was, of course, to accompany them to Rome, where he hoped to resume his rides, although he declined to do so in Hatty Hosmer's company on the score that she had been thrown thirty times.

Before she left, Mrs. Browning wrote to Fanny Haworth discouraging her from the idea of spending the winter in Florence, " so as to be near them." " We are rolling stones gathering no moss," she

---

[1] The Hon. Sir Odo Villiers Russell, K.C.V.O., K.C.M.G., C.B.

ROBERT BARRETT BROWNING (Siena 1859)

From a painting by Hamilton Wilde

p. 264

wrote, hinting, too, that it would be far wiser for her to return to England. "There's no use for anyone to run after us, but we may roll anyone's way. I say this penetrated by your affectionate feeling for us." Those who live abroad and have suffered from the same affectionate impulse on the part of free, unfettered, and often idle friends might well adopt the letter as a model. And, indeed, the Brownings were often rather overdone with people as it was, besides being then, as always, essentially self-sufficient.

Mr. Chorley dedicated his novel *Roccabella* to Elizabeth, but unfortunately he made the grave error of marrying his heroine to an Italian *birbante*, which, of course, annoyed her excessively. "You evidently think that God made only the English," she wrote indignantly. "Well, I have lived thirteen years on the Continent, and far as England is from Italy, far as the heavens are from the earth, I dissent from you, dissent from you, dissent from you!" She urged him to write another book, doing justice to our "sublime Azeglios, acute Cavours, and energetic Farinis." She ended with: "I persist in being in high hopes for my Italy."

She was then writing *Poems before Congress*, which embodied a little tediously her political views. For she did not really understand Italy or the Italians. Their deeply subtle, sharply logical mentality so destitute of all sentimentality, is not easy of comprehension at any time, and there was one extremely important side of the political situation—that of the Catholic Church—which was rigorously ignored or misjudged by her English mind. Nor can she be blamed for this. She had had so little contact with the world until she was in her forty-first year that it was difficult for her to acquire anything like a clear grasp of contemporary politics. There was something at once childlike and sentimental about her enthusiasms. But she was a poet, and everything she saw was touched with a poet's imagination.

None of them had any particular wish to spend the winter in Rome; indeed, Penini said that if he had to leave his Florence he should prefer to go to Paris. Their friends in Florence also tried to dissuade them from going, even assuring Penini that he would be massacred. Would it not be better, the child gravely asked, for Mamma to have a cold on her chest rather than a cannon-ball in her stomach? His parents had, however, no fear of revolutions and cannon-balls, and after a brief stay in Florence, during which Mrs. Browning had the threat of another attack, they left for Rome.

5

Instead of returning to their old rooms in Via Bocca di Leone, they spent the winter of 1859-1860 in a sunny apartment in Via Tritone. Probably the steep stone stairs of their former dwelling made it impracticable now for Mrs. Browning, whose health was rapidly deteriorating.

There was a movement on foot in Rome to give presentation swords to Victor Emanuel and Louis Napoleon, twenty thousand Romans having contributed a franc apiece to this end. Naturally the scheme met with the disapproval of the Vatican, and the swords had to vanish from the scene. Before they disappeared, Castellani—who had designed them—invited Mrs. Browning and her husband to see them, and she was fetched in a closed carriage to go to his house. The winter evening was wet but not cold, and on arrival the Brownings were received "most flatteringly as poets and lovers of Italy," and were pressed to give their autographs. They returned home "in a blaze of glory and satisfaction," but with the unfortunate result that Elizabeth caught a very severe cold. There was a swift return of all her worst symptoms—suffocation, irregular heart action, and a cough that tore her to pieces. The attack was not a prolonged one, and at the end of a week she was able to leave her bed. She had to drink asses' milk, a remedy then much in favour for persons of delicate lungs.   She was able to work at the proofs of *Poems before Congress*, admitting, however, that she expected to be torn in pieces by the English critics for what she had ventured to write.

Rome was comparatively deserted that winter, and apartments were unusually cheap, though wages had gone up inordinately.   Mrs. Browning's letters at this time showed her passionate preoccupation with the political situation, although she was annoyed with Mrs. Martin for alluding to Italy as her adopted country.   "I love truth and justice, or I try to love truth and justice, more than any Plato's or Shakespeare's country.   I certainly do not love the egotism of England nor wish to love it.   I class England among the most immoral nations in respect to her foreign politics."   All this could hardly have made soothing or acceptable reading for her English friends.   But perhaps, like Mrs. Jameson, they considered her fine intellect demented on the subject.

Among their circle of acquaintances at this time there was a young American girl called Kate Field, very pretty and charming and intellectual, whose acquaintance they had made the previous winter in Rome.   Both the Brownings were much attached to her.   She took herself very seriously and expected others to do the same.   "Mr. Browning," she wrote, "is the person whose good opinion I am most anxious for, and to whom I am already very much attached. He feels music, and I should like to sing before him. There is something about him that I fancy marvellous. Last night he said to me : 'You are very ambitious— —you are the most ambitious person of my acquaintance.'   I laughed and asked him how he had arrived at such a conclusion.   'Oh, I can tell by your eyes,' he said.   'How so ? '   I asked.   'I can detect it in their glisten.'   'Well,' I said, ' it is no great crime to be ambitious, is it ? '   'No indeed,' he returned, ' I admire it.   I would not give a straw for a person who was not ! ' "

On one occasion, when they were all assembled at Miss Blagden's villa, Kate Field arrived with her mother and was kissed by both poets. Mr. Landor, who was present, exclaimed : " What ? Do you intend to stop there ? " ; whereupon the young girl went up to him and kissed him. " This is the happiest day of my life," he declared ; " if I had been sixty years younger you wouldn't have kissed me, I'm sure ! " Small wonder that he told Mrs. Browning Kate was the most charming young lady he had ever met, " and you know, dear Kate, he has seen a great many," Mrs. Browning told her on repeating the praise. Landor subsequently commemorated the little incident in a poem which Browning had sent her from Siena in the summer of 1859.

> She came across nor greatly feared
> The horrid brake of wintry beard,

were its concluding lines. Browning's accompanying letter was full of delicate flattery.

" Dear Miss Field,
    " I have only a minute to say that Mr. Landor wrote these really pretty lines in your honour the other day. You remember on what circumstance they turn. I know somebody who is ready to testify to double the extent at the same cost to you and do his best too. And you also know.
                    " Yours affectionately,
                                " R. B."

But Miss Field was also in the habit of contributing articles to American newspapers and journals, and sometimes they were a little, just a little, afraid of what she might say or write. Thus, when Mrs. Browning sent her a copy of *Poems before Congress* from Rome, they heard through Miss Blagden that Miss Field persisted in believing that the *Curse for a Nation* (which really attracted more unfavourable criticism in England than even the anathemas of that country's foreign policy) was intended for America, not England.

Robert undertook to reply to Kate Field, which he did in the most obscure and cryptic manner imaginable so that one is not really much the wiser when one has read the letter.

" Do you really care to have the little photograph ? Here it is with all my heart. I wonder I dare be so frank this morning, however, for a note just received from Isa mentions an instance of your acuteness that strikes me with a certain awe. ' Kate,' she says, ' persists that the *Curse for a Nation* is for America and not England.' You persist do you ? No doubt against the combined intelligence of our friends who show such hunger and thirst for a new poem of Ba's, and when they get it digest the same as you see.

" Write a nation's curse for me, quote the anti-slavery society five years ago, and send it over the western seas. ' Not so,' replied poor little Ba, ' for with my heart sore for my own land's sins which are thus and thus, what curse can be assigned to another land when heavy sins are mine ? ' ' Write it for that very reason,' rejoined Ba's botherer ' because thou hast strength to see and hate a foul thing done within thy gates.' So . . . she wrote and sent over the western seas what all may read, but it appears only Kate Field out of all Florence can understand. It seems incredible. How did you find out ? . . . In short, you are not only the delightful Kate Field which I always knew you to be, but the perspicuous creature to whom I am suddenly found bowing before as the sole understander of Ba in all Florence. Kate persists, etc. . . . I can't get over it.

" To be sure the *Athenæum* pretended to make the same blunder for a private pique, but then it had the instinct of its kind, the crawlers, and took care to leave out of its quotation every word of the explanatory prologue I ,have been laying under contribution. But I thought the friends you ' persist '

against would read in plain English and were inclined
to pay a moderate attention to that of the divine
Mrs. Browning. They precipitated themselves against
this excruciatingly expected work. They read,
marked and thoroughly digested those precious
words above cited. They devoutly thanked God they
were not called upon to discuss any of the unintel-
ligible Browning . . . and they came to a conclusion
which Kate Field persists against. Browning the
husband means to try increasingly to grow somewhat intelligible to all of his intimates at Florence
with the sole exception of K.F., to whose comprehension he will rather endeavour to rise than to stoop
henceforth."

He ended by assuring her that the matter of
the present letter was not the annexation of Lombardy
and Nice. To this ambiguous and sarcastic missive
Mrs. Browning added a gentler postscript :

" My dear Kate, never say that I have cursed
your country. I only declared the consequence of
evil in her, and which has since developed itself in
thunder and flame. I feel with more pain than many
Americans do the sorrow of her transition time, but
I do know that it is transition ; it is crisis ; and you
will come out of the fire purified and stainless, having
had the angel of a great cause walking with you in
the furnace."

It is obvious, however, that they were both per-
turbed by the storm that had descended upon Mrs.
Browning's head. In Browning's letter there was
a sharp edge that must have cut, while his wife
sought to pour oil on the wounds. They both
possessed a horror of slavery, for both were descendants of slave-owners, and Elizabeth had long ago
learned from Treppy something of what that meant.
But they had many American friends in Italy,
friends from whom they had received unlimited
kindness and generosity, and it must have been

their very last desire in any way to offend them.

The *Curse for a Nation* inflamed alike those who believed it was intended for England and those who regarded it as a denunciation of American slavery. " Oh, Ba, such dreadful curses ! " Henrietta wrote from Taunton. Robert Browning was especially incensed against the *Athenæum* for adopting the view that it was meant for England. And very naturally her own relations were annoyed. George Barrett was furious and wrote her a letter to tell her so, and this upset her terribly. But Odo Russell comforted her. He told her the book had made a sensation, and that the offence it had given was due less to its objections to English policy than to its praise of Louis Napoleon.

Mrs. Browning wrote a long letter of remonstrance to Mr. Chorley, then musical critic of the *Athenæum*, in which she revealed a certain nervous tension. " Dearest Mr. Chorley, you have not been just to me, in the matter of my *Poems before Congress*. Why have you not been just to me ? You are an honest man and my friend. These two things might go together. . . . " She did not forget in writing to him thus that some of her earliest gladness in literary sympathy and recognition had come from him. But she did not write to please anyone, not even her own husband. . . .

One gathers that Chorley in his reply was apologetic and conciliatory; thus the review in the *Athenæum* produced no lasting rancour between these old friends.

It is interesting to note that in her preface to the *Poems before Congress* she makes use of the following almost prophetic phrase : " Freedom of the seas does not mean piracy."

6

George Eliot was to be seen walking in the Corso with Lewes that spring. Kate Field, who had met her at the Trollopes' in Florence, described her by

saying that " her whole face was of the horse make."
She had talked all the evening to Mr. Trollope amid
a company that waxed passionately enthusiastic over
Italian liberty. She had just then published the *Mill
on the Floss*. In Rome, however, the couple were
inseparable and visited no one.

Mrs. Browning was distressed that spring because
Mr. Page's pictures had been rejected by the Academy.
" Your Academy," she called it in writing to Miss
Haworth, the use of the pronoun " your " instead of
" our " being somewhat unpleasantly significant.
But she was tired ; her nerves were on edge ; the
adverse criticism of her book could hardly fail to
react upon a nature so sensitive. She was at work
on some lyrics, besides helping Pen to prepare his
lessons for the priest who was now his tutor, and she
had little strength for anything else.

They left Rome on the 4th of June, travelling
by way of Orvieto and Chiusi, through the beautiful
Umbrian scenery. But she confessed to feeling
tired. They only purposed to remain in Florence
about a month. Mr. Landor was there, still
faithfully tended by Wilson. The poor old dear
was, however, in a state of extreme wrath and
permanent indignation against the whole world,
with the single exception of Robert Browning. " He
has the most beautiful sea-foam of a beard you ever
saw, all in a curl and white bubblement of beauty,"
Elizabeth wrote. He was fairly amenable to Wilson,
and had only once thrown his dinner out of the
window.

Politics and spiritualism still occupied that fine
mind, injuring, one would think, its rare gift. Was it
true, she asked, that Lord Lyndhurst had been
lifted up in a chair ?   " I hear that Landseer has
received the faith, and did everything to persuade
Dickens to investigate, which Dickens refused."

But her hand had by no means lost its cunning.
The famous *Musical Instrument* was published in
Cornhill that year, and it is without doubt one of
her finest lyrics. The last two verses possess a

poignancy that seems to hint at something of the suffering she had herself endured as a poet.

> Sweet, sweet, sweet, O Pan !
>   Piercing sweet by the great river !
> Blinding sweet, O great god Pan !
> The sun on the hill forgot to die,
> And the lilies revived, and the dragon-fly
>   Came back to dream on the river.
>
> Yet half a beast is the great god Pan,
>   To laugh as he sits by the river,
> Making a poet out of a man :
> The true gods sigh for the cost and pain,—
> For the reed which grows nevermore again
>   As a reed, with the reeds in the river.

The deadly fatigue which was gripping her lent, too, an additional and almost painful pathos to her poem *My Heart and I*, which was also written about this time.

> How tired we feel, my heart and I !
>   We seem of no use in the world ;
>   Our fancies hang grey and uncurled
> About men's eyes indifferently ;
>   Our voice which thrilled you so, will let
>   You sleep ; our tears are only wet ;
> What do we here, my heart and I ?

Despite the unfavourable reviews, or even perhaps because of them, the *Poems before Congress* reached a second edition that summer, while *Aurora Leigh* attained to its fifth. There was thus no diminution of public interest in her work.

In July they returned to the Villa Alberti at Siena, but in the following month grave news reached Mrs. Browning from England concerning the health of her sister, Henrietta Surtees Cook, then the mother of three little girls all younger than Penini. She felt the anxiety all the more keenly because her own health prevented her from undertaking the journey to England.

Fortunately for her the summer proved an

unusually cool one and the weeks at Siena did her good. They had for neighbours the Storys, whose children were Pen's friends and constant playmates, Landor, who was then eighty-six years old, and Isa Blagden. Mrs. Browning led a very quiet life, lying for hours on the sofa, glad to be free of morning visitors and the sound of voices below her window.

Her last photograph, which was taken that year, shows her much as she must have been about this time. Thanks to the kindness of Mrs. Waldo Story, I have been able to reproduce it here. She was less black than she was painted, she told her friends, but there is no doubt that the hot suns of Italy had darkened her complexion, as so often happens in the case of brunettes. But Pen, standing by her side, was "lovely enough to satisfy her vanity." He was then eleven years old. "Pen is very like and very sweet, we think," she wrote.

Like all authors, Mrs. Browning was sometimes the recipient of abusive anonymous letters, and that summer she received one from an unknown source in which the writer said he had always hitherto regarded her as a " great Age-teacher, all but divine," but had now sorrowfully renounced her, first on account of her " immoral " poem (*A Musical Instrument*, published in Cornhill), and secondly because her brain had obviously been turned by the private attentions and flatteries bestowed upon her by the Emperor Napoleon III while she was in Paris, so that she had ever since devoted herself to the task of furthering his selfish ambitions !

Letters from England at that time brought little comfort. Henrietta, who had always seemed the strongest of the three sisters, and the one, too, who possessed the most vitality, was slowly dying. Sometimes Mrs. Martin wrote to give Elizabeth news of her, sometimes it would be one of her brothers or perhaps Arabel. Stormie wrote in August to say there was less pain, but always from the first the case had seemed quite hopeless. With this bitter anxiety in her heart—she described it

ELIZABETH BARRETT BROWNING WITH 'PENINI'

From a photograph
Rome, 1860

as a stone hung round her heart, and " a black veil
between me and all that I do, think, or look at "
—it was small wonder that Mrs. Browning felt ill
and depressed. She was so weak, too, that often she
was incapable of crawling out to sit on a cushion
under her own fig tree.

Still, the quiet place tranquillised in some measure
her uneasy spirit. It was very calm, this " great
lonely villa in the midst of purple hills and vineyards, olive trees and fig trees like forest trees."
She *could* have been happy there had it not been for
her ever-present anxiety.

Robert and Penini were well and rode out daily
together. As for herself, she said the best thing she
could do for others was to keep quiet and try not to
give cause for trouble on her account, to be patient
and live on God's daily bread from day to day. . . ."

CHAPTER XVIII

I

In the autumn of 1860 the Brownings returned to Rome and spent the winter in Via Felice. Mrs. Surtees Cook died after months of suffering, and Elizabeth's letters showed signs not only of grief but of a profound melancholy and dejection. " I have suffered very much, and feel tired and beaten," she confessed. We can trace the mood in which she had penned that saddest of sad poems *My Heart and I*.

She blamed herself for not having gone to England during that summer they had spent at Havre. After a life of close union she had only seen Henrietta for a total of about three weeks during the fourteen years of her own married life.

She lived very quietly in Rome, partly on account of her deep mourning and partly because of her own failing health. Robert kept people off. " Even now, when the door is open a little, gloomy lionesses with wounded paws don't draw the public." She did, however, receive Sir John Bowring, a Liberal with whom she had much in common. Both denounced the volunteer movement in England, which was deemed due to a fear of invasion by France, for even then the Liberal Party was violently opposed to any form of national defence, despite the fact that conscription has never been abolished in republican countries.

Robert was perfectly happy in Rome. He went out a great deal, which he had never done in Florence, and she was only too thankful to go to bed early, knowing that he was well amused. In the daytime he studied modelling under Mr. Story and made extraordinary progress, working with surprising energy for six hours a day at his new trade. He copied the busts of the *Young Augustus* and the *Psyche*. Pen, too, was well. As for herself, she wrote to Miss Haworth towards the end of the year, when she had only a few months to live, in words that sound to us now almost prophetic.

" I am weak and languid. I struggle hard to live on. I wish to live just as long and no longer than to grow in the soul. . . . "

Little things troubled and annoyed her. Her poem *De Profundis*, written more than twenty years before, and referring to the death of her beloved Bro, was published in an American newspaper about this time, greatly to her distress, since she feared people might believe that it had been written recently to commemorate the death of her sister. She had offered it to an editor some time before, on receiving a request for some verses, but it was unfortunate from her point of view that it should have appeared just then. " You know I never can speak nor cry, so it isn't likely that I should write verses. . . . It's not my way to grind up my green griefs to make bread of." The poem, she further explained to Miss Blagden, exaggerated nothing, and represented a condition from which she had already, when she wrote it, partly emerged after the greatest suffering—the only time in which she had ever experienced absolute despair.

There was snow once that winter in Rome, but for the most part the weather was mild, a condition that always favoured her. Their rooms were very sunny and warm. Penini had his pony there and rode regularly, went on with his lessons with the Abbé, and read a little German with his mother now and then, while Robert as usual superintended the music and arithmetic. But in a letter to Mrs. Martin, Elizabeth made the significant and poignant confession : *For the first time I have had pain in looking into his (Penini's) face lately—which you will understand.* . . .

Robert went to a grand ball at Mrs. Hooker's. All the Roman princes and many cardinals, he said, were present at it, and the Princess Ruspoli (a Buonaparte) appeared in the tricolour, thereby creating a sensation. He himself returned home at four in the morning.

Gaeta fell in January 1861. " One thing is clear," Elizabeth wrote, " that it wasn't only the French fleet that prevented ' our ' triumph."

Her mind was still occupied with politics, spiritualism and the situation in America. But her hold on these things was now ever so slightly relaxed. She no longer wrote of them with the same passion, and sometimes a sentence escaped her that revealed the most devastatng physical weakness.

" I have a stout pen, and till its last blot it will write perhaps with its usual insolence (as a friend once said), but if you laid your hand on this heart you would feel how it stops and staggers and fails. . . ."

Already she was beginning to shrink from the thought of their proposed summer journey to France —her real wish would have been to spend the year in a cave. But Robert would have to go if only to see his father, and he refused to do so without her. Arabel, who had been very anxious that she should visit England, now talked of meeting her in France.

2

She rallied a little during the early months of 1861 and was able to receive a few people, among them Miss Sewell, the author of *Amy Herbert,* who for so long kept an extremely select girls' school in the Isle of Wight ; and Lady Juliana Knox, pronounced *Nux* by the Italian servant, in whose mind it was associated with that favourite remedy of the Browning household. Lady Juliana had had an audience with the Holy Father, at the end of which he had prayed aloud in French, and after giving his blessing, added: *Priez pour le Pape.* This touched Elizabeth, who was always sensitive to sorrow in others, and for once she showed sympathy with that suffering figure. " Poor old man ! When you feel the human flesh through the ecclesiastical robe you get into sympathy with him at once."

I think there was never a heart more easily touched by any appearance of grief than that of Elizabeth Browning. Deep called to deep, and she was at once sensitive, alert, compassionate—her true self.

Her sense of humour had not even then been crushed by the successive blows she had received. Thus she was able to describe Miss Sewell as wearing " the nearest approach to a poky bonnet possible in this sinful generation," and to suggest that she evinced also a natural incompatibility with the crinoline (then apparently considered a not quite modest garment) so that Elizabeth forbore to glance at her lanky skirts. Then there was an unfortunate Mr. Massy Dawson, " who called upon me yesterday with moustaches and a bride," and maintained that her hero, Napoleon III, was ready to perish in defence of the Papacy. His bride meantime sat " in a delicate dove-coloured silk on the sofa, as tame as any dove, and not venturing to coo even." Jane Austen might have written that ironic criticism.

Penini, who was then nearly twelve, fraternised with the French troops on the Pincio, marching with them, discussing Chopin and Heller with the musical officers, and politics with all who were ready to listen to him. On one occasion he was brought home by a French officer who considered him too small to go alone in the crowd—he was still very small for his age and his long curls made him look even younger than he was. He invited his escort to come in and " see Mamma," but this was declined.

Mrs. Browning was annoyed with Sarianna for saying that Robert " looked old " in his new photograph. Of course his beard was whiter . . . but the women adored him everywhere, " far too much for decency."   In her eyes he was much handsomer and more attractive than when she had first seen him sixteen years before. And even when he was displeased with her (was he ever ?) he thought aloud with her and couldn't stop himself. Sarianna had evinced her disapproval of the modelling, as once before she had done about the drawing in Paris, but Elizabeth defended him with a certain energy. Reading hurt his eyes, and he simply *must* have an outlet for his active, restless, artistic temperament. She, too, had hoped that the poems would have been finished that winter, and he had a bright sunny room set apart for his own use in which to write, but it was of no avail ; he could only work when he felt inclined, and that winter he certainly didn't feel inclined. Perhaps he reacted a little to his wife's gloom and malaise, but in any case she was only too thankful that he should have discovered such a resource in modelling. He had the material for a volume, he told her, and would work at it in the summer. Mrs. Browning added with infinite wisdom : " The brain stratifies and matures creatively, even in the pauses of the pen."   And in the matter of sculpture he was beginning to show real talent.   One day he brought her back a perfect copy of a small torso of a Greek Venus, which was pronounced by the learned to be " wonderfully done."   He informed her that " all his happiness lay in clay now."   Although this was scarcely a compliment to her, he said it so sincerely and fervently that she " could not but sympathise, and wish him a life-load of clay to riot in."   It is in such little glimpses as these that we realise what a perfect wife she was to him.

Penini attended a *matinée d'enfants* given at the French Embassy by the Duchesse de Grammont. It was a very splendid affair, and he wore a crimson velvet blouse and met a number of little Italian princes, Colonnas, Dorias, Piombinos and many more, with whom he played leap-frog and discussed lessons and ponies.   Napoleon was, as ever, his hero, but he had conceived an immense, almost idolising admiration for the lovely young Queen of Naples, whom he pursued when out for his rides.   The little English boy with his flowing fair curls received many a smile from that sad, beautiful face.   Once she even stood up in her carriage to smile at him.   Pen, unwilling to arrogate all the attraction to himself, ascribed it in part to his pony and in part to a new jacket he had just acquired.   When charged with having fallen in love, he cautiously admitted " feeling an interest."

It was during those final weeks in Rome that Mrs. Browning wrote her beautiful last poem, *The North and the South*, offered to Thackeray for *Cornhill* in place of the rejected *Lord Walter's Wife*.   It was written to commemorate the visit of the famous Danish author, Hans Christian Andersen, to Rome. He called upon Mrs. Browning and she found him charming.   Penini's praise was slightly more qualified. " He is not really pretty.   He is rather like his own ugly duck, but his mind has *developed* into a swan ! "

There are unforgettable verses in that last poem of hers, and for once it was quite free from sadness.

" Now give us lands where the olives grow,"
    Cried the North to the South,
" Where the sun with a golden mouth can blow
Blue bubbles of grapes down a vineyard row ! "
    Cried the North to the South.

    .   .   .   .   .

" Yet oh, for the skies that are softer and higher ' ;
    Sighed the North to the South ;
" For the flowers that blaze, and the trees that aspire,
And the insects made of a song or a fire ! "
    Sighed the North to the South.

The introduction of Andersen's name in the closing stanza robs the poem of something of its purely lyrical quality.   But the perfect line, " And the insects made of a song or a fire " must appeal to all those who know Tuscany with its singing *cicale*, its wandering jewelled fireflies. It brings before one the breathless, burning summer days when the atmosphere resembles particles of dazzling white-hot crystals, and the still, warm scented summer nights when the fireflies flit among the trees like shining winged rubies.

Before they left Rome at the end of May they were in treaty for an apartment in the Barberini Palace, but this plan never materialised. Still, it clearly shows their reluctant realisation of the impossibility of Florence as an abode for Mrs. Browning during the winter months. Rome, with its larger stir, its growing coterie of artists, sculptors and writers, afforded, too, a more congenial atmosphere for Robert, while the milder climate had proved far more beneficial to his wife's health, which was, alas! so soon to be no longer a source of preoccupation to him.

Up till the end of her sojourn in Rome Mrs. Browning led the life of an invalid. " I go to bed at eight on most nights. I'm the rag of a Ba," she told Miss Blagden in a letter. " Yet I *am* stronger, and look much so, it seems to me." She had less than a month to live when she wrote those hopeful words.

3

Early in June, after their return to Florence, the project of spending the summer in France was definitely abandoned, to the deep disappointment alike of old Mr. Browning, his daughter, and Arabel Barrett.

Even before they left Rome the doctors had assured Mrs. Browning that to undertake such a journey would be a risk. Robert, as we have seen, refused to go without her, for which he must afterwards have been devoutly thankful.

" I can't let Robert's disagreeable letter go alone, dearest Sarianna" (she wrote to her sister-in-law on the 7th of June), " though my word will be as heavy as a stone at the bottom of it. I am deeply sorry you should have had the vain hope of seeing Robert and Pen. As for me, I know my place ; I am only fit for a drag-chain. . . . In fact I said almost too much at Rome to Robert, till he fancied I had set my self-will on tossing myself up as a halfpenny, and coming down on the wrong side. Now, in fact, it was not at all (nearly) for Arabel that I wished to go, only I did really wish and do my best to go. He, on the other hand, before we left Rome, had made up his mind (helped by a stray physician of mine whom he met in the street) that it would be a great risk to carry me north. He (Robert) always a little exaggerates the difficulties of travelling, and there's no denying that I have less strength than is usual to me, even at the present time."

In this, her last extant letter to Sarianna, she mentioned that they had returned home in a cloud owing to the death of Cavour—the man who, she had hoped, would fulfil all her dreams for her beloved Italy. His death was a sharp blow, which may even have hastened the end. But I think this is doubtful. All through the winter her keen enthusiasm for those things that had once so passionately preoccupied her had flagged a little. We can discern in her letters the kind of complete detachment from things of earth that is wont to characterise those for whom death is fast approaching. It was, indeed, as if in a sense she were beginning to fold up and lay away, one by one, her earthly garments. Where sorrow was still able to touch her sharply was when she looked at her child's face, which, as she said, she seemed to see then through a mist of tears. Their mutual love had been a very close and intimate thing. She never permitted it to interfere with her complete devotion to her husband, but maternal love was with her a quality no less strong and profound.

She was never well after they left Rome on June 4th. The journey fatigued her, and Cavour's death two days later struck sharply at her diminished vitality. She had a bronchial attack, which, however, did not particularly alarm anyone, for her powers of endurance and of recuperation were always astonishing in one of such striking physical frailty. Even her husband felt no special cause for alarm, though afterwards he said that, looking back on those past years, he realised that " they had been walking over a torrent on a straw."

Browning had intended to go to Leghorn to visit the Storys on the Sunday following their return, but on the Saturday his wife was attacked by a difficulty in breathing, and he had to fetch a physician in the middle of the night to attend to her. Dr. Wilson remained with her for the rest of the night and took a very gloomy view, which effectually convinced Browning as to the undesirability of leaving her even for a short period. She was better on the following morning, and, though visibly weaker, declared she was in other respects as well as ever. But there is no doubt that the severe attack had weakened the resistance of the heart.

Still, neither felt any particular cause for alarm, and they again discussed plans for the summer, deciding to go to Siena, which had proved so beneficial the previous year. They talked, too, of giving up Casa Guidi, of taking the proposed apartment in Palazzo Barberini at Rome, and perhaps of leasing a villa on the hills outside Florence as a spring and autumn residence.

During the days that followed, Mrs. Browning was able to leave her bed and go into the *salotto* every day, lying there on the sofa till it was time to go back to bed. Once she even went out on to the terrace, but this proved too much for her, and she returned to the sofa. This continued till the Friday, the 28th of June. On that morning Mr. Lytton paid Robert a long visit, so that she remained in her room all day and did not go into the *salotto*, since she was still too weak to receive visitors. But she saw her beloved friend, Isa Blagden, who came in the evening and remained with her until eight o'clock. . . .

After she had gone Mrs. Browning returned to bed, and later she and her husband had another talk about their summer plans. On the whole she felt decidedly better that day, had been able to read the *Athenæum*, and had enjoyed Isa Blagden's visit.

The servants went to bed as usual. Browning watched over her that night, as was his invariable custom when she was ill. Although there had not seemed any special cause for anxiety, he was troubled by certain symptoms that struck him as untoward. She slept heavily and brokenly ; every now and then she raised her hands in front of her, holding them long before her. At intervals, too, she wandered in her mind, but this he attributed to a somewhat larger dose of morphia prescribed by the doctor to ensure a quiet night.

This went on till three o'clock, when her changed, difficult breathing startled him. He woke her, but she was inclined to laugh at his anxiety, declaring she was better, and speaking so quietly about her condition that he was tranquillised even against his better judgment. He gave her her medicine and she fell asleep again. But at four o'clock an aggravation of those alarming symptoms caused him to awaken the servants and send for the doctor. He wanted to bathe her feet, whereupon she laughed and said : " Well, you *are* determined to make an exaggerated case of it ! "

The maid, watching them, thought by her earnest manner that she was aware of approaching death, but this could hardly have been the case since she never even asked for Penini, who was asleep in the next room. When her husband inquired how she felt she answered : " Beautiful. . . ."

" Then came," Robert wrote afterwards to Fanny Haworth, " what my heart will keep till I see her again and longer—the most perfect expression of her love to me within my whole knowledge of her. Always smilingly, happily, with a face like a girl's, and in a few minutes she died in my arms, her head on my cheek. These incidents so sustain me that I tell them to her beloved ones as their right. There was no lingering nor acute pain, nor consciousness of separation, but God took her to Himself as you would lift a sleeping child from a dark uneasy bed into your arms and the light."

It was St. Peter's Day, the 29th of June, 1861, little more than sixteen years after their first meeting in Wimpole Street.

" The cycle is complete," Browning told the Storys, who journeyed at once from Leghorn on hearing the sad news, as he looked round the now desolate rooms of Casa Guidi. " Here we came fifteen years ago, here Pen was born, here Ba wrote her poems for Italy."

After death she looked, despite her fifty-five years, like a young girl. " All the outlines," wrote Story, " were rounded and filled up ; all traces of disease effaced, and a smile on her face so living that they could not for hours persuade themselves she was really dead."

4

Browning was utterly unprepared for the terrible blow. He was heartbroken, and according to Kate Field, who wrote an account of the tragedy to the *Atlantic Monthly*, did nothing but rush about the house all night, broken-hearted with grief. Penini, too, wandered, sad and disconsolate, from room to room, scarcely realising his great loss.

Kate Field, who saw Mrs. Browning lying dead in Casa Guidi, said that all her hair had been cut off, and that the emaciated form was heartrending to look upon. I prefer to think of Story's version, which was not intended for publication, as the more accurate one.

The funeral took place on July 1st, the intervening day being a Sunday.   Elizabeth Browning was buried in the old Protestant cemetery, which was at that time outside the walls of Florence, in a grave that has since been an object of pilgrimage to thousands of English and American travellers.   The classic sarcophagus that holds her frail remains was designed by their friend Lord Leighton, and there on summer days the " insects made of a song " chant their ceaseless choruses, while on burning, breathless summer nights the fireflies tangle the groves of cypresses with their wandering ruby lights. . . .

At the funeral there were present, among others of the English and American colony, the Storys, Mr. Lytton, Mr. Trollope, Mr. Power, and Kate Field and her mother.

" It was agonising to look on Mr. Browning," Kate Field wrote to her aunt that same day.   " He seemed as though he could hardly stand, and his face expressed the most terrible grief.   The poor boy stood beside him with tears in his eyes, and when I glanced from them to the pall where their loved one's remains lay, it seemed as though the sorrow was too much to bear."

On the coffin there were two wreaths—one of white flowers and the other, appropriately made of laurel, placed there by Story.

" The service," he afterwards wrote, " was blundered through by a fat parson in a brutally careless way, and she was consigned by him to the earth as if her clay were no better than any other clay."

The American sculptor also wrote thus of her, in words of generous praise and appreciation :

" She is a great loss to literature, to Italy, and

to the world—the greatest poet among women. What energy and fire there was in that little frame, and what burning words were winged by her pen ! With what glorious courage she attacked error, however strongly entrenched by custom, how bravely she stood by her principles !   Never did I see anyone whose brow the world hurried and crowded so to crown who had so little vanity and so much pure humility."

Fifteen years before (as Story wrote to his friend Charles Eliot Norton) the doctors had given her up, yet she had lived to bear a child, to write immortal verses, evincing always an " amazing energy of spirit and intellect."

Miss Blagden took pity on the forlorn father and son, and carried them off to her villa on Bellosguardo, the scene of so many of their happy meetings with the *literati* of Florence.

Browning was very ill during the days that followed his wife's death. He had a severe cold, and was attacked with a kind of strangulation, when he believed himself to be dying. He rallied after a few days and was able to receive Kate Field and her mother, to whom he gave a shawl that had belonged to Elizabeth, while to Kate herself he presented a locket containing a crystal in which was his wife's hair shaped in two hearts. Before this meeting he had written the following note to the young girl who had shown her so much simple adoration :

"Dear Friend, God bless you and yours for all your kindness which I shall never forget. I cannot write now except to say this, and besides, that I have had great comfort from the beginning. I know you are truth itself in all you profess to feel about her.   She also loved you, as you felt.   I hope to see you soon and talk with you. Meantime ever remember me as

"Your affectionate

"R. B."

The Fields visited Casa Guidi and found everything in her room just as she had left it. The last issue of the *Nazione*, the copy of the *Athenæum* she had read a few hours before she died, were lying on the table. There was the little open desk on which she had written her poems. Nothing had been changed or moved. . . .

Meanwhile, Browning made immediate preparations to leave the place that had known his greatest happiness and his greatest sorrow. Miss Blagden, whose warm friendship for both him and his wife had never failed, made endless and astonishing sacrifices in order to be of use to him. She gave up her villa, stored her furniture with Mr. Trollope, and accompanied the desolate father and son to Paris a few weeks later. Pen was well, " very dear and good," as his father wrote of him, " anxious to comfort me, as he calls it."

To his friend Leighton, Robert wrote on the nineteenth of July :

" It is like your old kindness to write to me and to say what you do. I know you feel for me. I can't write about it—but there were many alleviating circumstances that you shall know one day—there seemed no pain, and (what she would have felt most) the knowledge of separation from us was spared her. I find these things comfort indeed. . . . Don't fancy I am ' prostrated.' I have enough to do for the boy and myself, in carrying out her wishes. He is better than one would have thought, and behaves dearly to me. . . . "

What his enduring love for her was has been set down best by his own hand, alike in the soft hushed music of *One Word More* and in the splendid, almost triumphant tribute that ends the first part of *The Ring and the Book*. It is an extremely well-known passage, but I cannot refrain from quoting it here because it shows so clearly that death could never quite rob him of that beautiful presence.

O lyric Love, half angel and half bird
And all a wonder and a wild desire—
Boldest of hearts that ever braved the sun,
Took sanctuary within the holier blue,
And sang a kindred soul out to his face—
Yet human at the red-ripe of the heart—
When the first summons from the darkling earth
Reached thee amid thy chambers, blanched their blue,
And bared them of the glory—to drop down,
To toil for man, to suffer or to die—
This is the same voice : can thy soul know change ?
Hail, then, and hearken from the realms of help !
Never may I commence my song, my due
To God who best taught song by gift of thee,
Except with bent head and beseeching hand—
That still, despite the distance and the dark,
What was, again may be ; some interchange
Of grace, some splendour once thy very thought,
Some benediction anciently thy smile :
—Never conclude, but raising hand and head
Thither where eyes, that cannot reach, yet yearn
For all hope, all sustainment, all reward,
Their utmost up and on—so blessing back
In those thy realms of help, that heaven thy home,
Some whiteness which, I judge, thy face makes proud,
Some wanness where, I think, thy foot may fall !

Never, perhaps, did Browning surpass that *cri de cœur*. Those famous lines :

That still, despite the distance and the dark,
What was, again may be ;

belong emphatically to the bereaved lover of all time, as well as to him who had once written : *" To the end . . . the very end . . . I am yours. . . . "*

" A soul of fire enclosed in a shell of pearl." That is perhaps the best-known description of Mrs. Browning by Hillard, an American lawyer who met the two poets in Italy. All agree as to that look of physical fragility which characterised her, and it is certain that none of her portraits or photographs give any idea of her charm and spirituality. " That pale, small person, scarcely embodied at all," was Hawthorne's description of her, and he added that she spoke with " a shrill yet sweet tenuity of voice."

Mrs. David Ogilvy, who visited the Brownings in Florence in 1848 armed with a letter of introduction from Elizabeth's cousin, Mrs. Martin Lindsay, wrote thus of her :

"With her profuse feathery curls, half-hiding her small face, and her large soft pleading eyes, she always reminded me of a King Charles's spaniel. Something unutterably pathetic looked out of those eyes. . . . She habitually sat in dark rooms. . . ."

William Wetmore Story, the sculptor, wrote of her thus to his friend Lowell :

" The Brownings and we became great friends in Florence, and of course we could not become great friends without liking each other. He is of my size but slighter, with straight black hair, small eyes wide apart which he twitches constantly together, a smooth face, a slight, aquiline nose, and manners nervous and rapid.   He has a great vivacity but not the least humour, some sarcasm, considerable critical faculty, and very great frankness and friend-liness of manner and mind.   Mrs. Browning used to sit buried up in a large easy chair, listening and talk-ing very quietly and pleasantly, with nothing of that peculiarity which one would expect from reading her poems. Her eyes are small, her mouth large, she wears a cap and long curls. Very unaffected and pleasant and simple-hearted is she, and Brown-ing says : ' Her poems are the least good part of her.' "

" A face plain in feature," wrote Harriet Hosmer, always such an intimate and beloved young friend of both the Brownings, " but redeemed by wonderful dark eyes, large and loving and luminous as stars. The manner ever gracious with a touch of shyness at times.   Small in stature and in form so fragile that the gentlest zephyr might have borne her away."

After her death Miss Hosmer wrote of her as follows :

" She lives in my heart and in my memory as the most perfect human being I have ever known. The calmness of her death was a fitting close to the beauty of her life, for after thanking her husband for all his devotion to her, she laid her head upon his shoulder and died as peacefully as if she were going to sleep."

Perhaps it has been given to few other authors to be so tenderly beloved and remembered in two countries as Elizabeth Barrett Browning will always be, both in England and Italy.   The tragedy of her girlhood, the faery-like development of her love-story, the romance of her married life, her unvarying tenderness as wife and mother— these things apart from her wonderful gift and lasting fame make their permanent appeal to the hearts of men.   The fierce searchlight that for so many years has illuminated every corner of her life, public and private, has revealed little that we could wish either unsaid or undone.   Our great loss is that all her letters to her own family should still be unknown to us, although we may hope that a future generation may see fit to publish what must necessarily be of so much value and importance.

For the rest, her epitaph was undoubtedly written by her husband in Pompilia's famous tribute to Caponsacchi in *The Ring and the Book :*

> . . . Through such souls alone
> God stooping shows sufficient of His Light
> For us i' the dark to rise by. . . .

5

It is no part of the purpose of this book to follow the father and son through the long years that elapsed before the death of the one in Venice in 1889, and of the other at Asolo in 1912. Browning's life was for many years dedicated most faithfully to his son. They lived in London, often spending the summer holidays abroad, generally in France with old Mr. Browning, who lived on until 1866, and Sarianna.

When able to settle down in a home of his own Robert Browning took a house in Warwick Crescent, so that he might be near Arabel, who lived close by in Delamere Terrace. His friendship with his wife's sister became a very close and intimate one ; they met daily, and there can be little doubt that her presence was an immense source of comfort to him during the desolate years that immediately followed Elizabeth's death.

Arabel Barrett died in 1868. Five years before she had seen her beloved sister in a dream, and asked her when she would be with her again. " In five years, dearest," was the smiling reply. The dream having been duly told to Browning, he made a note of it, and after his sister-in-law's death he related the episode to Miss Blagden. " You know I'm not superstitious," he added, " it was only a coincidence, but noticeable. . . . "

That his heart, despite many passing attractions (for the women still continued to " adore him far too much for decency," as his wife once said), remained essentially and permanently faithful to his beloved Ba, is confirmed by his fiery outburst of indignation when Fitzgerald's *Life* was published and the unfortunate extract from his diary was accidentally lighted upon by Browning. " Mrs. Browning is dead. No more *Aurora Leighs*, thank God ! "

Browning, in the fury of the moment, wrote a fierce little poem and sent it to the *Athenæum*, in which paper it was immediately published.

TO EDWARD FITZGERALD

I chanced upon a new book yesterday,
I opened it, and where my finger lay
   'Twixt page and uncut page, these words I read—
Some six or seven at most—and learned thereby
That you, Fitzgerald, whom by ear or eye
   She never knew, " thanked God my wife was dead."

Ay, dead. . . . And were yourself alive, good Fitz,
How to return you thanks would task my wits ;
   Kicking you seems the common lot of curs—
While more appropriate greeting lends you grace :
Surely to spit there glorifies your face—
   Spitting from lips once sanctified by hers ! . . .

More than a quarter of a century had elapsed since the death-scene in Florence when his beloved Ba had died in his arms, her face pressed to his cheek, when he took his pen and wrote those burning vituperative lines. He regretted afterwards that on the impulse of the moment he had given them for publication, but excused himself to his friends by saying : "I felt as if she had died yesterday. . . ."

Thus, " despite the distance and the dark," he had not even then lost the sense of her nearness, her beautiful presence that for nearly fifteen years had given him a joy and happiness such as it is given to few mortals to experience, when, to use her own words, " He of the heavens, brought us together so wonderfully, holding two souls in His hand. . . ."

THE END

APPENDIX

Letters from Elizabeth Barrett Browning to Mrs. William Wetmore Story.

I

Casa Tolomei,
Bagni di Lucca.
[About July 1853.]

MY dear Mrs. Story: I was very forgetful yesterday (only remembering that I wanted to see Edith and Joseph) when I asked you to send the children this evening. Unfortunately there was a previous engagement on our parts. May they come on Friday, instead ? To-morrow we go to you ourselves.

I must expose myself to your contempt by telling you that after all the *tea* didn't come from Florence. See how right Robert is about my ignorance ! Wilson tells me that the tea provided at the Baths of Lucca is better than any we have found in other parts of Italy and even France. It is bought at a little Italian shop close to our house where they profess to sell English goods and to which Wilson will direct your servant at any time.

I dreamt of the spirits last night. Is it all a dream from first to last ?

Ask Mr. Story if this is not curious, that I who pass among my sceptical contemporaries as being singularly credulous, am never liable to mistake or doubt about the suggestions of my own mind?—never in long tracts of mental agitation and bodily weakness, imagined that I saw or heard ghostly vision or sign?—never could in the act of writing or any other act, mistake a state of consciousness for one of unconsciousness?

I have been trying this morning with a pencil. Not a letter came—not the semblance of a letter—shaken from nervous movements of the hand . . . yes . . . but nothing articulate or intelligent.

Most truly yours always.
ELIZABETH BARRETT BROWNING.

I return with thanks the little " polka."
Wednesday evening.

2

[No date.]

My dear Emelyn: I write by Robert's command to explain that he has had a fit of remorse about leaving Mr. Perkins's table at nine, scarcely waiting for the dessert. He thinks that he has not the face for it, and all the more that it is a novelty to him to dine there at all.

Will you therefore, says Robert, have the great goodness to let Mrs. Lodge know, in case she should rely on him for walking? Plainly he is in a scrape, and runs away, throwing all the explanations on me! He will get to you afterwards, later in the evening.

Affly yours,
E. B. B.

Tell dear Edith to *believe* how much she pleased me to-day and Saturday.

3

[No date.]

I do hope, dearest Emelyn, you will be wise and kind to others as well as to yourself, and go to the Villa notwithstanding. It is, as you say, an exquisite day, good for soul and body, and Mr. Story won't have the benefit of it if you stay at home, so think of him and the rest of us, and be good and go.

As to the great controversy last night, I daresay I ought to beg everybody's pardon on bended knees for meddling with what doesn't concern me. I am ignorant, of course, and having certain impulses am the apter to trust to them on that very account of ignorance. So as nobody happens to *know* much on the subject let us hope at least for the best— that's all I venture to say on behalf of those same instincts.

For the rest there was not a call on you to *vindicate* yourself . . . nor is. . . . Vindicate ! . . . From what I wonder ? From being patient with

Your affectionate
E. B. B.,
for instance.

4

Thank you again and again, dearest Emelyn, for the beautiful present which will keep the thought of you close to me—

" Oh so fair, oh so white, oh so soft is she ! "—

you are too, too kind—" Oh so kind " should come after.

We are delighted to see dear little Edith back among us, and Penini has almost choked himself with pudding in the emotion of his haste to welcome her. How well she looks ! Wouldn't it do you good, dear Emelyn, to join

the walking party which Robert is to make one of ?
I am delighted for him to go. It is as desirable for
him as for Mr. Story to take exercise, and I can't
help thinking that, as a matter of duty and wisdom,
it would be good for you to go too.

Very affectionately yours,

BA.

5

Perugia[1]

November 18th, 1853.

Friday.

Dearest Emelyn : I snatch such paper and ink as
the gods here provide (niggardly gods, though) to
tell you that we have come half way, as far as Perugia
that is . . . to receive the blessings of your hands
and handwriting.

Thank you, thank you, you reconcile me even
to the third piano, if nothing lower is to be had,
even though Robert [frightens] me by proposing to
carry me upstairs. Certainly we must be reasonable
and accept the disadvantages with all the advantages
you speak of, and I expect to have an additional
lobe of lung to walk up steps with in the Roman air.
The room for Robert is worth waiting for besides,
isn't it ? How we thank you for all your deeds,
but for the feeling that prompted them, most !

Oh yes, of course having been filled with sinister
suspicions against me, you have supposed that we
should be kept at Florence *somehow*. In spite of
this, however, we have broken the chain. We set
out on Tuesday, arrived here yesterday, and finding
an excellent hotel resolved on staying a whole day
to see the pictures and the tombs.

---

[1] Written on the first journey to Rome. It will be remembered that
the Storys had taken the apartment on the third floor of No. 43 Via Bocca
di Leone for the Brownings, and that the first days of their visit were
saddened by the death of little Joseph Story on November 23rd, 1853.

Such an exquisite journey we have had!—
lovely warm weather—Penini (for one of us) describing
himself as "warm as a lion and alive as a nosegay"!
He however does not approve of our loitering here
at all. He wants to see Edith and *Blome* (Rome).

All this morning Robert and I have been spending
before the Peruginos, or wandering up and down
this romantic Perugia. How picturesque! ... It
seems lifted up in the sunshine to look at the mountains, and all the houses strain upwards. I scarcely
ever saw a town I liked better. We sleep to-morrow
at Foligno, the next night at Spoleto, the next at
Narni, the next at Città, and on Tuesday 22nd
shall be in Rome. So take our rooms—we trust
you entirely!—and remember unless by miraculous
interposition something better (that is lower) shall
offer itself we accept thankfully your third piano.
Will you let your tradespeople supply us with bread,
milk, coffee, sugar and eggs for our arrival? Thank
you, both of you, from us both, warmly and grate-
fully, and best of love to you both from Robert as
well as

Your affectionate

E. B. B.

6

To William Wetmore Story, from E. B. B.

Dear Mr. Story: I scarcely excuse to myself
(may I to you?) the delay of thanking you for the
gift of your volume of poems, by my desire to return
' Angela ' by the same occasion. At last I do thank
you, we both thank you, for this kindness done, and
this pleasure given: through verses—full of noble
and true instincts and touched everywhere with the
poetical sense of beauty.

Mrs. Marsh has not charmed me as much in the
book we return, but it is nevertheless an interesting

story, " though an old woman's tale rather than an *old man's,*" says my husband.

We unite in thanks and regards to Mrs. Story and yourself,

and I remain, your obliged

ELIZABETH BARRETT BROWNING.

Palazzo Guidi.
    Feb. 5.

INDEX